MIHAIA

MIHAIA

The Prophet Rua Kenana and His Community at Maungapohatu

JUDITH BINNEY

GILLIAN CHAPLIN

CRAIG WALLACE

AUCKLAND UNIVERSITY PRESS
BRIDGET WILLIAMS BOOKS

First published by Oxford University Press, Auckland, 1979
Reprinted with corrections, 1987, 1990
This edition published by Auckland University Press with
Bridget Williams Books, University of Auckland, Private Bag 92019,
Auckland, New Zealand

ISBN 1 86940 148 4

Designed by Lindsay Missen
Cover design for this edition by Mission Hall Design Group, Wellington
This edition printed by South Wind Production, Singapore

This book is dedicated to the Tuhoe,
and to Te Akakura and Puti,
who took Gillian and Judith
as their daughters.

Rua at Opotiki on his way to
Gisborne to meet King Edward in
June 1906. He is walking, a dog at his
heels, towards a policeman. Photo by
F. Braae. *Auckland Weekly News, 5
July 1906*

Contents

A map of places referred to in the
text.

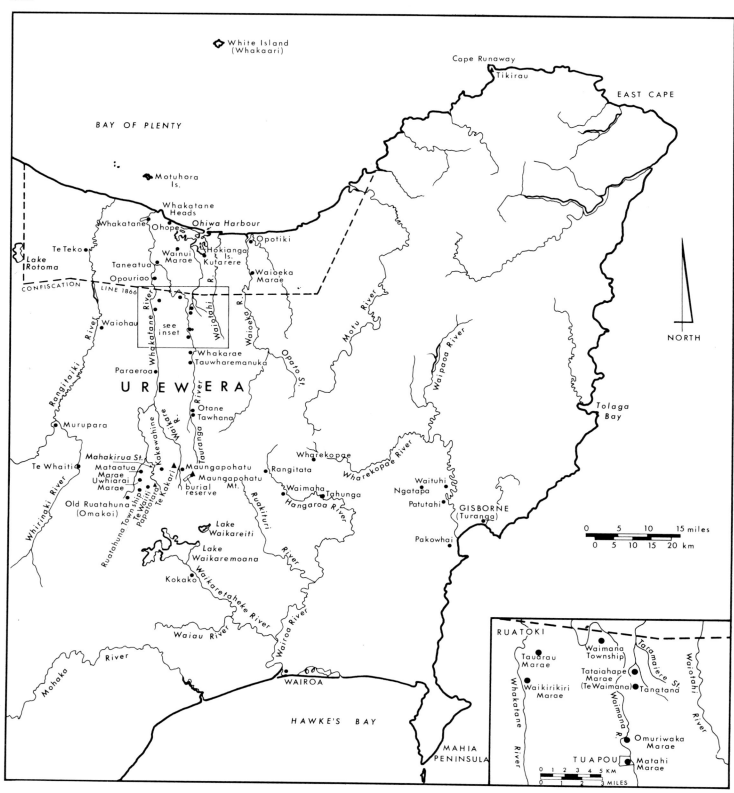

Introduction

Rua Kenana Hepetipa was one of many Maori prophetic leaders who arose in the nineteenth and twentieth centuries. He called himself *Te Mihaia Hou*, the New Messiah, and, like the others, owed his power to the great skill with which he applied the Scriptures to the day to day events in the lives of those who believed in him. His prophetic sayings (*nga kupu whakari*) gave meaning to a harsh existence, and offered hope for the future. Visionary and millenarian leaders have emerged in almost all non-Christian societies turned upside-down by European colonization and, indeed, in European societies undergoing crisis. But the details of such religious-political movements are infinitely varied and the role and achievements of each leader unique. Rua came from the most conservative section of the Maori people, the Tuhoe of the Urewera country, but his leadership proved to be highly innovatory. He attempted to create new systems of land ownership and land usage. He organized a strong communal basis in all the settlements he founded, but also emphasized the concept of family ownership of property. He cast aside all traditional tapu practices, but replaced them with new forms specifically associated with the faith in himself as the Promised Messiah. His methods and his teachings divided the Tuhoe irreconcilably, but he always worked closely with those elders who did give him support, and tried to reinforce their political and communal roles. His guidance and his judgments – for better, and for worse – directed his people through a most difficult period of adjustment, as the Pakeha gradually took control of their world. Though pacific, he was a disruptive force within the tribe and the larger society, as his protracted and controversial trial of 1916 revealed. In the end, he failed to realize his dream of economic independence for the Tuhoe, but the problems with which he wrestled were huge. If he was defeated in his aspiration, it was in part because Pakeha prejudice was given the power to act with the force of the law, which became the instrument of a prevailing hostility towards Maori local autonomy.

In the course of carrying out research for this book it became apparent that substantial differences existed between the published sources – mostly journalists' articles and contemporary Pakeha reports – and the Maori oral accounts and their manuscript records of the same events. There is a real gap between Maori and European perceptions as the symbolic quality of thought belonging to the Maori world view shifts 'reality' into forms unfamiliar to the European. At the same time, I found the elders with whom I talked very accurate in their knowledge not only of events but also, surprisingly, of the dates of those events, many of which I could verify from written records. Such a detailed recall of a past in which the person may not have been involved, or, if so, only as a child, is possible in small communities which have remained more or less intact over a long period of time. The oral cultural traditions are still strong in rural Maori settlements and the local history is passed on by being told. Significant differences emerged from individuals, but the core of the legend or event was constant. This kind of knowledge may not survive this century. In the Waimana valley, where we made most of our contacts, many people have left and the young, we were told, no longer want to know about the past. We felt that one reason why we were accepted was simply so that the names and the story could be recorded for the *mokopuna* (grandchildren), before all is lost. The old are dying; Horo Tatu, the oldest of Rua's followers when we commenced this work, is now dead. Some younger Maoris understandably protest against the intrusion of Pakeha historians, but at least something of Horo's knowledge has been recorded here. It is the people who remain in the rural areas who are the most conscious of these losses.

This photographic history was never intended to be a complete study of Rua, nor is it one, but it has grown in unexpected ways. At the beginning of 1977, when two women set out nervously for the 'heart of Maoridom', the Tuhoe country, they did not really expect to do much more than look at the places where Rua had lived and photograph them. Instead, because of the warm cooperation we were given, that limited concept was transformed. This book is the result, and it was possible only through the help of the people of Rua. We learnt that, while it was difficult for Pakeha to undertake Maori history, it was not because we were not made welcome. We met with unfailing generosity and friendliness. Because women conducted the field work, we learnt a lot from the women. Details of life at Maungapohatu came alive in their memories, and we were treated with endless patience when we failed to understand, or got it muddled. The mistakes which remain are not theirs.

Much of the help we received was in the identification of people in the photographs. These photographs possess powerful associations for those to whom we brought them and there were soon many things to talk about. Most importantly, we were thanked for coming. This was not simply because we summoned up happy memories, although that is what one old man said as he recalled one of the great hui. The photograph of Rua's arrest has been crumpled and stained with tears. Seeing the portrait of Rua's first wife, Pinepine, 'the mother wife', was for one woman as if Pinepine herself had briefly returned, and she conversed with her. Another woman, sunk in a reverie of pleasure at seeing the 'old faces' again, spoke to an image whose name she could not bring to her mind, 'Who are you? Who *are* you?' The past, and all it meant, was alive again.

Of the many photographs in this book, only those of the witnesses at Rua's trial came with identifications – and even these were not complete. Virtually all other identifications have been established by asking the people who once lived in Rua's settlements. There were problems, of course. In a few cases, particularly in the very early photographs, there were too many conflicting opinions for me to accept any suggestion with confidence and so these faces have been left unidentified. I would like to hear from anyone who can help to fill these gaps. No work of this kind has been undertaken before in New Zealand – nor, indeed, has much been done elsewhere. We have assembled a collection of over 350 photographs of Rua's people; they form an unparalleled record of a community through time. The best are reproduced in this book, but the entire collection will stay together and be deposited as a public archive for the Tuhoe. We also hope that the publication of the book will bring more photographs to light.

The text of this book has been written to the photographs. One day, a Maori – and I hope, a Tuhoe – will write a history of Rua, and it will be very different from this. I have tried to understand what I have been told, but in shaping the material in written form I have been conscious that I may be altering its values and the significance it has for the people with whom I talked. I have found explanation for most of Rua's actions in the Scriptures, parts of which he consciously attempted to re-enact. But there were other influences and sources of thought drawn from Tuhoe tradition, even though he cast aside much of that. Some of these influences I will have missed, and no-one will have thought to tell me, because everyone took them for granted. There are also the manuscript books in the hands of those to whom they belong. They include ledger books and account books other than the one to which we were given access, and there was a diary, which may still exist. I did not consider it appropriate to seek out these books, and I hope that, one day, a Maori scholar will have access to them.

In 1971, Dr Peter Webster, of Victoria University, completed a Ph.D. thesis, 'Maungapohatu and the Maori Millennium'. Since then, the thesis has been closed and despite a personal request to its author, I have not been permitted to read it. However, just before writing this introduction, I learnt that it is to be published under the title *Rua and the Maori Millennium*. Although I regret Dr Webster's decision, the publication of two discrete studies of Rua in the same year certainly adds spice to New Zealand historiography.

There is a particular problem on which I must comment. The Tuhoe were still using a patrilineal naming system, by which the child bore the name of the father as its second identifying name: thus, Te Akakura Ru is the child of Ru Hoani. There was no fixed 'surname'. In addition, many people were known by more than one name – sometimes a man would bear his wife's father's name, or his name would be changed in association with a particular event or acquired role in life. Though I soon became conscious of these difficulties, as the same person in a photograph was identified variously and at last I would discover that they were all names for the same person, some of the confusions which arose may not have been eradicated. In the index, the man or woman's first given name is treated, quite properly, as their formal name: thus, Teka Hekerangi, also known as Teka Te Rika, Teka Te Kaawa, Tekaumarua Teka, is indexed under Teka.

The sources for this book are many and varied. We were amazed by what kept turning up and, indeed, by what continues to turn up. For the written sources, two particular acts of generosity transformed this photographic history. The first was Dick Scott's loan of the Ledger book from Maungapohatu, which had come into his possession many years ago. The second was the decision of Noel and Eric Lundon, the sons of Rua's defence counsel, J. R. Lundon, to make available to me his papers and documents. This collection includes the entire Court transcript of Rua's trial, which has never before been studied because all the Auckland Supreme Court records of criminal trials before 1929 were destroyed by an outrageous decision of Mr Justice Callan in 1949. The newspaper accounts of the trial remain valuable, however, for they often quote question and answer verbatim, which the transcript does not. In addition, the Lundon papers include a mass of correspondence and notes; so much that the material could not be adequately incorporated in this study. I will be writing a further essay on the trials based on this collection.

The others we most wish to thank are those who talked with us at length. Most consented to be recorded, and the tapes will be preserved, although they remain closed for the present to protect our informants. For this reason, also, there are a few instances in the text where I have not said whom I am quoting; the context makes it obvious why anonymity has been preserved. All the interviews and conversations were carried out in 1977 and 1978. The following are those with whom we talked at length and to whom we are greatly indebted: Henry Bell; Robert (Boy) Biddle; Kino Hughes; Te Huinga (Jack) Karauna; Paetawa Miki; Puti and Mac Onekawa; Harimate Roberts; Heta and Te Paea Rua; Hillman Rua; Iraia Rua; Mau and Miria Rua; Mangere and Naomi Teka; Tawhaki Te Kaawa; Te Akakura Sherrin; Tuhimai Tiopira; Horo Tatu; Te Puhi Tatu. The particular contributions of these people will be seen in the text.

Our thanks are also due to three policemen who were with the expedition of 1916, and who have also given generously of their time and their recollections: Arnold Butterworth; Tom Collins; Harry Maisey.

Others with whom we talked, and whom we would like to thank for their help and hospitality, are: E. G. Armstrong; Paretai Biddle; Purewa Biddle; Mrs Sonny Biddle; Rev. and Mrs Lloyd Carter; Mary Evetts; Beryl Gollner; Jessie Howden; Catherine Ingram; Pita Kenana; Kelly and Kume Kereopa; Jim Laughton; Don Lochore; Ira Manihera; Taniko Miki; Norman Nicholls; Ata Nohotima; Peti Nohotima (Afemui); Nan Orupe; Rangi Rakuraku; Alfred Rimmer; Hira Rua; Te Mata Rua; Meri Taka; Nino Takao; Rata Takao; Makarini and Kiti Temara; Mei Tuwairua; Te Mamai Tuwairua; Winny Tuwairua; Wi Whitu. Many of these contributed in ways which may not be so apparent in the text, but their help and knowledge was most valuable.

I would also particularly like to thank Joe Te Maipi, Witi Ihimaera, and John Rangihau for their help and advice; Heather Beaton, Dr Michael King, Rev. Jim Irwin, and Dr Allan North for theirs; Hamish Keith and Richard Hill for keeping their eyes open when carrying out their own research; Michael Sims of the Colonial Ammunition Company, and Associate Professor Bernard Brown of the Law Faculty, University of Auckland, for giving advice on arms and the law to an innocent; H. G. D. White for his generous hospitality in Opotiki and his vast local knowledge; R. A. Creswell for his equally large local knowledge and the detailed map of the area which he drew for our assistance; Colin McCahon and the Urewera National Park Board for their permission to reproduce the Urewera mural; Peggy Smythe for her kind hospitality in Wellington; and Jeff Sissons for his enthusiastic exchange of ideas.

Others whom I would like to thank are those who made available to us photographs and documents from their own collections: Heather Beaton; Nancy Bracey; R. A. Creswell; W. C. Davies; Rowland Dickinson; Andrew Fuller; Flora Johnston; Hardwicke Knight; Alan J. La Roche; Mrs I. McHaffie; Mary McKenzie; Brent Mawson; Professor S. M. Mead; P. E. Murphy; Norman Nicholls; Rex Norman; Puti and Mac Onekawa; R. W. Petrowski; E. T. Pleasants; Olwyn Rudd; Mrs M. S. Satherley; Len Shapcott; Alan Smythe; George Stephenson; Meri Taka; Rata Takao; Sergeant John Taylor; Bernard Teague; John B. Turner; Brian D. Webb; H. G. D. White. To others who wrote to us with advice, or sent photographs not finally used, I would like to reiterate the gratitude which I expressed in correspondence. I would also like to add here my thanks to friends and colleagues at the University of Auckland for their patience with my obsessions and their helpful suggestions.

The Libraries and Museums must not be forgotten; indeed without them we would never have started at all. In particular, Anton van der Wouden of the Whakatane Museum; Roger Neich of the National Museum; Gordon Maitland of the Auckland Institute and Museum; John Sullivan of the Alexander Turnbull Library; and the Maori Schools' Officer, R. A. Miller, of the Department of Education, Auckland, deserve special recognition. The reference assistants at the Auckland Public Library answered many apparently pointless questions with great patience; as did the staff at National Archives; the Police College Library, Trentham; General Assembly Library, Parliament House; and the Hocken Library, University of Otago. Merimeri Penfold and Rangi Motu translated for us. Rangi wrestled with the very real difficulties of transcription and translation of the Ledger book, as well as passages on the tapes. A research grant from the University of Auckland helped pay the costs of her work; Merimeri laboured out of the kindness of her heart. All other costs were borne by the authors. And I would like to add an expression of gratitude to our editor, Wendy Harrex, whose experience has proved invaluable, and to Karl Peters who drew the maps. Finally, I wish to thank my father, Professor S. Musgrove, who took his red pencil to those stylistic oddities of his daughter which he had been unable to eradicate in her youth.

The project of the photographic history was conceived by Craig Wallace four years ago, when he recognized the dramatic potential of the material. He undertook the initial documentary and photographic research over a period of two years. At the beginning of 1977, Gillian Chaplin and I joined Craig and collaborated on further photographic and archival research. At the same time, Gillian and I undertook the field work. Gillian has contributed her own photographs and has also printed many of the old photos from copy negatives to obtain the best possible image. I have written the text and am solely responsible for it and the interpretation of the material we have jointly gathered.

JUDITH BINNEY
Auckland, January 1979

Rua Kenana, 1908. Photo by James
McDonald. *Alexander Turnbull
Library*

14

1 The Prophet Ascendant

Early in the year 1906, the newspapers of New Zealand began to notice a new Maori prophet, Rua Kenana. He caught their attention by his claims to strange and mystic origins: he was brother to Christ and son of the still feared visionary and guerilla leader, Te Kooti Rikirangi. He prophesied that within the month of June all the lands of the Maori would be restored to them. On 25 June, King Edward VII of England would meet Rua at Gisborne and, in exchange for diamonds, would hand over New Zealand into Rua's authority. Thus, by peaceful means, the longest standing grievance of the Maori would be remedied: their subjection to Pakeha rule would be ended at once.

These early visions of Rua's contained little appeal to European understanding, but his messianic dreams for his people incorporated other more pragmatic and comprehensible schemes. By 1908 he had built for himself and his followers a new community, at Maungapohatu, in the heart of the Urewera country. The few Pakeha visitors who undertook the arduous inland journey to the settlement praised the enthusiasm of the faithful, which Rua was directing towards the creation of a good life on ancestral Tuhoe lands.

These more recognizable goals made Rua into a person of note in the Whakatane district. Indeed, he became a very familiar figure as he rode down from the hills, with his disciples, on large-scale shopping expeditions to the general stores at Waimana, Gisborne, and Opotiki. Today he is not remembered with fear. Yet fear lay close beneath the surface of contemporary European commentaries and Pakeha children were hurried home from school when Rua rode by. Though pacific, he was a separatist leader of the last section of the Maori people who emerged from relative isolation into contact with European settlement – the Tuhoe of the Urewera country.

At the turn of the century, the Tuhoe were deeply suspicious of Europeans and, as Elsdon Best, their Pakeha historian, commented, they did 'not have very much use for Christianity'.[1] During the early part of the nineteenth century, they had been largely protected from direct European rule by the very nature of their land: remote, mountainous and densely forested. They had had only brief contacts with missionaries. The inland Anglican station which had been founded at Te Whaiti in 1847, had been abandoned with the onset of the Anglo-Maori wars and the Tuhoe had largely become followers of the prophetic leader, Te Kooti – or Te Turuki as he always called himself, and as the Tuhoe know him.★ They, who had sheltered him when he fled from imprisonment on the Chatham Islands, became a mainstay of the new faith he founded, the Ringatu.

The wars between Maori and Pakeha were fought largely in the Ureweras between 1869 and 1872, because Te Turuki sought refuge with the Tuhoe. Their principal grievance was the recent loss of their low-lying lands, across the mouths of the Waimana and Ruatoki valleys, which were taken in 1866 in the general Bay of Plenty confiscations. Fourteen thousand acres were appropriated from them (in the final settlement of 211,000 acres), as reprisal

'Te Kooti. Sketch made at Te Teko. March 29th. 1892.' Drawing by Henry Hill. There are no known authentic photographs of Te Turuki, who refused to allow his picture to be taken. *Misses D. and G. Hill Collection, Alexander Turnbull Library*

★He abandoned his Anglican baptismal name, Te Kooti (from the Church Missionary Society's Secretary, Dandeson Coates), and signed himself either Te Turuki or Te Turuki Rikirangi. Te Turuki was an older kinsman's name; Rikirangi his own given name.[2]

Note: in the photographs all identifications are from left to right.

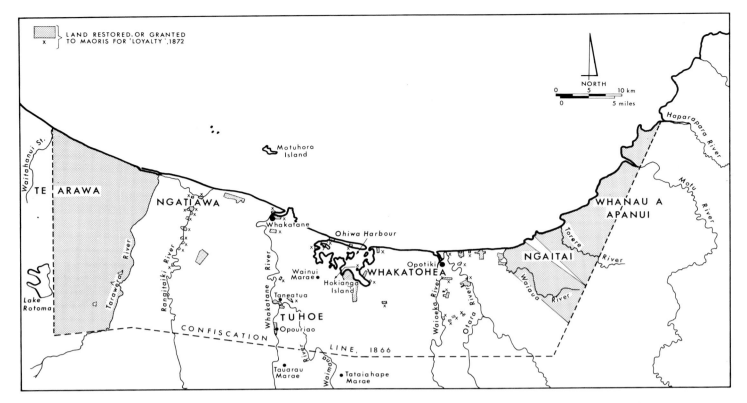

Confiscation of land, eastern Bay of Plenty (derived from the official map published in the *Appendices to the Journal of the Legislative Council*, 1873, with amendments deduced from written records).

The original confiscation border of 1866 contained 448,000 acres. In the subsequent settlements (most by 1872), some of the land was restored, or granted to Maori 'loyalists', or recognized as already being in European hands. In the end, 211,000 acres were confiscated from Ngatiawa, Whakatohea, and Tuhoe. Five hundred acres were restored to Tuhoe; 14,000 were confiscated from them. The very acts of confiscation, restitution, and grant created confusion and conflict of land claims between the tribes, while the records and the mathematics of the several confiscation reports, including the last (1928), leave much to be desired for precision.

for the so-called 'Hauhau rebellion' in the Bay of Plenty.[3] Those Tuhoe who committed themselves to Te Turuki did so because of the injustice which they felt they had suffered, and because his vision of the future gave back to the Maoris control of their own world. They emerged from the wars bitter against the Pakeha and the confiscations. In each valley, the boundary lines of the confiscation were marked by a carved post, the sign of separation between them and the white man and all his works. But by 1893, the year in which Te Turuki died, the relative isolation from Europeans in which the Tuhoe communities lived was beginning to be eroded. The first surveyors entered the Urewera country in 1892, and in the last years of the century the familiar phrase, 'bringing law and civilization', began to be repeated with heavy solemnity in Parliamentary discussions of the 'problem' of the Ureweras and its people.

Te Turuki's sudden death left his followers leaderless, and immediately the Ringatu faith was beset by the factionalism he had tried to prevent. Just before his death he had devised a hierarchical structure of government for the Church, focussing on a leader, *Poutikanga*, or 'Main Pillar'. But rivalry split the leadership and prevented the election of the first *Poutikanga* until 1914.[4] Te Turuki had also made predictions about the succession in a series of prophecies undoubtedly aimed at preserving the *kotahitanga* or unity of the people.[5] In a sequence dating from 1878, he foretold the emergence of a successor from within the Tuhoe. He foresaw the advent of two rival 'stars', and announced in 1885:

The two stars are still standing as they were. . . . I make it known that this leader is going to be from the east. He shall appear directly between Nga-kuri-a-wharei and Tikirau, no further.[6]

The boundaries he named are those of the Mataatua canoe district, from a point near Katikati to the hill on the eastern slopes of Cape Runaway – that is, the land of the Tuhoe, Whakatohea, and Ngatiawa tribes. The star from the east he had said, in 1880, was the force for good. In his last years, he reiterated these prophecies, some warning of division and rivalry, others stressing the hopes for unity and strength. In 1892 he said:

He tamaiti noa nei mana e huri te riu o to waka ki runga, mana ano hoki e whakakotahi nga Iwi ki te Whakapono.

There will be a child who will turn upright the canoe and he will unite the People through the Gospel.[7]

And he prophesied as he lay dying at Ohiwa:

In twice seven years a man shall arise in the mountains to succeed me. He shall be the new prophet of the people.[8]

Rua Kenana claimed to be this man. As the 'son' of Te Kooti he was naming himself the One who had been foretold. He was the next successor in the unbroken chain of *poropiti*, the Maori prophets, who had risen to lead their people 'in their time in the wilderness'. Te Turuki had spoken of the continuing function of these prophetic leaders in his book of teachings, written down in 1867 and 1868:

As it is written in the Prophets behold, I send my messenger before thy face which shall prepare thy way before thee.[9]

In the nineteenth century, faced with loss of land and an inexplicably high mortality among their people, many Maori leaders had turned to the story of the Israelites, desolate and lost in their land. The essence of their identification with them was the pain they shared: 'O God, if our hearts arise from the land in which we now dwell as slaves. . . . Do not Thou, O God, cause us to be wholly destroyed.'[10] The Maori prophets, men like Aperahama Taonui of *(Below) see p. 18*

Hokianga, Te Ua, Te Whiti, and Titokowaru of Taranaki, and Te Turuki himself, of Ngatimaru from Poverty Bay, adopted the Scriptural promises for their own people. This was the *wairua* tradition, or the spirit of prophecy which focussed particularly on the protection and recovery of Maori lands, and the preservation of themselves as the children of Israel, the chosen people.

For his Tuhoe followers, Rua was important because he was the Tuhoe prophet: 'He was different from Turuki; he was the prophet for us'.[11] But his claims to be the One foreseen by Te Turuki were not wholly accepted either by the Tuhoe or by the Ringatu generally. However, his earliest followers came from the three tribes who trace their descent from the Mataatua canoe: Whakatohea and Ngatiawa of Opotiki and Whakatane, and Tuhoe of Waikaremoana, Ruatahuna, Ruatoki, and Waimana. His strongest support came from his own hapu, the Tamakaimoana. To others of the Ringatu faith, the advent of Rua was the beginning of a disastrous major schism. They point to other prophecies of Te Turuki which foretold division and dissension. One spoke of a man who would trample underfoot the faith, divide the land, and leave the people poorer, fatally disturbing the calm waters of the Ringatu movement. The Tuhoe section of the registered Ringatu church see this prophecy as referring to Rua.[12]

Rua Kenana Tapunui was the posthumous son of one of Te Turuki's fighters, Kenana Tumoana, who was killed in battle at Makaretu in November 1868. Rua claimed he was born three years after his father's death: 'Kenana was only my father as Joseph was the father of Christ.'[13] He was, in fact, born in 1869, probably at Maungapohatu, the village lying at the foot of the sacred burial mountain of the same name. He was often said by Europeans to be of low rank, but in actuality he was a direct descendant, through his mother Ngahiwi Te Rihi, of Tamakaimoana, the eponymous ancestor of the people of Maungapohatu. His father, although of lesser lineage, was kin to the major Tamakaimoana chief at the turn of this century, Tutakangahau.

Rua was sent away as a child to live with Ngati Kahungungu, his father's people, at Napier, Pakipaki and Te Aute. Later, he used this childhood experience as an image of exile: 'My people rejected me, and I was homeless.'[14] He returned to Maungapohatu when he was about nine years old and again, he said, 'I was . . . rejected and despised by my people, so that the Bible words were fulfilled.' By 1895 he was well known as a figure among the Ringatu and about 1904 he began to experience the visions which set him upon the path of succession to Te Turuki. In 1906, on New Year's Day (one of the sacred days kept by the Ringatu), he first foretold the arrival of King Edward.

Rua had been working as a shearer and ditch-digger for Pakeha farmers in the Waimana and Gisborne districts for about eighteen years. He lived mostly in the Waimana valley, on the confiscated land. He leased a property south-east of Taneatua and continued to exist as though he was an outcast from the rest of the Tuhoe. He interpreted this isolation as the sign of God's purpose. One of his followers has described Rua's first visions: 'The spirit of God came to him and said, "Take up my work". [He replied,] "If it is the sick I will not do it. If it is the land, I will."'[15]

It was on the sacred mountain of the Tuhoe that Rua experienced the vision which confirmed him in his chosen path. Christ appeared before him on Maungapohatu and took him to the hidden diamond which, 'in days to come', will be the means of the redemption of his people. Heta Rua, the prophet's eldest living son, tells the story this way:

'Eripitana', the tapu house built for Te Turuki at Te Whaiti by all the hapu of Tuhoe in 1884. It was built specifically as a Ringatu house of worship. Te Turuki chose the name to allude to passages in Isaiah; it could be a rendering of 'Epiphany' (the manifestation of God) since the texts refer to the Leader and Saviour. The house is variously described as the 'House of God' or the 'Holiest of Holies'. By 1900, when this photograph was taken (Hamiora Potakurua of Ngatiwhare of Te Whaiti sits in front), Eripitana was derelict. In the carving, the lizard on the central post had been inverted and when Te Turuki came to open the house his horse shied. Observing the *hapa* (error), he prophesied the day when the people of Te Whaiti would lose all but their meeting-houses. Subsequently, Eripitana was considered extremely tapu and the house fell into disrepair. Ringatu services were held in the open air here, by the stream. A small whare was built at the rear of the house in which offerings of money were placed as a sacrifice to God. Rua used the whare as his 'House of God' (see p. 68): 'Wherever Te Turuki was, our father was', said Te Akakura, Rua's daughter, on revisiting Eripitana in 1978. The house was rebuilt in a much smaller form, using some of the original carvings, in 1938. Although there have been attempts to lift the tapu, it is still considered a strange place. Photo by Augustus Hamilton. *Alexander Turnbull Library*

18

Pinepine, Rua's first wife. After Pinepine had been on the mountain and seen the diamond, Rua declared her a tapu woman. This photograph was taken many years later by one of the missionaries at Maungapohatu. *Whakatane Museum*

It was at Tukutoromiro,† when he was first living there with Pinepine his wife. They'd built a whare, made out of ponga, and one day they were baking bread in the kitchen. *He* was doing the baking. He heard this voice, calling out. He turned round to his wife and asked, 'Are you calling me?' 'No', she says. It was the third time when the voice called, he knew it wasn't her. He went outside. It was an angel. It was an angel he saw. And the angel told him what to do, to go up that mountain. So they went to the top of that mountain. He told his wife, 'Don't hesitate, whatever you see on that mountain.'

† Tukutoromiro is a hillside above the Waikare river at Maungapohatu. See photograph, p. 139.

A portrait of Rua's favourite wife (right), Te Akakura, taken on the same occasion as the photograph opposite, which may have been her wedding to Rua. The cover portrait of Rua also probably belongs to the same sequence, since all were taken by James McDonald in 1908. Here, the two women wear huia tail feathers, indicating their high rank. The woman on the left is unknown, although it has been suggested that she may be Te Rau Miria Te Haunui, Te Akakura's mother. But Te Rau Miria is also remembered as being *kirikotea*, fair of skin. In marrying Te Akakura, a major chieftainess of Ngatirongo, Rua allied himself with his main opposition within Tuhoe. This was probably the reason for his formal (and therefore legal) marriage on the marae, for Ngatirongo were much opposed to the union. But Akakura's father, Ru Hoani, was a strong follower of Rua. *National Museum*

The track was narrow and hard to find; the mists closed in. Three times they stopped, exhausted, and three times a woman appeared before them, to urge them on and to point out the path. It was dawn when they reached the flat on the top of the mountain, and the woman's long black hair gleamed in the first shafts of sunlight. She was Whaitiri, ancestress of Tuhoe. Then the figure of Christ appeared beside her; he took Rua and brought him to the swamp where the diamond lay. Rua fetched Pinepine and both thus acquired the ability to see what others could not; through the protective veil of the swamp they witnessed what lay beneath.

The diamond's still there to this day, just as Te Turuki covered it up with the rainbow shawl.‡ It was still on it. He looked at it and covered it up again. Never took it, never touched it. Just as Te Turuki put the shawl on the mountain. 'Don't touch it!' It looks after the mountain.
Then he went down to the flat. It's got three lakes and each one is a different colour. And then this thing happened again. They saw the woman and she was in rags. When she opened it, it flows out. That's when they saw the wings. It was covered up. Of course, Pinepine hesitated. And then the snow came, it started to pour down.

They were isolated on the mountain for three or four days.§ But Rua's big Newfoundland dog, Darkie, who had gone with them, took them under the trees and brought them food. 'Darkie is the only dog who has been on that mountain. He's a dog who can tell you if you are doing something wrong.' He was a dog who could, thereafter, foresee death.[16] When Rua and Pinepine returned from their time on the mountain, everyone knew that Rua was the One who had been foretold. He came from the mountain sliding down a rainbow.[17] The rainbow is God's promise to man, the sign of the everlasting Covenant with Israel.

That's how that gift was given to him. That's how he started off. It was from this time that he prophesied the things to come. After that, he can tell you when it's coming. He tells you about things that people have never heard of.
The diamond? Well, it's still on Maungapohatu. There's a time when it will be seen again. You can't find it, but it's there. First story I heard was the people from overseas, well, they come half way to New Zealand and they see this bright star all the time. They would sail for it, knowing it was New Zealand. But when they get closer, it disappears. So they know it isn't a star, but it must be something. Every boat saw it, but as soon as you get closer, then you can't see it again. It's still there, but Te Turuki put his shawl over it and covered it up so that people couldn't find it. He knew in times to come people would fly in the air and find it. Sure enough, we get aeroplanes.

It was after this vision on the mountain, as the Lord had spoken to Moses, that Rua started to journey through all the land of the Mataatua canoe tribes, seeking their recognition. He built for himself a meeting-house on the tapu island in the Ohiwa harbour, Hokianga, where Te Turuki had lived. He called this house Te Poho O Mataatua, the Bosom of the Mataatua people.[18] In this way, he sought to rediscover the power of Te Turuki, which he thought might reside on the island. He drew to him men who had been with Te Turuki and were now leaders of the Ringatu. One of these was Eria Raukura, of Ngatapa, an elder of part-Tuhoe descent whom Te Turuki had baptized in 1881 as the major tohunga of the Ringatu. Eria was the guardian of Rongopai, the tapu house of Te Turuki at Repongaere near Waituhi, and an important figure among the Ringatu. By 1905, Eria had come to accept Rua as the man who had been foretold. In 1906, he baptized him as the Messiah, by Pakowhai, in the waters of the Waipaoa river, before a great crowd of people. Eria accepted Rua because of the strange *tohu* (portents) which had been seen over Maungapohatu: a shower of shooting stars, signalling the rise of the new prophet. Rua's gift for oratory and his changed life, eschewing the riotous

‡ *Horo*, the shawl. In some versions, it is a black shawl.
§ In other versions, they were six weeks on the mountain.

ways of his youth, were also tokens which convinced Eria.[19] Other elders who had lived with Te Turuki on Hokianga were similarly convinced. One was Te Hurinui Apanui, the leading Ngatiawa chief and considered the paramount figure of the Mataatua tribes. He became an articulate spokesman for Rua and was photographed in 1908 with other supporters of Rua, elders of the Tuhoe and Ngatiawa. In the photograph, both Hurinui and the younger man present, Hori Taia, wear the long hair which had become the distinctive characteristic of Rua's committed followers by the middle of 1907.

The acceptance of Rua's message that he was the New Messiah by such a man as Te Hurinui indicates that there were strong grievances among the people to whom it was brought. Rua belonged to the first generation of the upland Tuhoe who had begun to work as casual labourers for Europeans. Some European farmers today can still recall him working in his tattered dungarees on their parents' properties. For the Tuhoe, familiarity with Pakeha settlements meant exposure to their relative material wealth, in contrast to the deep poverty in which many Tuhoe lived as shearers and drain-layers. The conditions of the *kainga* drew the concerned attention of Elsdon Best, then sanitary inspector for the area.

Water supplies were often contaminated because of the absence of latrines. Between 1896 and 1901 (the last date when a tribal census was made), the Tuhoe population fell from 1400 to 1000. In 1906, when the next census figures were being collected in the district, the inspectors reported an unparalleled failure of the basic food crops, kumara, potato and maize. These were critical years for the Tuhoe, as they underwent the new experience of

This photo is labelled, erroneously, 'Rua and his Council'; Rua is absent. But the men are elders of Tuhoe and Ngatiawa, with the exception of the young Hori Taia.
Back: Te Horohau, Te Rau Miria's second husband and chief of Ngatikuri; Takuta Noema; Te Hurinui Apanui of Ngatiawa; Te Pou Papaka of Ngatiraka from Te Waimana; Tiopira Tamaikoha.
Middle: Hori Taia, one of the members of the ruling Council of Maungapohatu in 1908; Rangiahua; Te Wakaunua Houpepe.
Front: ? Te Rau Miria; Te Akakura Ru.
Te Pou, Tiopira, and Te Hurinui were staunch followers of Rua, but there is some doubt about the others. However, Te Wakaunua is known to have gone to Gisborne with Rua, and Te Horohau for a while followed him. Te Pou gave Rua the land for his first community in the Waimana valley. *National Museum*

A Maori family in the Ureweras, 1906. The makeshift *wharepuni*, sleeping-house, was not atypical. The child wears a patterned feather cloak, probably made of kiwi (brown) and kereru (white), the woman one of dogskin. *Auckland Weekly News, 15 February 1906*

settling and seeking employment in the coastal valleys. At the same time, they were exposed to the Pakeha belief that they had a moral right to expand their own settlements into the still closed lands of the Ureweras. In the early twentieth century, it was a common rumour that the Tuhoe controlled an area of fertile upland valleys, ripe for settlement and farming. Stories were told of an enormous potential wealth in minerals, especially gold.

The official survey parties sent out in 1895 had aroused such resistance from the Tuhoe that the Prime Minister, Richard Seddon, felt that he must receive a delegation of chiefs. They asked that the Tuhoe lands be set aside as a reserve, that all European settlers and prospectors be excluded, and that control be in the hands of tribal committees.[20] The government's response was the Urewera District Native Reserve Act of 1896, which set up a commission to survey the area, and to divide it into blocks owned by family groups. The considerable costs of the magnetic survey were to be borne by the Tuhoe. In presenting the bill to Parliament, Seddon offered it as an experiment in Maori local autonomy, for it provided for a General Committee (drawn from elected block committees) which had sole authority to lease or sell land, but only to the Crown. Though the primary purpose of the act was to prevent Tuhoe land being sold to individual Europeans, pressure exerted on the government whittled its effectiveness away. The General Committee was not set up until 1909; but in April 1906 the government decided to allow prospecting in the Urewera lands, and in 1907 they were brought under the scope of the Mining Act. In 1906 they were also included in a survey of 'Native Waste lands' suitable for settlement.[21] The Tuhoe had real reason to fear that, once again, the law would be used to take away the Maori land it purported to protect. Already they were being urged to improve their land rapidly, so as to prevent the government from seizing it.[22] Consequently, they were tempted to permit prospecting and milling, tempted indeed to sell land in order to raise the money needed to pay for the survey and the costs of development. The law did not unite, but divided them.

Rua was aware of these issues. Working as a labourer for European

Tuhoe chiefs meet Seddon and James Carroll (Timi Kara, extreme left) in Wellington, September 1895. The two politicians had visited the Urewera in 1894, hoping to stop obstruction of the Urewera surveys, but the opposition proved just as strong when government surveying began in 1895, and Seddon had to make concessions to Tuhoe feelings. *Seddon Papers, National Archives*

Below
'A Modern Canute and the Tide of Settlement'. This cartoon reflects the common European attitude to James Carroll's policy *taihoa*, or delay in the alienation of 'idle' Maori lands. The *New Zealand Herald* objected strongly to the 'privileged and entailed Maori landocracy' to whom Europeans were the 'rack-rented tenants' (Editorial, 1 November 1909). Drawing by Trevor Lloyd. *Auckland Weekly News, 25 March 1909*

A MODERN CANUTE AND THE TIDE OF SETTLEMENT.

Rua (on his white horse Te Ia) with some of his followers, at Taneatua. He is said to have been journeying to the Whakatane Heads, where he was to reveal his ability to walk on water. The first recorded account of this oft-told tale was on 2 May 1906 and it is possible that the photograph is from this occasion. (For one version of this story, see pp. 42-3.) This is probably the earliest known photograph of Rua. It was taken before he and his followers began to grow their hair, that is, before June 1907. A. J. Canning is seated in the buggy. *Whakatane Museum*

employers, he had seen much of Pakeha life, and asked himself why they were better off than his own people. He had come to value some Pakeha standards, particularly those of hygiene and housing. He had also recognized the root problem of Tuhoe poverty: although they were wealthy in land, they were totally without the means to make it productive. For the Tuhoe to achieve some Pakeha living standards, and to become self-sufficient again, they had to retain economic control of their land. Rua sought to develop the wealth of the Tuhoe so that the land could be used for their own advantage. If his movement was founded on a very considerable distrust of Europeans and their material pursuits, it also sought to use some of their ideas and skills. Throughout, he hoped to contain those acquisitions within the autonomous communalism of Tuhoe society. In this specific sense, Rua's intentions were separatist. He was to take his people back into physical isolation from Europeans. They were to seek refuge at Maungapohatu, adapting their lives and their land at their own pace and under their own leadership. Where perhaps Rua can be criticized, as some Tuhoe would now say, was that he gave his followers little real motive to emerge from that isolation. 'As a contribution to Maoritanga, in the long run Rua's movement is questionable.' 'Our people were very backward there. They didn't like white people.' But those who stayed with him also stress the moral basis of his teachings. 'This is what lives with us today.' It seems that, in providing a focus for energy and a faith, Rua helped his people at a period when little else was offered them. And when he considered the time ripe, he also attempted to end the isolation with which he had protected them.

At first, Rua's vision seemed to be one of immediate salvation. In May 1906, when the first newspaper accounts appeared, he was preparing to travel, with a following of a hundred or so, to Gisborne. That Gisborne was the place of deliverance accorded with Te Turuki's predictions. The young man who will be coming, he had said, 'te tamaiti a Te Kooti', would be known when he took the people to Gisborne. In this way, he would be recognized as the true one who would complete the work (*whakapono*).[23] For Turanga (Gisborne) had been the 'seat of hatred'. 'My religion there is harshly treated, therefore to lighten their burden is [an act] of love'.[24]

To establish his divine origin as the brother of Christ, and the son of the Holy Ghost, Rua claimed also to have the power of healing – a power which forms an attested part of the skills of all Maori prophets. By 1906 Rua was sought out by both Maori and Pakeha for his remedies. He used an infusion of tea in which he placed a coin or two, carrying his touch. The coins he put first under his armpit, then into the tea: the patient drank the liquid.[25] Healing with coins is still practised among the Ringatu. Rua would send a coin carrying a *karakia* of blessing and protection to those who were far away and could not come to him. Once, it is recalled, heavy snow prevented a sick man from reaching Maungapohatu. Rua, foreknowing his wish, sent him a coin bearing his touch, which made him well when he was rubbed with it.[26] Inexplicable sickness, *mate Maori*, is often attributed to evil forces living in the human body; their extraction, possible only by faith in the healer, is a major part of the role of a tohunga. The high mortality rate amongst the Maoris had bred numerous religious cults which concentrated on sickness and death. The problem, for which there seemed to be no explanation except divine anger, was the apparent fact that the Pakeha waxed 'fat and prosperous'[27] while the Maori were decimated. Rua stressed this dilemma: in 1906 he said 'that Christ was sent to save the pakeha, that since His advent the Europeans have flourished and multiplied exceedingly. Now he (Rua) had been sent to remove the tapu from the Maoris, and when this is accomplished the natives . . . will increase as the pakeha'.[28]

The same occasion at the settlement of Taneatua (built on the Opouriao block confiscated from Tuhoe). The big dog is probably Darkie (Paki), whose foresight is still remembered. (He chose one of Rua's wives, it is said.) This photograph was dated 1907, while the previous photograph, clearly taken on the same day, was dated 1905. One, at least, must be wrong. Rua is known to have visited Taneatua, with an estimated 200 followers, in 1906. *Whakatane Museum*

Defiling tapu and making *noa* that which had been sacred was a practice which had been adopted by earlier Maori prophetic leaders. The purpose was to destroy the power of the *atua Maori,* the old Maori gods, the supposed source of the sickness. The abolition of tapu, keeping only certain places of worship, was central to Rua's teachings.[29] He explained, 'I have seen the Maori inflict a great deal of mischief on himself in believing in tapu.'[30] In 1910, the well-known collector of carvings, Augustus Hamilton, was able to purchase Tuhoe work because, as he said, 'the Maoris have destroyed all tapu in the Urewera country and are quite anxious to sell anything and Rua has sent out the things that he can get hold of for sale.'[31] In the previous year James Carroll, the part-Maori Native Minister, had received a letter of complaint from Ruatoki:

The works that those people are doing are of a character new and strange. There is now a new system in connection with the burial of the dead, which has been adopted from the plan of Rua, and his people. The corpse is taken to the burial ground, without order or ceremony, as if it were a dog. They go on to the graves and actually eat food there. When they return from the burial a feast is spread, and a collection is taken up. These monies are for Rua. They come along here to do the same thing, but we send them off.[32]

This deliberate violation of tapu on the graveyards was intended to render harmless the malevolence of the *kehua*, the spirits of the ancestral dead who could destroy the living.

In both these incidents, the breaking of tapu was also specifically linked with obtaining money. This aspect of Rua's leadership caused much talk. For Rua, the money given him by the faithful or raised by the sale of what had been tapu was money for the redemption of those who were to be saved. As Moses, upon whose commands Rua based many of his actions, took up money from the children of Israel who were to be redeemed,[33] so Rua took his portion, which he would use to feed his followers. One of his basic teachings was that the food he and his followers were given on their journeys should be paid for, so that those who provided 'will no more be burdened'.[34]

Rua in 1906 also encouraged his followers to sell their possessions, stock and equipment. He explained that only without material preoccupations could they concentrate on the last days. With the millennium ushered in at Gisborne, all the land would be theirs and most Pakeha expelled. Only those who had been 'kind to the Maoris' – and a few tradespeople – would be left.[35] Elsdon Best was told that he might as well give up his stove, his glass washboard and 'that thing you peel potatoes with', as he would not be able to take them back to England with him when the time came.[36] The end to Pakeha rule was to be achieved by simple expatriation, not by violence but by lawful royal purchase. The land which had been ceded to a Queen would be returned by a King. Deliverance, as Te Turuki had said in 1893, would only come through the law: 'the canoe for you to paddle after my departure is the Law. Only the Law can be pitched against the Law'.[37] This vision was central for Rua. Against the 'rule of law' which had brought about the legal confiscation of much Maori land, Rua was to raise his banner: one law for both peoples, '*Kotahi Te Ture Mo Nga Iwi E Rua*'.

Early in 1906 Rua's legitimacy as Te Turuki's successor was first revealed. Two cycles of events occurred focussing on Gisborne. In March, he went to the sacred meeting-house of Rongopai, one of the few Ringatu houses of worship.[38] Rongopai, 'peace and good', had been built as a house for Te Turuki, but he had been prevented by the European authorities from ever returning to Gisborne and consequently never visited it. A tapu had been placed on the house by the elders, who had been shocked by its unconventional decorations of painted human figures and bright flowers, and it was said to be death to enter Rongopai. The door of

Rongopai was locked against Rua. When Ruatoto of Kutarere came to wake Rua in the morning, as he had been instructed, he found him gone, riding headlong on his white horse, Te Ia (the Crest of the Wave). With others, Ruatoto followed at full speed, but when they reached the house they saw that the horse was already inside, opening the door for him to enter. 'The *horse* had the golden key'.[39] 'They waited for him to die and he didn't die. But they still didn't know what he meant. They still didn't know that he was the King they were waiting for.'[40] Nor did they know what he had seen inside the house. Now it is said that Christ and Te Turuki greeted him as the King who would fulfil the prophecies.

From Rongopai he went inland to Maungapohatu, where he announced that he would return to Gisborne to meet the King. Rua's concept of legitimacy now concentrated on the exchange that would occur between them. He rode unarmed and carrying with him, it is said, a large box of precious stones which he would present to Edward.‖ These jewels – in some versions one huge diamond, in others gold and diamonds – had been obtained from a place known only to him. Elsdon Best was told that it was Paraeroa, on the Whakatane river;[41] others had heard that one diamond lay at the head and one at the mouth of the river, on the route which Rua took to Gisborne. In 1906, he intended to give it to Edward to compensate the Pakeha for their losses. This diamond would probably be part of the legen-

‖ There are other versions—that *Edward* was to bring the diamond (or £4 million) to buy New Zealand for the Maoris. On the debt owed the Maoris for the taking of New Zealand in 1840, see p. 42.

Rua, with some of his followers on Marine Parade, Wairoa: Te Hurinui Apanui; —; —; Rua; Wharepapa Hawiki (Te Kati), one of the twelve Disciples. *Bernard Teague, Wairoa*

27

This faded photograph shows Rua, in the centre, riding his white horse through the streets of Opotiki. *Whakatane Museum*

Opposite (top)
Rongopai: painted panels on the exterior porch. The panels have suffered from exposure, but the diamond design, which recurs at Maungapohatu with new meaning, is visible. There are notable parallels between Rongopai and Eripitana: both were built for Te Turuki as houses of worship. It is also said that Te Turuki entered Eripitana on his horse (through the rear window), while Rua's horse gave him his entry into Rongopai. The figures are of local people. Photo by Judith Binney, 1974.

Opposite (bottom)
Rua Tupua. A flag probably made for Rua by the Pakowhai people in 1906. The words mean Rua the Spirit, but *tupua* is not the Tuhoe form. The flag is now owned by the Urewera National Park Board. Photo by Gillian Chaplin, 1981.

dary 'hoard of Te Kooti', to put it in contemporary Pakeha terms; it is clear that it is not the same as the diamond of Maungapohatu, although both possess a redemptive purpose.

Rua travelled to Gisborne, it is still remembered, with the big box strapped to a packhorse by day and jealously guarded in a special tent erected for it at night.[42] It was, in effect, the Ark of the Covenant, or the chest carried by the Israelites of old, as they wandered in the wilderness, containing the tablets of law given by God to Moses on the mountain. The Ark bore the eternal Covenant made with Israel:

Unto thee will I give the land of Canaan, the lot of your inheritance . . . .[43]

The Covenant is, then, the symbol of God's plan and purpose for the Israelites. They brought the Ark to Jerusalem, the City of David; Rua would take his Ark to Maungapohatu like David before him and would build there the House of the Covenant. The Covenant which Rua possessed was a huge English-language Bible given to him by the Tuhourangi tribe of Te Arawa, when they recognized him as the One whom Te Turuki had foretold.[44] This Bible became the sacred Covenant of his followers.

Rua left Waimana on the last stages of his journey on 20 June, when King Edward's star had 'appeared in the East'.[45] He was accompanied by a carefully chosen 'guard', 'selected mostly from those who were the followers of Te Kooti.'¶[46] They were all old men, and unarmed to show their

¶ Forty-two had originally been chosen to accompany Rua, at a meeting held at Te Waimana on 27 May.[47] But all the chiefs of Tuhoe went — eighty-two — and as a consequence there is much confusion in the contemporary newspaper accounts about the 'body-guard' of forty and all those who went. Some Ngatiawa chiefs also went with Rua: Te Hurinui Apanui was one. Te Aitanga A Hauiti hapu from Tolaga Bay also came to Gisborne, converted by Timoti Maitai, a scholar from Te Aute college, who had been sent by Rua in advance to preach along the East Coast.

peaceful intentions; it was only because they were without weapons that they were allowed to pass at all. They entered Opotiki in state and then turned inland, coming down the Waioeka and Motu rivers. On 23 June they reached Pakowhai, near Patutahi, north-west of Gisborne.

Here their reception was distinctly unenthusiastic.[48] At the marae, Rua violated traditional etiquette: to some observers it appeared that he 'did not mourn the dead, for Rua did not acknowledge the dead of his Gisborne hosts'.[49] He adopted a 'pakeha stance' when he spoke, his hands clasped behind his back. None of the hosts at Pakowhai stood up to welcome their visitors, except Eria Raukura and Hukanui, who were both Tuhoe. Rua was forced to camp by the roadside.

At Pakowhai, he had told his audience that he was

the second Christ. He . . . had a messenger, a John the Baptist, in the person of Te Kooti. He reminded his audience that Christ took three years to be born and indeed, it took him [Rua] three years to be recognized. . . . The people were now living in bondage and he had come to deliver them. . . . Rua went on to say that Adam had two children – Cain and Abel – Cain being the pakeha and Abel the Maori. And so it is today that the pakeha continues to attack the Maori. . . . He went on to say that the world was not aware that King Edward had left his throne. Only he knew that the King had left in January to arrive here in Gisborne . . . .[50]

The expected date was now the 27th, two days late, and on this morning Rua and the people waited for Edward at the wharf. For three days they waited and each day the event was postponed. ' "When will the King come, Rua?" the

A PROPHET WITH HONOUR IN HIS OWN COUNTRY.

East Coast Prophet: Next year, King Edward come to New Zealand and spend four millions, and Mr Seddon go to England and take his place there.

King Dick: Why, they told me this prophet was a fool, but there's lots of method in his madness. Merciful Providence, let his prophecy come true.

'A Prophet with Honour in his own Country.' Cartoon by 'BLO', William Blomfield, from the *New Zealand Observer*, 19 May 1906.

Opposite

Eria Raukura (also known as Eria Tutarakauika), photographed here in July 1913. He wears his particular frock coat, which was edged with gold braid and upon the cuffs of which appeared the words 'Holy Church', while the same words in Maori, 'Hahi Tapu', were on the collar. (Ringatu tohunga usually do not wear vestments.) His right hand is raised in the act of homage to God, the gesture of the Ringatu worshippers from which they took their name: 'Ringa-tu', the upraised hand. *National Museum*

people said after three days.' He answered, ' "I am really that King." ' ' "Here I am, with all my people." '[51] In place of salvation ushered in by a King, Rua offered salvation through himself as that King.

By going to Gisborne with all the elders of the Tuhoe, Rua had fulfilled the task set him by Te Turuki. The Tuhoe, Te Turuki had said, had the God and the covenants; they needed only union, 'kia tawharautia ai a Tuhoe', 'that the Tuhoe may be sheltered'. Now the elders had come together and thereby the prophecy had been fulfilled. Or, as one Tuhoe elder put it shrewdly, the purpose in their being taken 'was in case Rua's word was in error – they could not with conviction belittle him.'[52] This union of Tuhoe was ritually sealed. Rua was baptized as the New Messiah, *Te Mihaia Hou*, by Eria.★ Then, in August, Rua and his followers went to Rangitata, on the uppermost reaches of the Hangaroa river, where he built his first circular 'booth' or chamber of unity, *te tawharau*, to complete Te Turuki's command. It was also an imitation of the rough 'booths' built by the Israelites. In this manner, Rua's identity was confirmed.

From the fulfilment of Te Turuki's command, Rua turned his attention to building the promised City of God, in the lands of the chosen people

★ 'Eria', exclaimed a Waimana informant, expressing the strong regional affiliations that still exist, 'What do you want to bring him in for? He belongs to the other side! He'll makutu you!'

Rua speaking outside the Commercial Hotel, Whakatane, probably 23 March 1908. The photograph was taken by H. Fortune, licensee of the Whakatane Hotel. *Auckland Institute and Museum*

themselves. In August 1906, before leaving Pakowhai, he let it be known that he would be returning home, 'when his time has arrived',[53] but it was not until June 1907 that he and his followers returned to Maungapohatu, to build there ' "a habitation for God and man" '.[54] In the intervening months, Rua wove together a disciplined group. By the middle of 1907, they had adopted the name by which they are still known, the Iharaira, the Israelites. They had begun to let their hair grow in imitation of the Nazarites of old. They had given up tobacco and alcohol: Rua neither smoked nor drank. At this time, he seems to have taken pleasure in speaking freely to his audiences, a feature of his prophetic role which seems to have declined in later years. There are many descriptions of meetings held at Pakowhai or on the roadsides, where he skilfully rebutted ribald comments and sceptical banter, and astonished hecklers with his detailed knowledge of the Scriptures.[55] In March 1908 he was photographed speaking outside the Commercial Hotel in Whakatane. His walking-stick is raised – firmly in the tradition of the Maori orators – and a hesitant crowd has gathered around him.

Rua's claims in these first years varied. Many derived from Christian as well as Jewish teachings. He performed the miracle of feeding the multitude – with two 'fifties' of flour.[56] He called himself the 'twelfth prophet',[57] twelve being the sacred number of the tribes of Israel and of the house of Christ, in Te Turuki's teachings. He was Moses,[58] to whom God had given the tablets of the law. But the name which he finally took for himself was Hephzibah – Hepetipa – the daughter of Zion. This he adopted in fulfilment of that prophecy of Isaiah which he had taken as his text: 'Thou shalt no more be termed Forsaken; neither shall thy lands any more be termed Desolate: but thou shalt be called Hephzibah, and thy Land Beulah: for the Lord delighteth in thee, and thy land shall be married'.[59] Hephzibah is the restored Jerusalem, when God's delight shall again be with her.

Soon he revealed the portents of the final days. From Rangitata, he announced that White Island would erupt; a great earthquake and tidal wave would destroy all those who remained in the low-lying valleys of the Whakatane area. In March and April 1907, many families in these districts sold off their stock and farming instruments – usually at low prices – and abandoned their work. The money they raised was required by Rua as their contribution to the founding of the New Jerusalem. They came together in one of the several camps which sprang up in the area, waiting for the second coming. In March 1907, Elsdon Best found many of the 'Native hamlets' to be deserted

of man, the people thereof having removed bag and baggage to the Messiah camps . . . . A great number of Rua's followers have been for some time past living at large camps – one at Haupapa, one at Te Waimana, and one near Te Teko. All Natives have been warned by Rua to leave their homes, sell all portable property, and go and live on the hills in order to avoid an appalling deluge which is soon to overwhelm all lowlying lands. At Te Waimana I recently found sixty tents full of Natives so living, besides numerous parties living in whares, cottages, &c. Many left Ruatoki, sold horses, ploughs, &c., and are now living at Kekataone,† as we term the Waimana camp. These people have ceased to work for Europeans, and are spending their money on food-supplies. . . . The few Natives left at Waikirikiri, Ruatoki, have cut a track from their hamlet up the range near by, through fern and scrub, so as to be able to quickly escape from the predicted deluge when it comes.[60]

Apirana Ngata recalled meeting two of Rua's converts, who had worked themselves into a ferment by reading the Scriptures and had become completely convinced that everything in the prophetic books, particularly Revelation, indicated that Rua was the One to fulfil the Scriptural promises. They had come to Opotiki to turn their milking cattle, calves, draught horses and farming implements into such money as they could get. They sold, he said, three horses worth £35 each for a total of £30.[61]

One Ruatoki family remembers this period now with some chagrin. Rua took them to Ohope and to the sea, for the first time in their lives. As the tide came up, higher and higher on the shore, they became afraid. Rua explained that it was the beginning of the last deluge, in which all the land from Taneatua to the Ruatoki valley would be drowned. They joined the migration to Maungapohatu. Some three years later they learned that their land had not been swept away and they returned home, only to discover that others of their kin were living on it and claimed shares by right of occupation. Rua they now cursed – 'pokokohua' – the worst curse possible, because of the violation of the sanctity of his head.‡[62]

In these ways the people gathered for the great migration. Some came up the Whakatane river, some from Ruatahuna, but most from the Waimana valley. On 16 April 1907 Rua delivered a formal message, sent from his camp at Rangitata, to the *Poverty Bay Herald*.

A Message from Rua. – Rangitata, Waimaha Nui-a-Rua, 16th April, 1907. New Jerusalem, the Holy City of God (Rev. xxi., 2).§

---

† Madtown: Best called Rua, 'Rua the Keka', or Rua the Madman.
‡ It means, literally, to put the head or skull, *upoko*, into an iron cooking pot.
§ 'And I John saw the holy city, New Jerusalem, coming down from God out of heaven, prepared as a bride for her husband.'

Poverty Bay Herald, 23 April 1907

At 3 o'clock in the afternoon of the above-mentioned date, the Israelites gathered together under a booth (Jonah 4, 5).ǁ
A question of land was brought forward by several persons for discussion, and in consequence the Leader Hephzibah . . . has finally determined the said question by having sworn and established before God, to be a habitation for God and man, the block of land known as Maunga-pohatu, containing 20,000 acres.[63]

From Rangitata, the prophet returned to the Waimana valley and from there he finally departed on 5 June, almost a year after the journey to Gisborne, with four hundred followers, on the inland trek to Maungapohatu.[64] At the foot of the sacred 'Mountain of Stone', Maunga-pohatu, he built the New City, Mount Zion, the City of Deliverance. Mount Zion also means the 'Mountain of Stone'; God's purpose was clearly revealed.

The decision to leave the camps in the Gisborne district seems to have been partly influenced by mounting criticism. There had been, from the beginning, strong local hostility. One who went with Rua, Parnell Titoko, remembered how short of food they were, when the chief at Pakowhai, Patoromu Ruru, refused to welcome them. Then, as a miracle, the river rose in flood and the waters rushed down upon them carrying corn, potatoes, and the small sweet marrows, kamokamo.[65] Everyone who was there knew now that Rua 'must be a true God'.[66] The *Poverty Bay Herald* made much of Rua's company of 'mighty eaters', and handed out standard advice on the value of plain hard work as the means of educating the 'Native' away from such cranks as Rua. The publication of a police report praising the discipline which Rua imposed on his camps[67] did little to silence the cries. Colonel Thomas Porter, veteran of the campaigns against Te Turuki, was sent to Rangitata, because of rumours that Rua was building a fortification; he was happy to report them completely untrue. But he also thought that he had managed to persuade Rua to leave the Gisborne district and return home.[68]

Perhaps the mounting hostility of the Takitimu Maori Council was equally persuasive. Their attempts to get him to move had fed a rising controversy among the Maori elders. The Takitimu Council were concerned about the many Maoris who were travelling with Rua and who would become a burden on the local marae. They considered his actions to be 'unlawful'. Their suspicions were heightened when he announced that he would take land here from the Pakeha (paying compensation) and subdivide it among his followers. To their surprise Te Hurinui, himself a principal figure on the Mataatua Council, argued forcefully against them. Rua, he said, had broken no laws: he had camped on private land with the permission of its owners; he had come not with a message of vengeance but simply as a teacher to his people in times of peace.[69] An anonymous but articulate supporter of Rua, 'Ngatiawa', also said in his account of this confrontation, 'Our main idea is to act within the scope of the law.'[70] Powerless to act, the Council could only grumble, but a new issue soon compounded their anxieties – the ban which Rua placed upon the attendance of the children at the Native schools.

At first, in May 1906, Rua took the children from the Waimana school, to 'remove' the tapu from them. He placed them on the bank of the river and splashed water up onto their faces with branches.[71] By June, he was asserting more: that there was no longer any need for the children to learn English, as the language would shortly not be used, when all the Pakeha were sent away.[72] Later he maintained the prohibition, arguing that at the schools the children had learnt only European vices.[73] At Maungapohatu, he said, they would learn some of the necessary skills, but without being exposed to European 'evils'. When the Waimana people followed him, in June 1907, the

---

ǁ 'So Jonah went out of the city, and sat on the east side of the city, and there made him a booth, and sat under it in the shadow, till he might see what would become of the city.'

local school closed for good. Others, at Ruatoki, Te Teko, Te Whaiti and Waioeka were also seriously affected and Kokako school, near Lake Waikaremoana, shut down. The schoolmaster wrote that Rua had not only persuaded the people to take their children away but also

2 Commanded that their land must be sold to the Europeans; & says:–
3 The King will be in Gisborne on 1st March [1908]
4 From 1 March 1908, God will teach their children in their homes.
5 God will give the Maoris more land, when they have sold the land they now own etc. . . . .¶[74]

These drastic commands and the closure of two relatively new schools gave fuel to the existing controversy over the harmful nature of Rua's influence upon his followers. This view, expressed by the Maori mediators in Parliament, led directly to the passing of the Act to Suppress Tohungas, in September 1907, though the powers given to the Native Minister, Carroll, were not, in actuality, large. Nor did he himself wish to foment trouble. By 1907 nearly all the Maoris of the Urewera and Bay of Plenty were followers of Rua.[75] Their political grievances were articulated by him. Carroll found himself, in 1908, having to mediate between the 'forces of order' and those of the Messiah, without any real increase in his authority. But if the Act itself remained a dead letter, the issues which provoked it were still very much alive. For in 1908 Rua took up the question of the Urewera lands; the methods of his leadership and the nature of his objectives brought the Tuhoe to the brink of civil war.

Rua insisted that any sale of land in the Ureweras, any right to settle there, and any grant of prospecting licences should be determined by himself, as the Messiah of the Tuhoe, and not by the Pakeha government in Wellington. In this stand he was making very clear the Tuhoe desire to direct their own affairs. There were, of course, other voices. In particular, there was Merito of Ngatiawa, the chairman of the Mataatua Maori Council, and even more prominently, Numia Te Ruakariata, known usually as Numia Kereru, a major Tuhoe chief from Tauarau, in the Ruatoki valley. Kereru had gone to Gisborne with Rua, but like Merito, nursed a very considerable distrust of Rua's activities and sought government support in opposing him.

In May 1907, Rua had first sketched out some of his proposals at a meeting at Ruatoki. They included a refusal to pay the dog tax, imposed by the government but collected in Maori areas by the Maori Councils and intended as a means of controlling the number of dogs in the kainga. It was much opposed in Maori communities and had fed the movement for political separation in other parts of New Zealand several years before Rua took it up. More important was his plan to sell a portion of the Tuhoe lands to provide capital to defray survey expenses and to raise money to enable them to work the lands fruitfully. He also argued that all the Tuhoe must follow his instructions so as to strengthen his cause.[76] To whet their appetites he later announced that the Governor was to visit Maungapohatu in October, after which, upon his return to Wellington, he would send boxes of gold to Rua for distribution among the faithful.[77] He had, he claimed, already received a letter from the Governor offering to buy the land at Rua's valuation. For those who still doubted, he also announced that the two-tiered chamber which he was building at Maungapohatu would soon replace the present Parliament in Wellington. He himself would occupy a throne and appear as King; his Twelve Disciples would sit in the upper chamber and eighty would sit below, as in the Legislature.[78] (When Parliament burnt down, in December 1907, his vision was seen as prescient.) Rua's prophecies reinforced his political

¶The authors have found no other reference to this revival of the notion of Edward's visit, although there are a number of references to the postponement of the original visit, as late as September 1906.

Numia Kereru (right), chief of Ngatirongo at Ruatoki and main opponent among the Tuhoe of Rua's movement. He is with Tutakangahau, major chief of Tamakaimoana and informant of Elsdon Best. To Best's great dismay, Tutakangahau became a follower of Rua. *Alexander Turnbull Library*

determination that the Tuhoe should exploit their lands for their own benefit, and to this end he proposed that he alone should issue licences to the gold prospectors and invite settlers, Maori and Pakeha, to the Urewera country.

It was this bid for undivided leadership which provoked the ire of other Tuhoe chiefs, particularly those who saw their best hopes in cooperation with the Liberal government and the relatively influential Maori members of Parliament, James Carroll and Apirana Ngata. Kereru, in particular, hoped that by cooperation, rather than confrontation, the provisions of the Urewera District Act might actually be implemented and the General Committee finally established as an effective body. By the beginning of 1908, the antagonism between Kereru and Rua had reached flash-point. Kereru had attempted to persuade Carroll to impose the Tohunga Suppression Act upon Rua, as a practising tohunga who had asserted that only those who followed him to Maungapohatu would live.[79] What was more, wrote Te Pouwhare of Ruatoki, a close associate of Kereru, in February 1908, Rua had now invited European prospectors to form a gold mining company with him. The *Rohe Potae*, the closed lands of the Urewera, were being 'ill-used by this mad tribe Tuhoe'.[80] The flood of protests to Carroll continued. Te Wharekotua wrote angrily from Ruatahuna:

The first of his words of strife-raising is that he take the whole of this land so that he may be the '*mana*', he will not agree that the policy of the Government shall touch this land.
Second word: That his Council is the permanent Council to administer the lands.
Thirdly: that a ring ('moria') be fastened to the noses of the chiefs who have remained aloof from his works.
Fourthly: On the day after the first meeting Rua handed the land over to Hiwa* principal man of the Gold Mining Company . . . .[81]

Kereru and Te Pouwhare, with government approval, summoned a meeting of all the Tuhoe at Ruatoki in March 1908 to discuss these issues and to elect a General Committee. Because conflict was expected, the Premier, Sir Joseph Ward, decided to visit Rua and Kereru before the tribal meeting was held. This dramatic encounter took place on Monday 23 March on the beach front at Whakatane. It was early in the morning and the town was crowded with people. Rua arrived at daybreak, seated in a gig with some of his wives and accompanied by a large group of followers. Distinguished by their shoulder-length hair, they gathered at one end of the narrow beach; at the other were the followers of Kereru, or the 'loyal group', as the *New Zealand Herald* insisted.[82] They stood gesticulating at each other. In the centre of a selected guard sat Rua, in a chair placed close to the water's edge. Three of his young wives were grouped behind him. He remained seated, displaying no emotion or curiosity as Ward walked down the beach towards him. He kept his eyes downcast and his followers stood silent. Kereru and his supporters greeted Ward with 'ringing cheers'. But as Ward approached Rua he acknowledged the Prime Minister with 'a bow of Chesterfieldian condescension'. His long hair was caught under a grey felt hat and fell in long 'waves down his back'. As he bowed, his hair hid his face from view. After some quiet words were exchanged, Rua agreed to a private discussion with Ward. According to the *New Zealand Herald*,

Rua came out from the conference a different chief. He walked down the beach and harangued his followers at some length. 'What's he saying,' whispered one of the white bystanders to a half-caste Maori linguist. 'He's telling them that it's no use trying to go against the Government. Their chiefs are too powerful . . . .'

*Perhaps Hiwi Make, or Hugh Macpherson, whose signature appears in an entry of 1908 in Rua's Ledger book for the Maungapohatu bank. He was a well-known local figure who succeeded his father-in-law, Andy Grant, as the District Constable at Te Whaiti, in 1923.

Some of Rua's followers on the waterfront at Whakatane beach, 23 March 1908. Rua has left his chair; three young wives remain seated. Notice the plaits worn by two of the men; it was their 'ordinary' style. The long combed hair was for special occasions and photographs. Photo by H. Fortune. *Auckland Institute and Museum*

Below
Sir Joseph Ward meeting Rua on Whakatane beach, 23 March 1908. Rua remains seated in what is presumably a pub chair. The pepper tree in the background still stands, opposite the Commercial Hotel. *Caisley Collection, Alexander Turnbull Library*

Rua talking with some of his followers after meeting Ward, 23 March 1908. Photo by H. Fortune. *Auckland Weekly News, 2 April 1908*

Then Ward addressed each of the factions publicly. He thanked the followers of Kereru for their loyalty and asked them to help to reconcile the differences in the forthcoming meeting at Ruatoki. To Rua's followers he said that he could not accept all that Rua had asked for. In particular, his request for his supporters to be placed on the European electoral rolls (presumably because they were outnumbered in the Eastern Maori electorate) was unacceptable, for Maoris have 'special representation of their own'. As to Rua's desire to have a separate Maori government, he said,

'I told Rua . . . that in New Zealand King Edward is King, and is represented here by his Government. There can be no other Government or king. . . . there can't be two suns shining in the sky at one time.'

Hereafter, this meeting came to be known amongst the Israelites as the 'Ceremony of Union'. From this time, Rua maintained, as the first principle of his political beliefs and his prophecy for the future, the maxim, 'one law for both peoples', *Kotahi Te Ture Mo Nga Iwi E Rua*, under the Crown. He would interpret the Union as a promise that they would enjoy the same laws as they enjoyed 'the one sun that shone above our heads.'[83] (Nowadays it is said that Rua replied to Ward, ' "Yes, there is only one sun in the heavens, but it shines on one side – the Pakeha side – and it darkens on the other." We have come to think of it that way, that the sun represents the two people, one who is in the light and one who is in the dark. But in the future it will end in one law for both, one law to govern all. We will not stay on the dark side.'[84])

There is little doubt that Rua was flattered by Ward's personal visit; on other issues and on other occasions he would refuse to deal with any but the highest. On this occasion he also agreed to go to Ruatoki and to 'fix it all up' at the planned meeting, which Carroll was to attend. Rua went to Ruatoki for the conference, which opened on the 25th, but deliberately left before Carroll arrived and camped about nine miles (fourteen kilometres) away. His spokesman was again Te Hurinui. The separation of the two factions was clearly evidenced by the cropped hair and traditional ceremonial dress worn by leaders of Kereru's contingent, while the Iharaira were conspicuous by their long locks and European clothing. They sat in a huge circle on the ground, facing each other. Rua had placed a tapu on the meeting-house so that none could enter it. Around the edges of the marae he had also set a boundary line, with a turnstile at each side. All who crossed had to sprinkle themselves from the containers of water placed beside them. In this way, the mana of the marae was protected. No Europeans were permitted to enter, because, it was argued, their pipes and tobacco would violate the tapu.[85] Inside the boundary the *korero* took place. A blast on the conch shell regulated all activities: the lighting of the fires, the emptying of the ovens, the summons to *kai*. About five hundred people gathered for the meeting and, while the men spoke, the women chattered amongst themselves (many of the younger ones displaying bright-coloured parasols) and the children played.

Rua, after the meeting with Ward. Photo by H. Fortune. *Jessie Tizard, Whakatane*

Hurinui spoke first for the Iharaira: a patriarchal figure who gestured firmly with a twisted wooden walking-stick, as he emphasized his points. He denied Kereru's charges of their disloyalty and asserted forcibly their recognition of the one King and the one government. They wished only for a separate local government for their own affairs.[86] Hori Tawaki, whose long black ringlets were decorated with combs, a common style among the Iharaira, then spoke on the contentious issue of gold mining. The revenue from the gold would, he said, help to pay the survey costs on their land. He read out an advertisement of Rua's offering to sell prospecting licences to Pakeha – for £11,400 – and fixing the fines for Maoris (£4000) and Whites (£5400), for prospecting without his licences. Kereru replied in anger. All that Rua's people were trying to do was to exploit the minerals for their own advantage, whereas it had been agreed that the country should be freely opened to all prospectors who carried government licences and not those granted by one section of Maori owners. He challenged Hurinui's professions of loyalty; for Rua to name himself ' "Lord of this world" ' was to set up in opposition to the government. Again Hurinui contended that they were not opposed to the government: ' "All we want . . . is simply to hold on to our lands. We do not want it to all disappear." '

Surprisingly, the mediation of Carroll and the powerful Taupo chief, Te Heuheu Tukino, brought about a reconciliation. At the end of the three-day meeting, Te Hurinui agreed that the Iharaira would send a party to Wellington to discuss the exact terms for opening the Ureweras for prospecting and settlement, within the frame of the existing law. Te Heuheu, who had himself been converted by Ngata to the policy of cooperation, persuaded them to accept the idea of a General Committee to take the decisions for all the Tuhoe country and urged them to begin by electing their local block committees.

The grievances voiced by Hurinui were part of a discernible pattern of dissent, found amongst the older Maoris in particular. They had learnt to distrust land legislation and suspected that European-established committees and councils were only surrogates for effective power. The *Rohe Potae*, the closed borders of Tuhoe, had first been broken by the Liberal government's decision to allow prospecting there and although the Iharaira in 1908 seemed to be seeking only their own benefit, they were afraid for the future. As Rua's followers had told the visiting geologist Dr James Bell in February, they were concerned that 'these rocks would serve as a pretext for the occupation of their country by whites'.[87] When Te Hurinui asserted at Ruatoki that the Treaty of Waitangi bound the government to give them assistance,[88] he was speaking with the knowledge that the only alternative source of capital that they had was the land itself, which Rua was seeking to control. At Ruatoki, Rua was kept notified of all developments by despatch riders, who carried messages to and fro,[89] and it was he who would go to Wellington in June. There he would seek again the 'right of administration' of the Tuhoe lands for himself.[90]

Rua's apparently contradictory behaviour in the succeeding years must be seen in this context. His objective, to gain control and capital, led him to attempt to sell a portion of the Tuhoe land directly to the government. In November 1908, after gathering nearly 1400 signatures in support, he offered 100,000 acres, regarding this act as his part of the fulfilment of the Ceremony of Union.[91] But Carroll insisted on dealing only with the General Committee, as the collective voice of Tuhoe, and refused to negotiate directly with him at any stage, causing him to withdraw the offer.[92] Instead, early in 1910, Rua joined the protest movement for a separate Maori government under the 'rights' of the Treaty of Waitangi, which had been initiated the year before by old Tana Taingakawa, the former Premier of the King Movement.† Taingakawa's petition to Edward VII, which the Iharaira signed, was directed specifically against Apirana Ngata's policies and the land laws, which had been 'expressly enacted for the purpose of plundering and otherwise forcibly taking the small residue of the lands remaining to us'.[93] This message was brought to the Tuhoe in terms directly reminiscent of Rua's first vision. Tupara Tamana of Ruatoki warned Carroll:

The laws of Taingakawa are here in the boundaries of Tuhoe. . . . Taingakawa claims to be able to restore the confiscated lands of Tuhoe, that is; that the Law and Edward will restore them.[94]

The restitution of the confiscated lands, which Te Turuki had prophesied would be recovered, was only one issue raised by Taingakawa. The 'laws' also sought a restitution of control, or the 'Chieftainship' promised to the Maoris in the 'covenant' they made with the Queen of England, the Treaty of Waitangi.‡ For Rua's followers, the main issue was the restitution of control over their lands. Among the tribes, Ngatitawhaki, Ngatikoura, and Te Urewera, 'the people of Rua',§ were committed to Taingakawa, and the Tuhoe, once again, almost came to blows. In an act of deliberate rejection of the General Committee, the three tribes began to lease portions of their lands. They would, they said, never accept the regulations of the Committee; they had 'taken hold of the Treaty of Waitangi, which has reached us, – the articles in which have been adopted by us in regard to ourselves, our lands, our cultivations, and all things belonging to us, so that their laws will in no way apply to us. We wish to retain to ourselves the power to lease our cultivations (clearings) to Europeans . . . . The General Committee have announced that the power to lease our cultivations lies with them. . . . If you confirm it we will never consent, never, never.'[95]

Finally, Apirana Ngata determined that Rua must be brought onto the General Committee if it were to function. In June 1910 Rua and Paora Kingi, an old follower of Te Turuki and now a leading supporter of Rua, were appointed to the Committee. As a consequence of this recognition, Rua,

† The King Movement had originated in 1858 as an attempt to unite the tribes, but after its defeat in the Anglo-Maori wars of the 1860s, it became largely an association of the Waikato people. From about 1892, there began a revival of attempts to make the King Movement the voice for Maori grievances, partly instigated by Tana Taingakawa, the Premier and second Kingmaker. However, in 1909, he split from the then King, Mahuta, and attempted to lead a wider Maori 'federation', seeking a 'Government for themselves upon their lands'.

‡ Clause ii of the Treaty reads, in a literal translation of the Maori text, 'The Queen of England agrees . . . [to give] to the Chiefs, the Hapu, and all the people of New Zealand the full chieftainship (rangatiratanga) [of] their lands, their villages and all their possessions. . . .'

§ Elsdon Best placed Ngatitawhaki (of Ruatahuna) and Ngatikoura (of Waimana and Ruatoki) as major sub-tribes of Tuhoe. Te Urewera was used both as a title for the whole tribe and as the name of a section of Tuhoe. In this context it was apparently used as a sectional name, the Te Urewera chief being Anani Te Ahikaiata. Sectional divisions were quite clear in these disputes, Ngatirongo (of Ruatahuna and Ruatoki) being strong supporters of Kereru, their principal chief.

under the authority of the General Committee, sold, in 1910, some of the lands of his followers to the government at its nominated price.[96] Forty thousand acres in the Maungapohatu district and in the basin of the Tauranga river (now usually called the Waimana river) were sold for £31,000. In this way he raised the capital for the support and development of New Jerusalem.‖ The land surrounding his community was to be a reserve.[97] The Tauranga river block, however, he hoped would be opened to settlement, to create a stock route through the Waimana valley to Maungapohatu.[98] In fact, it too became part of the Urewera national reserve, which had been Ngata's primary purpose in acquiring this land. The long-term result was much as Kereru had foreseen in his original discussions with Seddon. The initial debt for the costs of surveying the 650,000 acres of Tuhoe land was £7000; and the effect of the land sales was only a 'temporary prosperity', which he deeply distrusted.[99] Between 1910 and 1921 more than half the Tuhoe land would be alienated to the Crown.

Rua's actions were dictated by his conviction that, as the prophet, he was an independent authority. He had protested against the fact that only the Committee had the power to sell: 'what I object to is that the mana goes to the others'.[100] But in 1910 the mana of transaction with the government had come to him and so he accepted it. When he visited Wellington in 1908 he had insisted on his right of control and reminded the reporters that he had foreseen that the 'pakeha runanga house (Parliament) would end in flame, four days before the great fire came'.[101] But violence was not in his own nature. The journalists who visited him in his lodging-house at Molesworth Street found him to be a gentle, quietly-spoken man, 'who was not the least 'aggressively inclined towards European settlers and pakeha methods.'[102] He had come to Wellington, he said, 'partly to try to draw the European and Maori together'.[103] He received his visitors in a little sitting-room which had been set apart for him in the lodging-house, because he and his followers did not smoke. The reporter for the *Otago Witness* found there a 'happy family party of about a dozen, including two or three Maori ladies, comfortably seated around a pleasant fire'.[104] When he walked through the streets of Wellington, many turned to watch, for 'his dark flowing locks and calm tranquil expression would make him conspicuous anywhere.'[105] Only the waterside workers jeered.

Rua's dealings in land had taken him to the capital, but his prophetic mission also led him to new places. He is still remembered preaching in the side streets of Auckland, his hair tied in two long plaits and accompanied by some of his wives.[106] A particularly significant event, closer to home, was the *hahunga*, or ritual cleansing of the bones of the dead, held at Waimaha in February 1915. On this occasion, he and about fifty followers rode down from Maungapohatu to Hukanui's settlement there, with the intention of exhuming the bones of some who had died in a typhoid epidemic about seven years before. He joined up with Eria Raukura, who had ridden from Waituhi wearing his long black coat and carrying before him a large portmanteau.[107] The episode seems important because of the meeting of the two men and the portmanteau of human bones which Eria brought; it is said, by some, to have contained the bones of Te Turuki. Eria, according to the Gisborne people, was one of the four men who knew where Te Turuki's bones had been taken, when they were secretly excavated from Te Horo, near Wainui. The others, all of whom died with their knowledge, were Rikirangi Hohepa, Huri Te Ao,

‖ The land within the Maungapohatu block was sold at 12/- an acre; the Tauranga block was sold at 15/- an acre. The transaction was completed in March 1912; of the total paid, £31,353, Rua said he received £100 as his portion. In fact, he took 'tithes' from the shares sold by his followers.

Lord Plunket at Tauarau, Ruatoki, April 1909. This visit was intended to show government support for Kereru, as the major Tuhoe spokesman at the 1908 Maori Congress. But Rua, who had already met Plunket on his tour of the Ureweras, came down to Kereru's marae with about two hundred followers and insisted on talking with him there. In this photograph, Kereru is seated next to Plunket in the centre of the group. The house, Rongokarae, then possessed paintings as well as carvings on its porch. *Auckland Weekly News, 8 April 1909*

and Wi Kotu.[108] It is possible that this episode, disrupted by the Gisborne police, was to be a ceremonial cleansing and polishing of the bones of the prophet. Eria had been seen some years before with the unusual portmanteau, near the Ohiwa harbour, and it was said then that he was taking the bones of Te Turuki for polishing.[109] On the Gisborne coast it is believed that Eria brought Te Turuki's bones to Rongopai, when Heni Materoa, James Carroll's wife and the leading figure in Poverty Bay, finally gave her permission. It will probably never be known if this occasion, when Rua and Eria met at Waimaha in 1915, was a sanctification of Rua's descent. Later, Eria was to deny Rua's claims and to become the leader of his own section of the Ringatu faith, called by its original name, Te Hahi O Te Wairua Tapu, and was, in his turn, considered an apostate by members of the registered Church.

Most of the time Rua travelled within the borders of the Mataatua country, visiting the marae up and down the valleys. He denied that he was inducing the people to become converts; he merely visited according to Maori custom to exchange greetings.[110] But in this way he maintained constant contact with the different communities. In 1909 he made sure he was on Kereru's marae at Ruatoki, when the Governor, Lord Plunket, called. But when the formal photograph recording this visit was taken, Rua had absented himself: he would not be part of the 'endorsed' leadership. For he still maintained, at least in 1908–9, that the government was in bond to the Maori, under the Treaty of Waitangi. Five million pounds were still owed.[111] He held out hope, in what seem to be crude terms: one million of this debt had been promised immediately to Rua, as part-payment. But in offering hope, Rua was also generating energy in men whose lives were otherwise bounded by desperation. The faith which he had created in himself is perhaps best illustrated by a favourite story of these years, told and retold. Hepetipa went to Lake Waikaremoana (or to the Whakatane Heads) with a large crowd of followers, who came to see him fulfil his claim that he could walk on the water. Standing on the shores of the lake, he turned to them and said, ' "Do

Rua with some of the Iharaira on a visit to Lake Waikaremoana, 1909. The little girl beside Rua is his eldest daughter Whakaataata (Meri Tukua), by Pinepine. Te Akakura stands on Rua's left. Teka Hekerangi, one of Rua's twelve Disciples, stands at the right, foreground, wearing a long ribbon from his lapel. Tauru Tuhua, another of the Disciples, is third from the left. The men have thrown their hats to the ground and all have the long hair of the Iharaira.
On the same occasion, in the lower photograph, are Te Wairama Taoho, also one of the Disciples, and born a hunchback; Makarini Te Ahuru, Rua's chief secretary; Te Akakura; Hori Taia. (The three men may also be identified in the previous photograph, dressed in the same clothes.) Rua stands on the rock in the centre. *Hardwicke Knight Collection, Dunedin*; *Dr Riley Album, National Museum*

you truly believe I can walk on the water?'' ''Yes,'' they cried with one voice. ''Then there is no need for me to do it,'' he replied, and walked away.'[112]

The prophet had won nearly all the Tuhoe to him. He claimed to have 1400 followers (on the basis of his land petition), and even those who were hostile conceded that the Urewera were now Rua's people. For them, he built a new City, in their ancestral lands. To this City, the Pilgrims went.

Rua, boating on Lake Waikaremoana, 1909: the same occasion as the previous two photographs. Te Akakura is seated beside him. Te Wairama is just visible in the little boat following. *Dr Riley Album, National Museum*

Below
Some of the Riwaiti, April 1908. Their youthfulness – and their poverty – is apparent.
Back: Pita Te Taite (Pita Te Rika; Pita Te Wharenui), who was Pinepine's brother; Teka Hekerangi (Tekaumarua Teka; Teka Te Rika; Teka Te Kaawa); —; —; Tuhua Pari (Tuhua Te Taite; Turei Tuhua); —; Tauru Tuhua.
Middle: Tatu Horopapera; Wharepapa Hawiki.
Front: Te Wairama.
Photo by George Bourne. *Auckland Institute and Museum*

44

2 The New Jerusalem: The Community at Maungapohatu

And many people shall go and say, Come ye, and let us go up to the mountain of the Lord, to the house of the God of Jacob; and he will teach us of his ways, and we will walk in his paths: for out of Zion shall go forth the law, and the word of the Lord from Jerusalem.   (Isaiah 2, iii.)

And Rua said to them, the Iharaira must hold fast and the Riwaiti must stay in Maungapohatu here, for that is the Mountain of thé Lord and of our Forebears. In the olden days our ancestors had their own mountain. But it was not like this; this is the Mountain of the Lord, the sacred Mountain. Even though he went away, Israel must remain. He likened it to the era of Moses.[1]

The migration of the Tuhoe to Maungapohatu from the coastal valleys and from the interior began in earnest early in 1907. From his camp at Rangitata, Rua had sent forth the twelve Riwaiti, or Levites, each to his own area, to gather their people for the exodus. These men were Rua's Disciples, sent out to teach the Scriptures and to make known the words of the prophet. Their number was twelve, in imitation of Christ's Disciples (and they were often called, in consequence, *Te Tekaumarua*, the Twelve), but they were actually modelled on the order of Levites which Moses had set up by God's command: 'thou shalt appoint the Levites over the tabernacle of testimony . . . and over all things that belong to it . . . and they shall minister unto it'.[2] They were drawn from different groups from within the *Rohe Potae*, so as to represent the nation of Israel, or the twelve tribes.[3] They were a disciplined body, bound by such strict rules of tapu that they could not, for example, enter any kitchen, for fear of contamination from the food prepared there. They were also bound by strict codes of sexual restraint, and in particular, their sergeant (*haihana*) was required to be celibate. The first group had been formed in 1906, before Rua went to Gisborne, and their primary duty was to study the Scriptures and to take the religious services which were held twice daily – at 7 in the morning and at 3 in the afternoon – as well as on the Saturday Sabbath. These men Rua sent in advance, 'everyone, everyone to his own place,'[4] to initiate the pilgrimage. From Ruatoki, from Te Teko, from Te Waimana, from Waioeka, from Ruatahuna, and Te Whaiti the people came: about five or six hundred by the middle of 1907.[5]

They arrived at Maungapohatu as the winter set in. Those who were there can still remember the harshness of that first year: the potato crop failed and there were no wild pig to be had. Tatu, one of the Riwaiti, had to go back to Te Whaiti to collect six sows to start their own breeding colony. At least fifty people died that winter, most of them children, from the inadequacy of the houses, an outbreak of typhoid which came from the valley camps, and a measles epidemic which devastated the community.[6] Sometimes there was nothing to eat but huhu, and the coarse toi leaves, normally used only for clothing.[7] But from this inauspicious beginning, the community struggled on to a first summer of great plenty.[8]

Two groups had come together to build 'te pa tapu o te atua', the sacred pa of the Lord: the Tuhoe, about half of the entire tribe, and the Whakatohea, who through confiscation were almost landless. Their leader, and one of the early Riwaiti, was Ngakohu Pera. With him came the young girls Whaitiri Rewiri, who married Rua's eldest son, Whatu, and Taupaki Te Kora, who

Ngakohu Pera, chief of Waioeka and one of the Riwaiti. With him are Heeni Tawhaia; Teratahi Matiu; Raiha Kahika. *Whakatane Museum*

Hiruharama Hou, April 1908. The building was stained a dark yellow-brown, with the posts and other features picked out in white paint. The emblems were in the same colours. On the post to the left there was a framed picture of a two-tiered and double-roofed temple, perhaps an image of the Temple of Solomon and the model for Hiona, Rua's meeting hall. The roof of Hiruharama Hou was covered with rubberoid and was unfinished when this photograph was taken, as were the windows, still covered with calico. But the glass, transported unbelievably on packhorses, was waiting to go in. The boards were all pit-sawn at Maungapohatu, and the nails were said to be wooden. The house had sixteen rooms and measured 40 feet by 40 feet, equal in breadth and width, like King Solomon's, and of about the same proportions (II Chronicles 3, viii). At this stage, there was only a verandah at the gabled ends; by 1916 there was also a verandah on the northern side. Standing on the front verandah are

Continued, p. 47

married Rua's second son, Toko. To signify this union of the two Mataatua tribes, Rua constructed the house of the Lord, Hiruharama Hou (New Jerusalem), built with two gables. One side was for Tuhoe and the other for Whakatohea.[9] There were two entrances and two corridors, and on the front verandah there were also pillars, in imitation of the house which King Solomon built for the Lord. The decorations were different for the two sides. Whakatohea, on the right, was plain; on the left hand column Rua placed the emblems of his kingship over the world. Between the Crown (on the top), and the World (the open sphere), was an emblem for the Church, Te Wairua Tapu (the Holy Spirit), which was the first name of the Ringatu faith. This name Rua kept as the name for his Church. The Ringatu emphasized the role of the Holy Ghost as the universal spirit which spread the gospel and thereby united the people, and Rua sometimes called his the 'third religion', as the religion of the Holy Ghost, the third Person in the Trinity.[10]

Hiruharama Hou was built in conscious imitation of the house built by Solomon,[11] according to the pattern given him by his father David. This visual parallel was intended to confirm Rua's lineage as King and Messiah. From David and Solomon sprang the Son of God:

I Jesus have sent mine angel to testify unto you these things in the churches. I am the root and offspring of David, and the bright and morning star.[12]

This mythology was emphasized also in the construction of the gaily coloured meeting hall and court-house, Hiona (Zion), which was virtually complete by the end of the first winter.[13] This was modelled after Solomon's court-house, the house of the King and the place of the 'throne of mercy'. Hiona was a

completely circular building. The upper storey was set apart for the prophet, his wives, and the two chiefs who at first formed a 'council of three' with Rua, to pass judgments in contentious local cases.[14] This level could be entered only by an outside staircase, upon which Rua also built a round platform, where he used to speak to the people and commune with the Holy Ghost. The upper storey measured about twenty feet (six metres) across and twelve feet (four metres) high, while the lower storey, 'the great court', was about sixty feet (eighteen metres) across and about twenty feet (six metres) high. The entire building was built of totara sawn at the pit, with a split-paling roof. It had been made circular by soaking the framing timber in the river and hammering it into place when wet.[15] The lower chamber was lighted by windows with wooden shutters, the upper by a skylight. There were two doors, on opposite sides, into the lower chamber, and in the centre there was an elevated rostrum, above which was a large circular opening into the upper chamber. At a later date, a 'fireman's pole' was put in between the two storeys. Originally there was no means of passage between them from inside, and the fireman's pole maintained the separateness of the two, being a one-way means of access! The body of the people met in the lower chamber and there, too, a larger 'council of twelve' met for hearings and judgments.[16] On these occasions, above them in the upper gallery, out of sight and listening to all that went on, sat the 'uplifted and glorified one' – to quote the Reverend John Laughton.[17]

Outside, Hiona was brightly painted, the background white, with diamonds of yellow, and clubs of blue. Its forerunner had been the round house at Rangitata, but that booth, constructed in imitation of the tabernacles of the Israelites, had not been ornamented and was built of split palings and canvas.[18] It is possible to interpret the significance of some of the designs painted on Hiona. Playing-card emblems were used in the nineteenth century

Continued
Rua, some of his wives, and some of the Riwaiti: ? Whirimako; Pinepine; Rua; Whakaataata, his daughter; Te Akakura; Mihiroa; Pehirangi; Wairimu; Whaitiri, Whatu's wife; Te Aue. Of the men, only Te Wairama is identifiable, with his short stature. Photo by George Bourne. *Auckland Weekly News, 23 April 1908*

Above
Hiona, Rua's court house and meeting-house. It was also known as Te Whare Kawana, the House of the Governor. When the *Auckland Weekly News* reproduced this photograph, on 23 April 1908, it commented that the designs were taken off the aces of the club and diamond suits. The kowhaiwhai panels painted each side of the lower part of the doorway consisted of red, black and yellow ochre.
Back: Te Akakura; Te Aue; Rua; Whaitiri; Whakaataata; Mihiroa.
Middle: ? Whirimako; Pinepine.
Lower: Pehirangi; Wairimu.
Photo by George Bourne. *Auckland Institute and Museum*

as mnemonics to the Scriptures by those who could not read. Te Turuki had devised such a system for the Ringatu, and Rua followed his example on the walls of Hiona. The club was the emblem to stand for the King of Clubs. He is the King who is yet to come: the last King in the line of David, or 'the bloodline of the Lord'. The Kings in the other suits have been 'played', but the King of Clubs is 'the Coming King': Rua.[19] He is the King with the power to command, the last King, who will bring everlasting peace, 'maunga-rongo'.[20] 'He is the King we are waiting for'.[21] Rua claimed to be the 'mystic fourth' in a line of Maori prophets: Te Whiti, Titokowaru, and Te Turuki. Three had fallen, as prophesied, but the fourth would stand:[22] the King of Clubs.

Linked with the emblem of the clubs was that of the diamond. It represented the Holy Ghost,[23] and it was also the diamond of Maungapohatu. 'It is hidden now. When the right time comes – when he comes back . . . . That is the time.' The diamond was one of the twelve stones allocated respectively to each of the tribes of Israel. The diamond was seen as Rua's stone; and 'Rua is the diamond of Maungapohatu'.[24] Hidden jewels, as here, often stand figuratively for knowledge or energy which is to be recovered and used for a specific purpose.

The bright colours of Hiona were derived primarily from the Bible. They are the colours of the royal vestments of Israel, blue and white, with a crown of gold. They were worn by Mordecai, who was considered 'great among the Jews', as one who led them out of captivity. He came 'seeking the wealth of his people, and speaking peace to all his seed.'[25] Mordecai came from Babylon with Zerubbabel, the rebuilder of Jerusalem, from whom Te Ua, the founder-prophet of the Pai Marire religion in Taranaki, had taken his identity. Rua said simply that he himself resembled *all* the prophets of Israel.[26] Rua also used the royal colours of Israel on his later houses. It should be added, too, that blue (rare in the Bible) is a favourite Tuhoe colour and is seen as the colour of life.[27]

Rua also placed the emblem for the King of Clubs on the large entrance gate on the eastern side of the pa enclosure. Alongside it he wrote his own sign, 'MIHAIA'. In Ringatu belief the Trinity is seen as consisting of separate entities, each one of the Three being the Word of God. Rua often spoke of himself as the mouthpiece of the Holy Ghost – the power through which the Wairua Tapu spoke[28] – or as actually identified with the Holy Ghost. 'He said, "I am the Holy Ghost." ' 'He is the Wairua Tapu, higher than the sun'.[29] He is 'coequal with God' in a Trinity consisting of 'God, Christ and Rua'.[30] But the four-pointed star at the centre of the entrance gate carried the emblematic sense one step further. It is the emblem of the Star in the East, prophesied by Te Turuki: the star which was seen over Maungapohatu, showing that the Son of Man was born again. 'It was just like in the old Bible. There was a star like that.'[31] The four points symbolize the Trinity completed, with Rua himself as the 'mystic fourth', the Word made flesh again. (Wiremu Ratana similarly adopted the four-pointed star for the emblem of the Trinity with himself, the *Mangai* or mouthpiece of God appointed by the Holy Ghost. Later, his emblem was changed to a five-pointed star, to include the Ministering Angels.) The four-pointed star and the diamond are both quaternary: emblems of completeness.

On the eastern gate there also appeared the signs of the comet and the morning star. The comet seems to be seven-pointed, while the star possessed eight points. Four and eight-pointed stars are traditionally signs of warning and change,[32] as is the comet. The comet, here marked by a chevron on its tail, was Halley's comet (Hare Kometi), which was due to reappear in May 1910. Mangere Teka explains the meaning of the two stars in this way:

The Dome of the Rock, Jerusalem. The pattern of yellow diamonds, made of tiles, probably provided an image for Hiona. This mosque was often called the Temple of Solomon in nineteenth century Biblical literature.

Opposite
'MIHAIA': Rua standing beneath his sign in painted wooden letters over the eastern entrance gate to the *wahi tapu* enclosure.
In this photograph, the club or trefoil is clearly established as Rua's emblem. It should perhaps be noted that the trefoil had been used by Te Ua and Te Whiti to represent the Trinity and it would be adopted with the same symbolic reference by Wiremu Ratana. It is possible, therefore, that it carried a double significance for Rua.
The two stars are moving in opposite directions and only the back of the comet is seen here. There is a design in the centre of the morning star, but it cannot be deciphered.
The containers standing at either side of the gate held water for washing, on entering and leaving. Notice the turnstile.
There are wildly varied statements about Rua's physique (he was a boxer as a young man): on police records, he was five feet, eight and one quarter inches tall. Photo by George Bourne, Christmas 1908.
Auckland Institute and Museum

These three photographs were taken in 1908 by George Bourne. In the first (above), taken in April, the rawness of the newly felled timber and the sheer size of the community are the conspicuous features.

The second (top right) was taken at Christmas and shows the main street looking from the northern entrance into the *wahi tapu* enclosure.

The third (lower right) was taken in April and shows the main street and Rua's house, at the top of the rise, its roof still unfinished and calico over the windows. Some tent houses, visible here, have vanished in the Christmas photo. This photo was taken looking down from Hiona and standing in the street are some of the Riwaiti. Below Rua's house is the double storey building which was both bank and office. The lower storey contained the savings bank, 'Moni Peeke o Rua Hepetipa'; the upper, the office for Rua's secretaries, who kept the record books. *Auckland Weekly News, 23 April 1908; 14 January 1909; Auckland Institute and Museum*

There are two main stars, Hare Kōmeti and Kopu [Venus]. Those two stars are the two Sons of God. We believe there are two Sons of God. . . . The Father, Son and Holy Ghost are three people, but they all came from the Father. He had two Sons. This is how we believe.

Venus is the morning star, the emblem of Christ. The comet is the promise of the New Messiah, the fulfilment of the Covenant with God.★

Hare Kometi was also emblazoned on one side of the north-eastern door into the lower chamber of Hiona. As well, there appeared a pair of monograms, C A on one side and A V on the other.[34] These monograms were dictated by Rua but their meanings were left unexplained, even to those who built Hiona. The signs remained part of his secret knowledge, as prophet.[35] Neither 'C' nor 'V' are letters in the Maori alphabet. The monograms could be emblems for Alpha and Omega, the First and the Last, 'the beginning and the ending', 'which is, and which was, and which is to come'. Occasionally, Alpha and Omega were depicted by these monograms, which could have been copied from illuminated letters in Rua's large English-language Bible. They could also be Masonic. Hiona itself was inspired from an image of the ancient mosque, the Dome of the Rock, illustrated on the previous page. This bright blue and gold building is said to be built on the site of Solomon's temple, and in illustrated Bibles of the late nineteenth century it was often labelled the 'Temple of Solomon'. The temple was also a Masonic icon. The mosque was decorated with friezes of golden diamonds. Although its base is octagonal, in many Scriptural illustrations it appears to be circular. But Hiona still retains its mysteries. As Kino Hughes of Ruatoki said, in explanation of the cryptic letters, 'what is in my heart you cannot see, only myself knows what I've got in my heart'. Rua kept this knowledge in his heart.

In these, and other ways, Hepetipa wove the Old Testament legends into the daily lives of the Tuhoe. He had built their place of deliverance. It was at the foot of the mountain of the Tuhoe, which itself possesses strange powers. The clouds which forever move and swirl over its rock pinnacles traditionally give warning of its moods and guidance to those who live below. The presence of important strangers in the valley is known to the people of Maungapohatu long before they arrive at the settlement; the descent of the mists on the mountain gives warning, in a land where visitors have usually meant danger. It is a *maunga tipua*, a mountain of power, a mountain to be feared. For the cloud is watchful, as it was for the Israelites in the wilderness: 'where the cloud abode, there the children of Israel pitched their tents.'[36]

Hepetipa built his city in these ancestral lands, 'Beulah' (*Peura*) as he now

★ 1910 came and went apparently without a murmur in the press about Rua and the comet, although other Maori prophets used Halley's comet as an image of destruction, which would sweep the Pakeha away, and 'so dispose of the lands question, noxious weed inspectors and all the other barnacles of civilisation'.[33]

termed them, the lands which had been but were no longer forsaken. He divided the City of God into two parts. Both the house of the Lord, in which Rua lived, and the Court of the King were placed inside the tapu pa enclosure, along with a number of other buildings, including the bank, the general store, and the council room for his secretaries. This inner area, the *wahi tapu*, was demarcated by a fence, the wall of separation, which set apart the sanctuary from the profane.[37] No food, and for a while, no fires were permitted inside the enclosure. There were two main entrances, one on the north side, the other on the east. Beside each entrance, containers of water were placed for washing, upon entering and leaving, so that the tapu of the place was preserved, and its contamination in turn removed. As well, everyone had to change their clothes by the entrances; work clothes belonged outside.[38] All the

kitchens and eating places were located beyond the enclosure, one by the
eastern entrance being used by Rua and his wives.

By April 1908, the community had taken on its essential first shape. Seven
hundred acres (two hundred and eighty hectares) had been cleared and about
fifty houses built, a mixture of tents and split-paling structures. There were
two streets within the *wahi tapu* area, both lined by rows of houses. The streets
were lit with oil lamps made from a slow-burning dried tree lichen, *pangi*,
which formed the wick.[39] Old or insanitary houses were burnt and replaced.

All the visitors to the community were impressed by the strict standards of
hygiene imposed by Rua. Each family had its own whare. Water was supplied
from several springs and pools, which had been brought down through the
township by diverting a nearby stream. They were grouped in a series, like
those built by Solomon in Jerusalem. The 'topmost' pool was generally
reserved for cooking needs, the second for domestic washing, and the third for
bathing, all located outside the *wahi tapu* area.[40] There were also basins at
frequent intervals so that the people could wash before eating. Initially, a clean
towel was also supplied daily at each basin by the sanitary committee, which
acted under the Council's direction. What was maintained for a much longer
period was the twice-weekly inspection of the houses, on Wednesdays and
Fridays. Dust – even on the outside fireplaces of blue clay – brought a 3d
fine.[41] The wood-piles had to be neatly stacked, the chips swept up, the
latrines clean, the domestic animals, pigs and fowls, penned. All dogs had to

Maungapohatu, city of the mist, April 1908. Photo by George Bourne. *Auckland Institute and Museum*

be tied up as a matter of course. Horses were allowed on only one of the two streets and then they had to be walked and not ridden. The usual fine for breaking any of these community rules was 3d, but a 1/- – a large sum – could be imposed. These laws Rua carried with him outside Maungapohatu when he visited other communities. One Ruatoki marae committee complained in 1910 that Rua was imposing similar rules upon them while he held a hui there. These laws, posted under the ordinance of the 'Council of the Lord of this World', Hepetipa, included a £5 fine for the selling of liquor. The Council also reserved to itself the right to fine anyone an undefined sum for causing trouble in the pa.[42]

By these rules, Rua attempted to impose discipline and some degree of 'Europeanisation' upon the Tuhoe communities. The photographer George Bourne, writing for the *New Zealand Herald* in 1908, described Maungapohatu as a kind of 'half-way house',[43] for those to whom the European world gave no place, except through the exploitation of their physical labour. Maungapohatu, he said, would help them to leave behind some of the 'primitive' aspects of their past and also stop them drifting. At Maungapohatu they would gain knowledge of some European ways – 'where', as Rua put it, 'such ways were of a beneficial character'.[44] Meals could be bought, for example, at the cost of 1/6, and platters and cutlery were in daily use; orchards had been planted, and breeding cattle brought in. At the same time, the people were maintaining their autonomy. Rua seems to have seen the community,

with all its rules, as the means of transition into the wider community in which he recognized they must participate. For those who did leave, and who returned for advice and guidance over the years, he would say, ' "I have prepared you so that you must seek for yourself." '[45] Those who were brought up at Maungapohatu as children remember particularly the orderliness which he achieved. They remember the ways in which he divided the food he had purchased for them – flour, sugar and tea – equally among the families. They remember how the too-scarce meat was portioned out each Saturday, after the services. When the carcase had been cut, one of the elders would call out for each portion, 'Who will have it?' Each family took a share without knowing which portion it was that they had called for; in this way the good and the poor cuts were allotted without favouritism. Discipline was the essential pillar of the Maungapohatu community. Achieved by the force of faith, it was maintained by the family's power to approve the actions of individual members. This discipline was continually reinforced through the religious services.

Each family would gather to say its prayers and worship twice and sometimes three times a day. Every family had its own particular prayer, *panui*, a text memorized from the Bible, and hymns and *waiata*, also taken direct from Scriptural verses, would be chanted. There were no books, only the teaching of the Riwaiti to instruct them. On Friday evenings the children were given their passages, which they must learn by the following week. The Saturday services began on the evening before, and lasted from 9 at night until 10 or 11 on the following morning, during which period the people went without food.[46] Early on Saturday morning, the entire community would assemble inside the *wahi tapu* enclosure, standing in the open air before Hiruharama Hou to worship. These services were always taken by the Riwaiti; often Rua did not appear at all. The family services he visited as he felt inclined;[47] on Saturdays he sometimes spoke from the verandah of the House of the Lord, when filled with the power of the Holy Ghost.

The services followed the essential forms of the Ringatu church, and indeed the people insisted that theirs was the religion of the 'uplifted hand'.[48] But Rua introduced certain changes which, in actuality, set the Iharaira apart. From the penultimate *karakia* (prayer) of the Ringatu service, he removed one critical

Morahu, the young follower of Rua who acted as a guide from Waimana to Maungapohatu in April 1908 for the *New Zealand Herald* photographer, George Bourne (nicknamed 'Taipo' because he was also a magician). Morahu agreed to go with Bourne only after a lengthy discussion among a group of Rua's people, whom Bourne found camped at Waimana and who at first objected to his proposed journey into the interior, thinking that he had come to prospect for gold. Morahu carries a case which probably contains photographic equipment. *Auckland Institute and Museum*

word: *pokaikaha*, which expresses the troubled and unhappy nature of man. The Ringatu pray to God, 'Lord, look down upon us, perplexed and in doubt'. Rua took out this word, saying that it belonged to the past and the times of Te Turuki. Now the Son, whom Te Turuki had prophesied, had come and there was no longer cause for confusion and doubt. Instead, lasting peace, *maungarongo*, had replaced division and uncertainty, and this phrase was used instead at Maungapohatu. The times of *pokaikaha* were at an end. This fundamental change in worship was to separate forever the Iharaira from the Ringatu. Up the Waimana valley, to this day, 'we do not use the *pokaikaha*',[49] and this is seen as blasphemy by the Ringatu church.

Hepetipa also brought to an end the observance of the Twelfth, the sacred day of the Ringatu, which commemorates 12 May 1866 (or, variously, 1868), when God revealed the Covenant of Israel to Te Turuki, and 12 February 1883, the day of his pardon, the day 'he came back from the other side'. †[50] This change in ceremony was one of the earliest introduced by Rua, who also abolished the four other sacred days in the Ringatu year – 1 January, June, July and November – keeping only Saturday as the Holy Day, in accordance with the teachings of the Scriptures. The 'first essential' of his faith was to be 'Religion as directed in the Holy Scriptures'. ‡[51]

† The Ringatu give many different explanations for the setting aside of the twelfth of every month, including, particularly, the mystic nature of the number twelve, for the twelve tribes of Israel and the twelve gates, one for each tribe, in the walls of the New Jerusalem. Te Turuki's Twelfth encompassed all these symbols.

‡ Directly contradictory evidence on the observance of the Twelfths (and of 1 January and July) was given both by Rua and his chief secretary, Makarini, at Rua's trial in 1916. Rua stated that the Scriptures instructed his people to observe heavenly and earthly rites on the twelfth of every month. 'They sought to make the 12th a Holy Day, so that they could perhaps reach some means of salvation. January 1 marked the division of the years, and, therefore was kept holy.'[52] (The Ringatu keep 1 January to celebrate the entry into the New Year, 1 June to mark the start of planting, 1 July as the middle of the year and thanksgiving, and 1 November (or December in some regions) for the gathering of food. These are the 'four pillars' of the faith.) Our informants however support the *earlier* documentary evidence: 'the Twelfth is nothing – the Iharaira don't take the Twelfths'; 'the Waimana people won't take the Twelfths'; 'Rua stopped the Twelfths because he is the Son of God'. Were Rua and Makarini then asserting their Ringatu orthodoxy, in 1916?

Portrait of Rua, April 1908. George Bourne said this photograph was the first posed study Rua had allowed. *Auckland Weekly News, 23 April 1908*

Opposite (bottom)
'Rua's people gathering for one of the frequent services held at the settlement'. Photo by George Bourne. *Auckland Weekly News, 23 April 1908*

Below
The people of the Messiah pose on part of the main street of Maungapohatu. This photograph may have been taken on the same day as that opposite (bottom). Photo by George Bourne. *Auckland Weekly News, 21 January 1909*

At a later date (exactly when it is not known), the Messiah instituted his own sacred Birthday, choosing 23 December.[53] From the 20th the Iharaira would gather for Scriptural recitations, when they told their own story and held their services for a period of four days. The 25th they also kept as the day set aside to celebrate Christ's birth. But on the fourth day of the Iharaira celebrations the gathering would break up and everyone would leave for other marae for the occasion of Christ's day. When it came to the time to cut the Christmas cake (tame), Rua always absented himself, for to cut and eat that cake meant that the next Christmas celebrations had to be held at your own marae.[54] 'Rua never touched that cake.'[55] The 23rd, as Rua's 'name day', is still maintained by the remnants of the Iharaira.

The sacred day of worship was Saturday, the Jewish Sabbath, which had been adopted by Maori *poropiti* before Rua. The choice of Saturday rejected the most emphasized element of Christianity as taught by the early missionaries: the sacredness of Sunday. Saturday asserted the identity of the Maoris as the chosen of.God, those to whom he has promised to return, and those to whom the land of Canaan will be restored. Saturdays are remembered, by all those who were brought up at Maungapohatu, as the focus of their week. But Makarini's statement, made at the trial of Rua in 1916, that all days were holy days and Sabbaths to Rua, was also true.[56] Treating all days as holy similarly rejects the heavy sabbatarian emphasis of the missionary teaching, and permits faith and life to intermingle. The followers of Pai Marire had practised a similar duality, stressing both the sacredness of Saturday and that of each day.[57]

If Rua abandoned the Twelfth in respect of worship, because of the particular associations with events in Te Turuki's life, he kept its importance as a Biblical number for guidance in another respect: the matter of the number

'The rising generation of Ruaites': children at Maungapohatu, April 1908. Photo by George Bourne. *Auckland Weekly News, 23 April 1908*

Rua with some of his wives, on the verandah of Hiruharama Hou, April 1908. This study was taken on the same day as the formal portrait of Rua on p. 55.
Back: Pehirangi; Whakaataata, Rua's daughter; Te Aue; Whaitiri, Whatu's wife; and in front of her, Wairimu.
Front: Mihiroa; Rua; Te Akakura.
Photo by George Bourne. *Auckland Weekly News, 23 April 1908*

of wives appropriate for a prophet. Rua was fond of referring to Solomon as his example in polygamy: 'I am a poor man', when compared with him.[58] Rua's first wife, Pinepine Te Rika, had already borne him four children when he emerged as prophet in 1906. Whatu, or Tane, was his eldest son and was then in his late teens. Toko, his second son, was about three years younger. His eldest daughter was Whakaataata, or Meri, his second daughter, Keita. §[59] All in all, Pinepine, 'the mother wife', bore him seventeen children.[60] By April 1908, however, Rua had taken seven wives, thereby, as he said, fulfilling the vision of Isaiah.[61] Altogether, Rua took twelve wives, most of them from different segments of the Tuhoe and Ngatiraka of Ngatiawa, who lived intermingled with them and were considered as Tuhoe. His purpose was to unite each part of the people to him. According to Cowan, Eria Raukura married him to many of his new wives, in 1908.[62] Pinepine was of Ngatikuri, from Te Uwhiarai marae, Ruatahuna. His second wife was Pehirangi of Te Hamua, from Ruatoki, who was, in 1908, about sixteen; she was a woman of whom he became very fond. His third and favourite wife was Patu, or Te Akakura, a young widow from Ruatoki, who married him as her legal husband in 1908. She was from Ngatirongo, Kereru's people, and from Tauarau, his marae. Te Aue was his fourth wife, of Ngatikoura, from Ruatahuna. Mihiroa of Ngatikuri was from Ruatahuna, and his sixth wife was Wairimu, or Martha Vercoe, a half-caste of the Hamua tribe of Ruatoki. (Akakura, Pehirangi and Wairimu had all been pupils together at the Ruatoki school.) Whirimako, from Te Hamua of Waikirikiri, Ruatoki, and Ngapera

Rua, with four of his wives at Opotiki, about 1908.
Back: Te Akakura; Waereti; Kiha.
Front: Te Aue; Rua.
The women are wearing greenstone set in gold as brooches; Rua, buttoned jodhpurs and a grey felt hat. *Hocken Library, University of Otago*

§The ages of these four older children were given in the list of the shareholders in Maungapohatu and Tauranga in 1901 and again in 1907, but there are internal discrepancies, due to the different times when the lists were compiled, but also to the fact that the Tuhoe, and the Iharaira in particular, refused to register their births. The ages given were approximate and often exaggerated.

57

'Patu', portrait of Te Akakura, in 1908 when she was about sixteen years old. This photograph was taken on the same day as those on pp. 20–21, and may be her wedding portrait. Rua, who was skilled with the *taiaha* weapon, fought for her after her first husband died, with Rakuraku, her husband's father. It was said that Rua had killed the young man by makutu, as the couple had been married for only two months. Photo by James McDonald. *Alexander Turnbull Library*

Opposite (top)
Ngapera, with her mother, Rahia. Ngapera left Rua, but bore him twin sons, Hira and Te Mata, in 1910. This photograph is from the Rewarewa marae, Ruatoki, copied by kind permission of Hira Rua. Photo by Gillian Chaplin, 1978.

Opposite (bottom)
The hand-coloured photograph of Marumaru and Pinepine, which hangs in the present meeting-house, Tane Nui A Rangi, at Maungapohatu. Photographed, by kind permission of the Tuhoe of Maungapohatu, by Gillian Chaplin, 1978.

from the Mahurehure of Te Rewarewa marae, Ruatoki, soon joined them, together with Kiha of Whanaupani of Ruatoki, and Waereti of the Ngatiraka tribe of Ngatiawa living at Te Waimana. His eleventh wife was Te Arani, also from Ngatiraka of Te Waimana, and his youngest and twelfth wife, whom he married much later, at Matahi, was Piimia of Ngatiupokorehe from Kutarere, who were a segment of the Whakatohea living with the Tuhoe since the confiscation of their land. Not all of Rua's wives remained with him. Five, Whirimako, Ngapera, Waereti, Wairimu, and Te Arani, left. Some were jealous. Some found new husbands, as Rua had always intended.[63] Those who remained with him, however, established strong bonds of friendship among themselves. Akakura was the dominant one, the 'rangatira wife', – and the spoilt one, some say. They named her the Queen of Sheba, to whom Solomon gave all she desired. Rua often consulted her; she could be disobedient to him. A song (*pao*) he wrote when imprisoned in Mount Eden jail suggests the strong influence she possessed over the community and him:

> Moe hurihuri ai taku moe i Mautini,
> *I toss and turn in my sleep at Mount Eden,*
> Ko taku tau tonu kei taku manawa i ora!
> *My darling always in my heart who lives!*
>
> Whakaarorangi ai te rere mai a te manu –
> *Straight towards me flies a bird –*
> He karere mai koe na Te Akakura i ora!
> *You are a messenger from Te Akakura i ora!*
>
> Koi ana, Wairimu! Hunaia to poriro,
> *Therefore, Wairimu! Hide your orphan,*
> Kei rangona nuitia e Te Iharaira i ora!
> *Lest the Israelites hear much of him i ora!*
>
> E rere ra, nga wai o Mautini!
> *Flow on, you waters of Mount Eden!*
> Maku hei inu iho hei manawa ra i ora!
> *I will drink to sustain myself who lives!* ‖[64]

If Akakura dominated, Pinepine was the *wahine tapu*, the sacred wife who had been on the mountain. She lived in a separate house of her own, on Rua's decree (as did Pharaoh's daughter, King Solomon's wife). Pinepine's house was built inside the tapu enclosure. Before entering the house every person had to take their clothes off and sprinkle themselves from the water vessels placed at the doorway, so that she should not be contaminated and so be made *noa*, and they in turn not be harmed by her personal tapu. Clothes had to be left outside her house. On leaving, the clothes and the body had to be sprinkled again.[66] When the community built their new meeting-house, in 1914, Pinepine could not enter it. Sometimes at night they saw her peeping in through the rear windows at the assembled company. Nor did she enter the kitchens, or handle food, until very late in her life. Instead she had a friend and servant (*hawini*), Marumaru (Te Kuini) who was always with her, and cooked her food for her. (Much later, it is said, when Rua lifted the tapu upon her and she cooked for herself, as an old lady at Matahi, she invariably burnt her food.)

‖ In 1928, when Rua sang this *pao* he explained it to Arapeta Awatere as follows: Wairimu had borne him a son, for which he was much pleased. *To poriro* is, literally, 'your bastard', but here it is used affectionately, as the 'fatherless child'. The Iharaira did not approve of Rua's favouring Wairimu, because she was not of high rank, and he tells her not to do anything that will attract their attention and annoy them. (Wairimu, as a part-European, was nick-named Patu Pakeha; Patu Maori was Te Akakura. They were often quarrelling.[65]) In July 1917, while Rua was in prison, Wairimu had a child by another man. In his later explanation, Rua may have concealed this original meaning.

Hiruharama Hou, with the four flags flying before it, Christmas 1908. The uppermost flag is Rua's:

KOTAHI TE TURE
MO NGA IWI E RUA
MAUNGAPOHATU

The second flag is the new national flag; the third, the red ensign, commonly flown over a marae. The lowest flag is the *tipuna* or ancestral flag which Rua flew, TE TAHI O TE RANGI.

As well as these flags of joy, the people of Maungapohatu possessed a black flag, called Te Wairua Kino, the evil spirit, which they flew as a flag warning of hostile visitors. Rua stands in his check jodhpurs, at the base of the flagpole. Te Wairama, the woman, and a man whose face is hidden by the flag, are wearing ceremonial cloaks of different styles. The old man may be Te Wakaunua; the little girl on the right is Whakaataata. The small house (to the right) was Pinepine's house; it was later replaced by another, on a different site. Photo by George Bourne. *Auckland Institute and Museum*

Marumaru used to feed Pinepine, in the same manner as those who had recently handled the dead had to be fed.

It is clear that certain forms of tapu were practised at Maungapohatu, but these were the laws of the 'new tapu', imposed by Rua. It was the old 'hoodoo tapu', as Mangere Teka puts it, which he abolished: 'he had a ministry to rebuke all that'. Consequently, although Rua lifted the tapu from the old graves, tapu practices connected with death were observed as a part of the law of the community because a Nazarite was polluted by the dead. At another level, these were basic 'laws' of hygiene. (The feeders, often children, took great delight in teasing the hungry men, holding pieces of bread flat on the sticks before them so that it was virtually impossible to take the food.) The uncut hair of the Iharaira restated the tapu nature of the human head. Rua himself was tapu. On festive occasions, he would put on a little blue and yellow cap, with a tassel, which freed him from tapu. The cap was in imitation of the decorative pins made from the feathers and head of the native parakeet, *porete*, which the people often wore for gay occasions.[67] Rua's bright cap allowed him to behave as an ordinary man.

Tapu was also associated with certain objects. Rua's large English Bible was deemed especially tapu because it was the Covenant of the Iharaira with God.[68] Rua built a house for it, Te Whare Kawenata, at the south-west end of the pa enclosure. Pinepine looked after the Covenant and only she could enter the house. The Bible was large, about eighteen inches (forty-six centimetres) thick, with an embossed velvet cover; Rua claimed it weighed 77 pounds – for the 77 sins of mankind.[69] (It was said to be so heavy that it could not be carried with ease except by straps on the back.) The Covenant was believed to have come originally from Israel; it had been given to Rua in 1906 by the Tuhourangi, when he came to them as Te Turuki's successor. They, who had refused to give it to Te Turuki and thereby, it was believed, brought about the Tarawera eruption which had destroyed much of their land, now gave it to Rua.[70] It was an act of conciliation by those who had fought in the wars against Te Turuki. In the Covenant, Rua kept a red ribbon marker inscribed with a Scriptural message of peace.[71]

His other message, the union of the people under the one law, he inscribed on the flag for Maungapohatu. The words, 'KOTAHI TE TURE MO NGA IWI E RUA MAUNGAPOHATU', were stitched onto a Union Jack. Rua devised this flag as the symbol of the 'Ceremony of Union' with Joseph Ward. The flag itself had been given to Tutakangahau by the Governor, Lord Ranfurly, in 1904.¶ Rua explained that it was, with its inscription, the 'symbol on our part' of acceptance that 'the authority of the Government extended over native lands.'[72] With this flag Rua flew another at Maungapohatu – the new national flag, upon which he had had stitched 'TE TAHI O TE RANGI', denoting his descent from the miracle-working ancestor of the Tuhoe of that name. Te Tahi O Te Rangi protected his descendants, particularly from the wrath of the sea, and his task was to succour his people in times of trouble. He had prophesied that he and his descendants would acquire 'fame by means of mercy', not by revenge.[73] In this way, Rua linked the ancestral traditions with his mission, while *Kotahi Te Ture*, in turn, looked to the unity of Edward's people (and later, George V's people) under the law. These words became the political centre of Rua's movement and it is for this reason that Rua Hepetipa remains a living force for the Tuhoe, when his messianic claims have largely faded. For the law, many Maoris would argue, is not in practice equal.

Rua was not, in any sense, a seditious leader, as his own iconography makes plain. But he was deeply concerned about the law and about concepts of legitimate autonomy, under the Crown, in much the same way as the

¶ All marae were given flags, upon which they inscribed their own words.

'God Save the King', 1920. The drawing of George V and New Zealand, which hangs inside the meeting-house at Maungapohatu. Photographed, by kind permission of the Tuhoe of Maungapohatu, by Gillian Chaplin, 1978.

Inside Hiona, April 1908. The tiered seats filled the space between the inner rostrum and the outer walls. The emblem of the club can be seen over the door. Photo by George Bourne. *Auckland Weekly News, 23 April 1908*

nineteenth-century leader in the King Movement, Wiremu Tamihana, had been. Tamihana had found no conflict with the 'law of God and the Queen', and that of the new Maori King.[74] At Maungapohatu, Rua established his own court-house, Hiona, and dealt out his own justice. The 'council of twelve' acted as jury. They sat on the elevated rostrum in the centre of the lower storey, at the famous circular table which Rua had built so that it would revolve at a touch. Documents were kept in a rotunda-shaped cabinet, possessing twelve compartments, built in the centre of the table; the twelve men sat in their appointed places, the table was revolved, and each drew, by the lot of revolution, the name of an apostle – such as Matthew, or Mark – for the session. Two witness boxes, one half-moon shape and one square, stood on opposite sides of the rostrum, at the head of two stairways which led up to it. According to the district constable, Andy Grant, who visited Maunga-pohatu quite regularly – and who had sympathy with Rua in the early days – Hepetipa insisted that the jury must not see the prisoner but only hear him speak, lest by his magnetism they were persuaded against their better judgments. After the evidence had been given, the first of the twelve wrote down his opinion, in silence, then pressing lightly on the table, revolved it so that the paper passed to the next. When all the verdicts were written, they were sent by a pulley up to Rua where he waited in the upper storey, with two chiefs who acted as his advisers. After examining the evidence and the verdicts, this 'council of three' pronounced judgment.[75]

Hiona was the seat of Rua's earthly rule. In 1907 he asserted that it was to be the means of abolishing the Parliament in Wellington. Early in 1915, he was still using the same idea. With the advent of the millennium, 'when his hair was at its full length', he said, all the kings of the world would congregate at Maungapohatu. He had built Hiona with thrones for them all. The highest of the royal thrones was for George V, the next for the Kaiser, and there were others for lesser monarchs. But the highest throne of all would be his.[76] More immediately, Hiona was the parliament or council chamber for the entire community. There, all matters were discussed, the people gathering for the *korero*. On these occasions, Makarini acted as usher. The larger Council of the elders, which included some of the Riwaiti and others in the settlement, also met there. Maungapohatu was run very much as a cooperative community.

The Council of elders, called the Council of the lord of this world ('te Kaunihera o te ariki o tenei ao'), was established early, and Rua seems to have

Ledger transcript, 8 May 1909. Transcription and translation by Rangi Motu (minimal punctuation has been added). *Alexander Turnbull Library*

Maungapohatu
8 Mei *1909*

Ko te Ra tenei i tukua motuhaketia mai ai e te ariki te mana motuhake ote whakahaere o nga mahi ki te kaunihera me nga whenua katoa ara nga Tikanga katoa. A ko te ra hoki tenei i uru mai ai a Wiremu Tepou ki te kaunihera

A ite 6 karaka ite ahiahi ka tuhera te whare o te kaunihera.
Ko nga mema i tenei hui

Ko	1	Kirihi		2	Ko Tuhua
Ko	3	Tu tewharau		4	Ko Mahia
Ko	5	Teroihe		6	Ko Kahukura
Ko	7	Puriri		8	Ko Wiremu Tepou
	9	Ko Pita	Tiamana		
	10	Ko Te Makarini			

A i tu Te ariki a hepetipa i homai ite moni ki Runga ki te teepu a te kaunihera £10.0.0. A i whakamarama ia i mea ko tenei moni Hai kaha mo koutou hai Timataranga ma koutou ki te whakatiputipu. Ite mea kua ka haere koutou ki te Rapu haere i to koutou huarahi e puta mai he tika kia koutou ina hoki ta koutou hui imahue ake mo a koutou Taonga Taputapu Taonga kararehe. Heoi Noreira ka homai e au te moni nei Hai kaha mo koutou ite mea kua kite mai ahau Kua kaha haere [a] koutou ki te whakahaere i to koutou huarahi. No te mea kai te pau i au to koutou oranga te Whangai ma nga rawakore Kaati ko tenei whakahaere a te ahua o te moni nei. Whiriwhiri hoki tetahi tangata tika hai whakahaere ite moni nei ina ra hai tiaki ahakoa kino a waho i roto kia pai. Heoi tena Kai au ano to koutou ora e mau atu ana ara nga moni o a koutou mahi. A kaati ki te kite mai ahau ite kaha ite tika o ta koutou haere Na ka homai ano e au
Heoi aku korero

Maungapohatu
8 May 1909

This day the lord gave over complete control and administration of all things; land, and all future plans, to the council. Also, today Wiremu Te Pou became a member of the council

At 6 o'clock this evening the house of the council was declared open.
Members present at this meeting were

1	Kirihi		2	Tuhua
3	Tu Te Wharau		4	Mahia
5	Te Roihe		6	Kahukura
7	Puriri		8	Wiremu Te Pou
9	Pita	Chairman		
10	Te Makarini			

The lord, Hepetipa, stood and gave a sum of money on to the table of the council, £10.0.0. He then explained and said 'This money is to strengthen you and for a beginning for you to multiply. As you are going to go your own ways you will benefit as at your previous meeting to discuss your belongings and animals. Well this is the reason I give you this money to give you strength because I can see now you are getting more confident to organize your ways. As it is I have used your wealth to feed the needy so this is the way this money is to be used. Decide on a person of integrity to control this money, that is to look after it, even though his outward appearance may not be pleasing yet 'tis the inner self which will matter. Enough of that I still hold your wages that you have earned for the work. So if I am satisfied you are trying hard and am pleased with your efforts well I will give you more
This is all I have to say'

attempted gradually to pass over to them much of the decision-making for the actual community. He set up the savings bank, 'Moni Peeke o Rua Hepetipa', and the 'well-stocked' general store, but both came under the Council in their daily operations. The first leader, *kawana* or *kai whakahaere*, of the Council, was Te Miini Kerekere, who came from Pakowhai. He kept a Ledger book for the bank and in it he put the records of the first deposits – and the withdrawals – as well as the sales in the shop. In May 1909, Rua apparently transferred all authority in the secular affairs of the community to the Council, save the payment of wages which he kept within his own control. He instructed them

Aperira 12 1908

Te ra tenei i Rui ai i nga Karaihe o Kake Wahine nga tangata Rui

———————————— Kotahi ra ————————————

Rau Karaka	utu ra	7/	. 0
Tuhua		7/	. 0
Wharepapa		7	. 0
Hitaua		7	. 0
Toko		7	. 0
Whaatu		7	0
Miki		5/	0
	Ko te Huinga	£ 2 . 7	. 0
Tame		. 7	0
	Koia nei te turu	£ 2 . 14	0

April 12 1908

This day grass seed was sown at Kakewahine. The sowers were

———————————— One day ————————————

Rau Karaka	*day's remuneration*	7/	. 0
Tuhua		7/	. 0
Wharepapa		7	. 0
Hitaua		7	. 0
Toko		7	. 0
Whaatu		7	0
Miki		5/	0
	Total	£ 2 . 7	. 0
Tame		. 7	0
	This is the true total	£ 2 . 14	0

to choose a man of integrity to handle money and seems to have directed their votes in a curious manner, with a reference to one whose 'outward appearance may not be pleasing', but reminding them that it was the 'inner self' which mattered. At a later date, probably in July 1909, a meeting of the Council and all the Iharaira was called 'to vote for a governor, a man to lead and organize according to the correct rulings of the laws' ('Ara he hui pooti i tetahi kawana tangata hai whakahaere ite ahuatanga o nga mahi irunga ite tikanga o te ture').[77] Te Miini Kerekere was voted out and the term decided for the new *kawana* was seven years.★

Miini's Ledger book records many of the early activities of the community. The first entries date from September 1907, and deposits in numbered accounts (24), in the names of many of the elders, including Te Akakura's

★An incomplete record shows votes ('pooti') for the new governor going to Wiremu (? Wiremu Te Pou, husband of Marumaru), and Makarini. Te Miini Kerekere was governor and leader 'under the great lord of this world, namely Hepetipa', from the latter part of 1907 until at least December 1908. In 1908 Makarini was the chief secretary (as he was in 1916). There are three lists of the names of the members of the Council of the lord of this world from the early period. One is undated, but is of this period, and is presumably the Council of twelve, for it contains eleven names and that of the head, 'Te Miini Kerekere'. These names include some of the Riwaiti: Tatu; Wharepapa; Teka; Te Wairama; Ngakohu; 'Piita' is probably Pita Te Taite. It also includes Makarini; Hori Taia; Te Ihi Paerata, who was one of Rua's secretaries ('Kai Tuhi') and the storekeeper in 1908. The other two names are Hori Marohirohi and Maui Marohirohi. Another list of the Council of the lord of this world, dated 27 April 1908, contains twenty names. Miini Kerekere does not appear, although the handwriting seems to be his. This list includes all the above named, and in addition, Tuhua (who by then was one of the Riwaiti); Tame; Kahukura [Pari]; Hitaua [Heurea]; Te Erani (?); Tahu Tiopira; Timi Ereatara; Roihe; and Tarau Hone. The list of May 1909 also includes some of these men. There is no record of the 'council of three' in the Ledger book, but there is one judgment recorded, concerning a damaged gun, on 26 July 1908, which carried Miini Kerekere's signature as governor ('Kaiwhaka Haere') under the great lord, 'te ariki nui'.

father, Ru Hoani, were made in the latter part of that year. Rua also ordered from Auckland, through Andy Grant, 250 bank books for them to use and an official seal.[78] On 23 January 1908, when quite a number of accounts had been whittled away, a grand total was drawn up of 'the money belonging to the people banked in the Bank of the Council of the lord of this world' ('nga mooni a nga tangata Kai te Peeke a te Kaunihera o te ariki o tenei ao'): £455. James Bell, visiting in February 1908, was told that a liberal interest was being paid on all investments and indeed there is a record of twenty percent interest being paid – and of ten percent being charged – for a loan. But Rua said later that he only paid interest on ten-year deposits![79] The bank seems to have been used as a community pool, whereby at least some of the money, put in by wealthier individuals, was given out according to need. The bookkeeping was kept fairly systematically until June 1908, when the regular records for this early period finish (at least in this book). The money was used by the Council to purchase the basic needs of the settlement – flour, cabin bread, sugar, cartridges – and smaller quantities of luxuries, butter and tinned meat, for the privileged. In practice, it seems, Rua controlled the purse and bought the bulk stores, which were distributed among the families. Otherwise, they were expected to provide for themselves. Many remember the shortages of clothing; trousers were a rare item for the boys – one pair of pants a year, if you were lucky. In 1916, when the shop was closed after the police attack and everything in it removed, only the second-hand clothes were left behind because, as they said, 'the coats were disgusting anyhow' ('he weriweri nei nga koti').[80]

In its early days the store did a roaring trade. Between 10 November 1907 and 14 April 1908, the Council received from the shop £394.4.10. The records cease after this, though Hohene Te Kaawa celebrated his success in cutting his account, on 12 April 1908, thus:

This is the day that Hohene Te Kaawa gave one pound to halve Kaawa's account to the shop of the Council of the lord

This is the account	1. 6. 6
Paid this day one pound	£1 0 0
Good!	
Left to pay	6 6
	£1. 6. 6

This account received the official rubber stamp of the bank:

The Maungapohatu families earned their money largely by selling cocksfoot grass seed to the European storekeepers, such as the Bell family of Waimana. The poverty of these families contrasts with the elegance of the clothing in Rua's household. European visitors speculated endlessly on the sources of Rua's money and on the ways it was spent. Rua liked to stress to his visitors that he was running the settlement on a 'business-like' basis,[81] while, at the same time, he constantly urged upon his followers the worthlessness of money. Henry Bell, whose family has run the general store at Waimana since 1906, still remembers the blackened coins which accumulated in their shop from the first years of the Maungapohatu settlement, when Rua used to 'burn the coin' to demonstrate the valuelessness of the money. † The Bell family sent half a sugar bag of blackened coins which Rua had spent in their shop, to the bank at Opotiki. Rua was also said to have burnt banknotes, but Wharepapa Hawiki, one of the Riwaiti, revealed to Bell that it was by sleight of hand, for Rua used only one note on the outside.[82] Rua announced that he intended to burn all the banknotes which came in the first payments for the Tauranga block, as a 'sacrifice'.[83] It was probably this money which he kept. He was also reputed to change the 'worthless' paper notes of his followers for 15 shillings in coins.[84] It is certain that Rua's followers also gave him money. Some earned it by seasonal shearing, others by the lease and sale of land. From these, Rua took a portion or a 'tithe': perhaps £20 from a shearer's seasonal packet of £50. One woman remembers giving him the first money she ever earned, £4, because he had healed her swollen leg. He took the money in his right hand, crossed his arms and placed his hands under his armpits. When he opened his hands the money had gone. For this money, Rua gave, to the Maungapohatu community at least, physical sustenance and personal direction in every aspect of their lives. For those who lived elsewhere, he gave advice and guidance and offered them, through their faith, a 'new spirit'.

At Maungapohatu, Rua also paid the men for their labour. In December 1907, when many were away shearing and the community had dropped to about 150 souls, Rua was paying those who remained 8/- a day, or 30/- an acre, to clear the bush and take out the stumps. The *Poverty Bay Herald* considered this to be a 'very fair price indeed'.[85] In March and April 1908, he was paying a daily wage of 7/- for sowing grass seed at Kakewahine, their neighbour valley on the way to Ruatahuna. Toko and Whatu were both employed, with others, in this work. Rua also actively encouraged the division of the Tuhoe lands into family shares, which had been completed by May 1907.[86] The shareholders could then lease their portions to the government, in cooperation with others. But at Maungapohatu itself, after the land had been cleared and sown in

Preparing for winter: making bedding in a *kainga* in the Ureweras. *Auckland Weekly News, 4 February 1909*

†It is possible, rather, that the coins were those Rua had used in faith-healing because, as the saying goes, 'you can't use the money for sores'. Coins used in healing were often put in the fire as a sacrifice to God. This was a practice from the times of Te Turuki.

Supplies for Rua and his followers being taken from Te Whaiti to Maungapohatu, 1908. Makarini was in charge of the purchases, and for 1907 records exist in the Ledger of the substantial sums given him by the chairman of the Council to make purchases there.
Observe the deeply worn nature of the old track from Ruatahuna, which is still like this in several parts. One visitor, in 1908, commented on the huge numbers of whitening bones and carcases of horses on the Gisborne track, victims, he said, of their masters' zeal. Photo by George Bourne. *Auckland Weekly News, 23 April 1908*

pasture, it was vested in Rua who sold this Tuhoe land back to the people of the settlement, at £2 and £2.10.0. an acre. He urged them that, in this way, they would ensure that the land would never be taken by the government. This manipulative device provoked an irate letter to Carroll from Kereru, one of the Maungapohatu block shareholders, and a member of the block committee.[87] But some of Rua's supporters waxed enthusiastic about the scheme. They said, in this way the land could never be sold to any except a Maori, although it could be leased as pasture to Europeans.[88] By 1909, some of the Urewera lands had been leased, some illicitly to individual Pakeha and others more correctly, under the law, to the government. Eric Ramson, the son of the storekeeper at Whakatane, recalls the visits of the Native Land Commissioners to make payments for the government leases. The two commissioners set up their table outside the Whakatane Hotel, and Rua and the local policeman would join them while the rents were paid out. Once Rua's followers had drawn their portion, they filed up to Rua's table and paid him a percentage.[89] Then Rua would buy all the foodstuffs in bulk, the saddles and horsecovers, (and the rolls of dress fabric, and petticoats, 'panekoti roto', for his wives). On one occasion, Rua spent £900 in the Ramsons' store. Then the supplies, together with the window glass and the sewing-machine and the rubberoid roofing, would be loaded onto the packhorses to be taken back to Maungapohatu.

A portrait of Christ, in the style of late nineteenth-century Scriptural illustrations. This picture was found in Rua's house at Maai, Maungapohatu; it is an image of Christ as the 'Good Shepherd' of Israel, used frequently by Rua. *Anonymous private collection*. Photo by Gillian Chaplin.

Two followers of Rua exchange the traditional greeting, the *hongi*, Christmas 1908. The man on the left is Miki (Wati Te Wakaunua), one of the senior *rangatira* of Maungapohatu. Photo by George Bourne. *Auckland Weekly News, 14 January 1909*

Rua also visited the Tuhoe family communities, the small *kainga* scattered in the valleys of the Bay of Plenty. Here he would set up a tent, or find a little whare, where the faithful could visit him. From the brief-case which he always carried with him, he would take out coloured Scriptural pictures, cut from magazines, and pin them around the walls. One portrait of Christ, with the flowing locks and long robe which were popular in the later nineteenth-century European image of Christ, was his favourite. He would point to it and comment upon his remarkable likeness to the Saviour.[90] His room inside Hiruharama Hou was decorated with many such Scriptural portraits. At the tents or whares which he used as wayside 'shrines', and which were called 'God's house' (such as the one at Eripitana), Rua sat 'in "tapu"' within, while a rope or boundary line was drawn without.[91] A tin wash-basin was placed nearby to be filled with money given by his followers. One of those who witnessed such an occasion remains adamant that for all his dubious methods, Rua used the money he got from his followers to look after their basic needs. 'No one went hungry with Rua'; 'with their money, Rua bought for the whole community'. This is Henry Bell, to whose family store Rua came every two months or so to buy. He would always know when Hepetipa was coming, for the little hunchback, Te Wairama, would appear in the valley on his horse, calling out in his shrill voice, 'Bell, Mr Rua coming'. And Henry and his father Frank would wait outside the shop with their goods displayed, in order to serve Rua, who being tapu in his person, could not enter such premises.

In these early years, Maungapohatu was a relatively wealthy community. Much of the money came from the leases and, later, sales of the land. In these years the pasture was laid, the cattle brought in, and the cocksfoot grass sown, which were to be the bases of the earning income of Maungapohatu. The work was hard and the discipline strict. Tobacco, alcohol, and gambling were banned, in accordance with the laws of Moses for the Nazarites.[92] But this community of 'saints', as they were scathingly called in Whakatane, also knew how to enjoy themselves. Hiona was used as a hall for traditional dances; those who were children before the First World War can remember it, lit up with candles, for such occasions. The dances took place in the centre of the lower chamber, inside the ornamented balustrade. The children also used to play a game, four on a specially-made sprung roller, jouncing around together in the centre arena.[93] By 1914, a separate little dance hall, the *whare kanikani*, had been built, near to Hiona. And there were all kinds of spontaneous games – hand games, games with throwing-sticks, stretching games, jumping games, and running races, which the children played outdoors.

One of the great festivities, which happened to be recorded in photographs, was the Christmas party of 1908. Rua sent Miini Kerekere to Gisborne to invite both Maori and Pakeha to the feast. By Christmas Eve (the 24th), about two hundred followers had assembled, as well as a few Pakeha, including the photographer George Bourne. Rua's wives had brought in bunches of evergreens to decorate Hiruharama Hou. On Christmas Day, the four flags were flying before the house and the greenery was tied to the verandah posts. A long dining-house had been erected just outside the precincts of the *wahi tapu*. Wild pig and cattle had been slain and there were many different kinds of bird: kereru, white eye, and kaka being the favourite of the Maungapohatu people. They served plum pudding, sweet cakes, and aerated waters. In the afternoon, sports were held. There was pole-vaulting, wood-chopping and handicap racing. The bookmakers did a roaring trade. Rua, dressed in check riding-breeches and gaiters, his hair bound up in a roll over his forehead, watched the proceedings with his eight wives, from 'an elevation within his wahitapu fence'.[94] He gave out cash prizes for each event, as well as gifts of finely woven mats, kits, silk handkerchiefs, and money. Those who received

the mats were expected to return the feast the following year. There was, consequently, some reluctance among the visitors to accept them. Before the visitors ate, Rua had addressed them from the balcony of Hiona. The *Poverty Bay Herald* reported, 'After expressing the hope that a number of Europeans would be settled upon the lands that he had placed under offer to the Government, the speaker launched into what may be described as a Biblical preamble, wherein his claims to being the real and only "Messiah," his resemblance to all prominent old Scriptural characters, and his prowess generally, figured largely.' The 'frequent ejaculations of admiration or conviction from his listeners' gave witness to their faith.[95]

Above
Rua's wives bring in the evergreens and flowers on Christmas eve, 1908, to decorate Hiruharama Hou (top photo).
Mihiroa; Te Akakura; Pehirangi; Waereti; Te Aue; Pinepine. Photos by George Bourne. *Auckland Weekly News:* (above) *14 January 1909*; (top photo) *8 September 1910*

The bookmakers at work during the Christmas day sports gathering. Toko Rua stands with his 'squeeze box' accordion, for which he is still remembered. Photo by George Bourne. *Auckland Weekly News, 7 January 1909*

Below
The start of the hundred yards handicap. Photo by George Bourne. *Auckland Weekly News, 7 January 1909*

Opposite (top)
The Christmas feast being prepared: pork, beef and many different kinds of native birds. 'The wahines worked like Trojans, preparing and cooking the food, which vanished in record time before the hungry onslaught of visitors and the inhabitants of the settlement.' Photo by George Bourne. *Auckland Weekly News, 14 January 1909*

Opposite (bottom)
The women, dressed in white for Christmas day (25 December) 1908, bringing in flax mats and pillows for sleeping. Or were these some of the fine mats Rua gave as gifts? Te Akakura, in front, also carries the washing-pails for the *wahi tapu* area. Te Akakura; Pehirangi; ? Mihiroa; Pinepine; Wairimu (at the back); Waereti; Whaitiri; Te Aue; — . Photo by George Bourne. *Auckland Institute and Museum*

Rua at the entrance to the upper storey of Hiona, Christmas 1908. Photo by George Bourne. *Auckland Institute and Museum*

Right
Rua preaching from the platform of Hiona. Photo by George Bourne. *Auckland Weekly News, 28 January 1909*

Opposite (top)
David playing the harp to Saul, from the folio of seven picture sheets from the Scriptures hanging inside Tane Nui A Rangi at Maungapohatu. Each is about 70 by 90 centimetres. The meeting-house is decorated with painted boards and in the last third of the house the club and diamond emblems are used. The clubs are black, the diamonds alternate red and yellow, with black being reintroduced in the multiple diamond image in the centre of the diamond pattern which runs down the wall. Photographed, by courtesy of the Tuhoe of Maungapohatu, by Gillian Chaplin, 1978.

This festivity in some ways marked a high point in the Maungapohatu community. Already, observers noted, the settlement had ceased to expand, though the new pastures were verdant with growth and the slopes below the village divided neatly into paddocks of potatoes, maize and melons. Each family had their own plots, although the work was shared. But the numbers of the population did not grow after this date (until a much later period), and indeed by 1916, Maungapohatu was a considerably reduced community, as photographs reveal. There had, in fact, been periods of internal crisis. One critical point was the death of Whaitiri, Whatu's wife, about 1911.[96] Rua's inability to prevent her death provoked a crisis in the faith of her people, the Whakatohea from Waioeka. It was at this point that they left the community. Others also departed, as it proved difficult to feed the large numbers in the harsh Urewera winters. Nevertheless, in 1915, visitors to Maungapohatu could still be impressed by it and by the elegance with which they were treated. The daughter of the schoolteacher at Te Whaiti, Beryl Bressey, recollected the meal they were served, the table set with white cloths, the silver cutlery, the finger bowls, the serviettes embroidered with Rua's monogram, and the cut glass dishes. Grace was said before the visitors ate – one of Rua's binding rules. Rua himself had changed from his blue dungarees for the meal and, she remembered, seemed very pleased that she and her father had visited. He told her the whole story of the New Testament, illustrating it with linen picture sheets which were laid out on the ground, one after another, by two of his wives. Each time he came to a portrait of Christ, he pointed to him, with his long hair and beard, and said ' "I am that fella." '[97]

Strongly prejudiced views about Rua and his followers were common among those who had never visited Maungapohatu. They were thought 'peculiar' because the children rode behind their parents on horseback standing erect. Any incident which involved Pakeha property or stock brought an hysterical response in the press, with demands that 'outlaws' be treated like 'any other person', by which was meant, with great severity.[98] Rua's 'doings' were kept under regular surveillance by the local constable stationed at Te Whaiti, Andy Grant. In December 1907 he rode in to deliver the first summons to Rua – for evasion of the dog tax.[99]

Hiruharama Hou, with Rua's followers gathered before it, Christmas morning 1908. Photo by George Bourne. *Auckland Weekly News, 7 January 1909*

Another view of the community, Christmas 1908. Some of the smaller houses have been demolished and the space opened up in front of Hiruharama Hou since April. The substantial nature of the buildings inside the *wahi tapu* area contrasts with the scattered dwellings on the eastern side. Photo by George Bourne. *Auckland Weekly News, 14 January 1909*

This episode was the first of a number of examples of official harassment of Rua, and others, in the community at Maungapohatu. The dog tax was widely resented, not only because the fee was large (2/6), but because it was collected by the Maori Councils, who were seen thereby to be puppet agents of Pakeha rule. Rua's refusal to pay this tax in August had led to the issuing of the summons for evasion. Grant was instructed in May 1906, 'to watch the movements of a native named Rua Tapu. suspected of acting as a Tohunga.'[100] In fact, he found his task uncomfortable. In the same month in which he finally served the summons on Rua – and had it torn up in his face[101] – he had given an interview to the *Poverty Bay Herald* in praise of this 'remarkable man' and of his 'social work'.[102] In the end, Rua agreed to pay the tax and visitors to Maungapohatu were impressed by the relative absence of dogs and by the fact that those that were there were kept under firm control. But almost immediately after these events, Grant was again sent to Maungapohatu, this time to remove Wairimu, who was under fifteen years of age. Her father, Harry Vercoe, a European surveyor from Ruatoki, had taken the matter to the police and Detective John Cooney was sent from Wellington to 'assist' Grant. They went to Maungapohatu in June 1908 while the prophet was visiting Carroll in Wellington. After being threatened with 'troops' who would destroy the community,[103] Whatu handed Wairimu back to her father. She returned to Rua, as his wife, before the year was out.

Despite such incidents, Rua's mana remained high. Grant maintained regular contact with Maungapohatu and observed, in 1916, that Rua always kept 'great control' over his followers.[104] This control derived essentially from the faith he had generated in himself. Sometimes, fear was the motivation. Certainly, some believed that he possessed the power of makutu.

The death of a rival, Tamawaka, one of the early Riwaiti who attempted to claim too great powers for himself, was attributed to a makutu placed on him by Rua.[105] Some say that Te Akakura's first husband, Hena Rakuraku, died because Rua desired to take her as his wife and therefore placed a 'taipo' (goblin) upon him.[106] A suicide in 1906 was also attributed to a makutu placed by Rua on one whom he had labelled the cause of the 'recent calamities of the Maoris'.[107] One European journalist writing in 1908 noted his use of 'superstition'. 'Rua', he said, 'has taken up by far the most effective weapon that the situation affords.'[108] If Rua used fear to manipulate his people, it was for a particular end – the creation of a community, and a religious faith, which needed to be fortified by fear of the unknown in order to defeat present despair. The Scriptural texts fed his prophecies of the imminence of the Apocalypse, in which the chosen, the faithful, would be saved. He talked of the ten kings, with feet of base metals, who ruled the earth in 'these latter days';[109] they were, presumably, the ten kings for whom he built the thrones in Hiona, the Kings of the threatened conflagration in Europe. But out of this fiery second coming, God would return to him in whom he delighted –

The wedding portrait of Whaitiri and Whatu, which hangs inside the meeting-house at Maungapohatu. Photographed, by courtesy of the Tuhoe of Maungapohatu, by Gillian Chaplin, 1978.

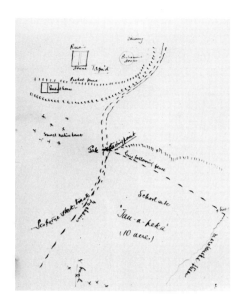

This diagram of Maungapohatu was drawn in March 1914 by the Native Schools' Inspector. While this drawing suggests that the houses had been removed from the inner enclosure, the accompanying report added that there were 'other buildings' on the 'enclosed hill top'. Tane Nui A Rangi, which bears the date '1914' at its apex, has not yet been built. By 1916, Hiona, the *whare kanikani*, and the meeting-house were all fenced off from Hiruharama Hou. (The school site, marked here, was given to the Education Department in 1914, but never used.) *Maungapohatu Native School File, E44/4, I, Department of Education, Auckland*

Maungapohatu, about 1912-14. The first changes are already visible. The new house for Pinepine can be seen above Hiruharama Hou. In the far corner of the enclosure is the Whare Kawenata, the House of the Covenant, its upper part stained a dark colour. *Judith Ellmer Collection, Whakatane Museum*

Hepetipa. In these ways, Rua wove the fabric of prophecy into the details of daily life. The white horse he rode was the white horse of the Messiah.[110] (Te Turuki had also ridden a white horse, said then to be a symbol of resistance to the Pakeha.) The long hair of the Iharaira was a sign of those who had taken the vow to dedicate themselves to God, one which he had required of the Nazarites.[111] There were 'two Jacob's ladders' to heaven: one was for the 'dark-coloured people', who now had their own Messiah.[112]

Such a community, bound by strict rules because the 'consecration . . . of God' was upon it,[113] was impossible to sustain in its pristine enthusiasm. The first relaxation was on the use of alcohol, though not tobacco. By 1910, spirits were being consumed by the Iharaira, the Ruatoki decree notwithstanding. Other changes could be observed at Maungapohatu itself by 1914. The most obvious was the erection, late in that year, of a new and much more traditional meeting-house with a much more traditional name, Tane Nui A Rangi (Great Tane of the Heavens). It was used as the community dining-hall, in direct contradiction of most Maori practice, for food renders *noa* that which is tapu. Rua lifted the traditional tapu from all the Iharaira meeting-houses. The house was built in what had been the *wahi tapu*, but was fenced off from both Hiruharama Hou and Hiona. When it was opened, a great hui was held and among the many visitors were those of the Arawa who followed him.[114]

This change was part of a complete reconstruction of the whole settlement. All the buildings which had been inside the tapu pa enclosure were pulled down, with the exception of Hiruharama Hou and Hiona, while a new house was built for Pinepine. Both Rua's and Pinepine's houses were tapu and were fenced off from all the other dwellings and buildings of the community. The dwellings were grouped around the gully on the eastern side and the kitchens moved down in a cluster around Tane Nui A Rangi. These physical changes were a part of the lifting of the tapu upon the community.

The sequence of events is not entirely clear. A rough diagram of the settlement drawn in March 1914 suggests that some of the buildings have already been demolished inside the *wahi tapu*. In August, the original 20,000 acres were divided and half set apart. Finally, late in 1915 a great gathering was held, when the tapu was lifted from the Riwaiti and from the people and Rua told them that they could all go where they wished.[115] The major reconstruction of the pa also took place late in 1915. It took place in three days, suggesting the deliberate 'resurrection' of a new and more perfect community: 'I am able to destroy the temple of God, and to build it in three days.'[116] An entry in Rua's Ledger book, dated 11 Sep-

tember 1915, records that the pa was to be built by one hundred men of Ngatikuri between 16 and 18 September, working for three hours on each day: 'Ka taati te mahia ote pa ite 16 otenei marama, kia oti i nga ra e toru . . . . E toru haora ote ra kotahi hai mahi. Ma te hapu kotahi ma Ngati Kuri, e mahi kia oti ite 18 onga ra o Hepetema nei; tau 1915. . . . 100 na tangata hai mahi itenei Pa'.[117] Te Puhi Tatu explains, 'during the war, about 1915, the fence was taken down from around the pa;‡ he left it, and so the pa was closed for two years then he returned and restored it with his people.' She was not referring to the period of Rua's long jail sentence in 1916–17. Rather, the dramatic changes which took place late in 1915 were the consequence of his first prison sentence beginning in May of that year. In August he returned, after spending three months in jail for the sale of whisky, with his long hair shorn. His personal tapu had been violated by the prison experience and his hair cut by the police.§ As a result, the Iharaira cut off their locks. The days of their separation unto God were brought to an end at a great ceremony, held in accordance with the laws given by God to Moses, when their hair was shaved and put 'in the fire which is under the sacrifice of the peace offerings.'[119] The cutting and offering of the hair was seen as the fulfilment of the days of separation. Our informants told us that Te Akakura cut the sacred hair of Rua and his locks were burnt.[120] At the same time, the tapu was lifted on the Riwaiti and on all the sacred places.[121]

The ceremony of the lifting of the tapu on the Riwaiti meant that 'they were not encumbered any more. They were free to go where they wished, and to work where they wished, there were no more ties. All the laws of his long-haired people were finished.'[122] The Riwaiti could now enter the kitchens and places where food was prepared, for the first time. The ceremony marked the breaking of their strict order; from this time the Twelve would no longer be replaced, should any of their number die.

Until this time, the Twelve had been maintained in number. The names of the Riwaiti who are still remembered include some who were amongst the earliest: Pita Te Taite, who was their first sergeant (*haihana*); his brother Pari (Te Ahuru Te Rika); Te Wairama, the 'humpy back'; Ngakohu of Waioeka, who left when Whaitiri died; and Wharepapa, who stayed with Rua to the end.

‡ In the first stages of the reconstruction of Jerusalem by Zerubbabel after the exile, there were to be no walls. Walls (and gates) were then added again.
§ The local constable at Whakatane stated that Rua asked for his hair to be cut before he returned, so that he could give the locks to his wives, but Rua said that it was cut as he entered jail.[118]

Maungapohatu, the same period as the previous photograph. Within the *wahi tapu* area several houses have been removed. The new dance hall can be seen beside Hiona. *Judith Ellmer Collection, Whakatane Museum*

Tioke Hakaipare (Te Kaharoa) at Matahi, in the early 1920s. *Sister Dorothy Keen Collection, Mrs Olwyn Rudd, Christchurch*

Tatu Horopapera became their *haihana* when Pita refused to leave his wife, thereby disobeying Rua's decree for the 'high priest'. Tatu was particularly gifted in the powers of healing (and a rough man on the horses). Teka Hekerangi was learned in the Scriptures. Te Naiti acted as the all important 'policeman' at the services, controlling the start of the sessions of worship and gathering the people, 'who are the house', by the ringing of a bell.[123] Others were Tauru Tuhua; Tamati Rautao; Tioke Hakaipare (Te Kaharoa); Tuna Mokomoko, who was one of Rua's 'physicians', an expert in traditional herbal remedies; and Manuka Ereatara, who was similarly skilled. One of the main functions of the Riwaiti was to help the sick; nursing the suffering was one of the essentials of Rua's teaching, as his advocate 'Ngatiawa' stressed in 1906,[124] when the order of the Riwaiti was first established. Te Amoroa Te Hira and Pari Te Taite's son, Tuhua Te Taite, joined the group after it was first formed. Both of these men were still alive when the prophet died in 1937, as were Tatu, Wharepapa, Te Wairama, Tioke, and Teka; all were still considered to be Riwaiti and carried out the tasks of healing and interpretation of dreams through the Scriptures as they had always done.[125] The breaking of the order did not end its ministry.

When Rua lifted the tapu from the Riwaiti, he also took the tapu off the sacred places. At Maungapohatu, only the houses of Rua and Pinepine remained tapu and it was probably at this time – in the three days – that the steps were taken down from Hiona. He now often lived at Maai, the little community beside the river, or the place 'freed from tapu'. The tapu was also lifted from Tawhana, or the region they called the Promised Land. Tawhana lies high up the Waimana valley, and had been named the Promised Land by Te Turuki. One elder, referring to Te Turuki's flight to the Ureweras, explained:

While the war was going on . . . [Te Turuki] entered into a covenant with the Tuhoe people, at Te Tawhana: it was to rest on the chiefs of Tuhoe, i.e. Kereru . . . Te Ahikaiata, Te Tutakangahau . . . [and] these people gave their mana to be under the guidance of Te Kooti; and a piece of land including this block [Ruatoki] & extending from Waimana to Maungapohatu, was given over to Te Kooti. . . . Te Kooti said: 'Under this oath, let the people be one.'[126]

Or, as Horo Tatu put it:

Tawhana was a very sacred place, more so than Maungapohatu. The Land of Promise to God. That is the name of Tawhana. The Promised Land for all of us. And Rua cleared even that, the most tapu place round here.

In this series of ritual ceremonies, Rua thus ended the separation of the people and the places unto God. But the lifting of the tapu did not end their faith; rather, it marked the beginning of their return from isolation into the world. It was the beginning of a new era. At Tawhana some years later, a meeting-house called Tauemaha, or the Many Years that they had waited, was erected.[127] Many of the families who had made the original pilgrimage to Maungapohatu now left, as they determined for themselves. 'You can go to your own place, no tapu, nothing', explained Horo Tatu.

In this way, the Iharaira scattered. In fact, of course, the movement had begun long before. Many had gone to live on their newly defined blocks in the coastal valleys, and the development of subsistence and cash crop farming there was dramatically altering the life of the Tuhoe. Rua had encouraged the building of these settlements by his followers and indeed had earlier started a new community in the Waimana valley. This was Te Waimana, or Tataiahape as it was also known, which was founded as a deliberate settlement of the Iharaira in 1909. The Ngatiraka chiefs, Te Pou and his brother Taura Papaka (or Haturini Papaka), gave Rua a hundred acres of land and by the beginning of 1911 the new community was well under way. Rua sold quarter acre sections, at 10/- each, to the forty or so families who came to live there.[128] Soon, little nikau and totara bark houses sprang up, alongside the existing meeting-house. Rua built for himself and his wives a large house with a verandah. The township had a general store, which Toko ran, a smithy, and a billiard room.[129] The meeting-house, Takutai O Te Rangi, had been built four years earlier, to welcome Rua on his way to Gisborne. It had been opened on 14 May 1906 and shortly afterwards a hui was held when the forty-two were chosen to go with Rua to meet King Edward. Like all the other Iharaira houses, the tapu had been lifted from it by Rua, and food was eaten inside.

But in 1912 Rua was driven out of Te Waimana.[130] Te Pou's son, Wi Kamaua,‖ returned and claimed back the land his father had given. Wi Kamaua's anger, it is said, stemmed from jealousy, for the crops were flourishing and the people had a surplus to sell.[131] The underlying reason was the fact that Rua had sold the sections. In this way he had raised money for building the community, but Wi was hostile to the device and successfully asserted his ownership claims over the 'shareholders', when he took the case to Court. The community broke up, and many went to the other new settlement Rua had founded in the valley, Matahi. They took their houses with them.[132]

Takutai O Te Rangi, the meeting-house at Te Waimana. Photo by Gillian Chaplin, 1978.

Rua also went to Matahi, but soon returned to Maungapohatu to live.[133] By 1916, 'New Jerusalem the Golden', as Elsdon Best scathingly called it, was a very different community from what it had been at its inception, nine years before. From the beginning it had drawn much comment and criticism, not least from the young Maori leaders. Te Rangihiroa (Peter Buck) was particularly concerned with the ignorance of Rua's people in matters of health, which the prophet's emphasis on faith-healing would not alleviate. Numia Kereru was also very disturbed by the 'works of madness' which had occurred in the first harsh winter, when in strict observation of the tapu of the pa, the people going out stripped off the clothes they wore and left them inside the fence, regardless of the weather.[134] He attributed the high number of deaths that winter to this practice, along with the fact that they ate their food in the open air, having no dining shelters. But other voices were raised in praise of Rua. James Bell argued that he had brought a peace and plenty 'rarely seen in any Maori community'.[135] Maungapohatu had been characterized by a 'wonderful enthusiasm for work',[136] and this quality was transferred to the other settlements associated with Rua in the Waimana valley. He also remained alert to new ideas that could benefit his followers: he was singled out by Europeans for his cooperation after the 1913 smallpox epidemic, as he worked to ensure that all his people received the vaccine.[137]

Rua was the leader because he was the prophet. As prophet to his people, he foretold literally hundreds of events that were and will be part of the lives of those who believe. He had great skill in keeping the people aware of the possibility that perhaps he really was the Messiah: he would say, ' "Well, there were three, after all, and I could be one of those three. I could be one of the others. I could be the Holy Ghost." ' Or when the people asked, ' "Is Jesus going to come back, Rua?", he would reply, "If you got a hiding in a paddock, would you return to the same paddock? But there might be another man going to come . . . ." '[138] He had a gift with words, never seeming to be at a loss; he had a manner that was gentle, and he did not lack humour. He was a kind man – on this all who remember him agree. And he was a moral man, in that the essence of his teaching was to care for others, to look after those who could not look after themselves. He taught above all, not to seek greedily for oneself; to conserve food so that there would be enough; to give grace in thanks for the food that there was. These qualities, he stressed, were those which the people must take with them into a changing world.

‖Not to be confused with Te Pou's adopted son, Wiremu, who married Marumaru.

Maungapohatu, April 1916. This photograph was taken by the *Auckland Weekly News'* photographer who was with the police force in the assault of 1916. Several members of the constabulary are visible on the knoll at the edge of the marae. Hiruharama Hou is fenced off; the paddock has become 'Rua's enclosure'. The stairway into the upper chamber of Hiona has been removed. The kitchens are clustered on the northern and eastern sides of the marae. Photo by A. N. Breckon. *Sergeant John Taylor, Auckland*

The ending of the laws of separation unto God was a deliberate decision. It marked the beginning of the attempt to return to this world, for those who had set themselves apart. The introduction of alcohol into the community was one such decision, for abstinence had been a specific sign of their consecration to God. In actuality, Rua was forced to accept it in the Waimana valley, where ease of access made it impossible to prevent spirits being brought in; he then began to use the issue to urge their right to equality before the law. The Tuhoe, like all Maoris, were prohibited the use of alcohol in their own settlements. Rua hoped to introduce it under the control of the community. But the European government was distrustful of any separate authorities and particularly distrustful of anything that looked like Maori separatism. A leader who had gathered a large section of one tribe to himself in the relatively isolated territory of the Ureweras; who had rejected the government schools, with their policy that only English could be spoken in school grounds; who saw the Maori Councils as mere playthings invented by the Pakeha; and who now defied the paternalist and retrogressive legislation banning liquor at home for Maoris, would inevitably draw the wrath of those who prided themselves on strengthening order and conformity to law in this society. 'Sly grog' would give the pretext and the opportunity to break the separatist community of Maungapohatu. The irony was that Rua was already attempting to end that very separatism. 'Sly grog', instead, ushered in what the people of Maungapohatu still call 'The War' of 1916: the police assault, whose memory remains as bitter as gall to this day.

3 The Law Against the Prophet

The clandestine sale of spirits among the Iharaira began regularly when they acquired wealth from the sale of land. Rua was forced to accept the introduction of alcohol among his people, although earlier he had been unequivocally opposed:

While strolling through the streets of Hastings yesterday, accompanied by a pakeha, the Maori prophet Rua, pointing to a Maori woman, who was evidently under the influence of liquor said, 'See that! you are responsible for that disgrace.' 'Not me,' replied his companion, 'I have nothing to do with it.' 'Well, your countrymen have,' said Rua, 'you will see nothing like that in my Kainga, but wherever Natives mix with Europeans harm comes of it.'[1]

He accepted alcohol in order to control its sale. It was well known that the local publicans brought up the bottles and hid them at pre-arranged spots. From 1910, Toko sold square gin and whisky from his little store in the Waimana community. In that year, Rua approached Apirana Ngata, as M.H.R. for Eastern Maori, for a licence for Waimana, but this Ngata was in no position to provide. Knowing that he could not prevent the smuggling of liquor, Rua thought it better to control it. As he said at his trial, ' "I did not like whisky being sold there by others. Liquor is an evil whether licensed or not. . . . [But] why should we be treated differently from other people?" '[2] ' "That is what hurts most." '[3] The inequality which forbade Maoris to drink at home preyed on his mind, and led him to defy the law. He reminded others that it was Sir Joseph Ward who had first introduced him to alcohol when, in March 1908, he had taken him into the Commercial Hotel at Whakatane to seal their 'Ceremony of Union' and the understanding that Maori and Pakeha 'should enjoy the same laws'.[4] Rua construed the continuing inequality as a betrayal of the 'Ceremony'. He had sealed it, for his part, with the offer of the lands, or so he came to believe.

In 1911, when he was first fined for illicit trading in whisky, alcohol was not a problem in the lives of the Iharaira, though perhaps their new wealth was; but heavy drinking became characteristic of their communities, and would continue to be so long after Rua's death.

At first the introduction of spirits was gradual. Rua prohibited it at Maungapohatu when he accepted it in Waimana. But he began to use it himself because, like Te Turuki, he discovered that it could extend his visionary and prophetic powers. Te Turuki claimed 'second-sight' when he was drunk and could see, he said, who was seeking to destroy him by makutu.[5] By the 1920s Rua was drinking on Saturday mornings before the services. His oldest followers stress that it was not he who brought the liquor to sell, but others, whom they have named to the writers; in the early years, they argue, he did not use it much himself. But, as he said, he came to like it.[6]

Rua was first fined, on 21 February 1911, on five charges relating to selling whisky, and one further charge was held over. Four years later, on 18 May 1915, he was summoned again on five new charges, all originating from a big hui held at Maungapohatu in March as part of the bone cleansing ceremonies. He was charged because he acted as head of the community. Toko, Whatu and Maka Kanuehi, Pehirangi's brother, who ran the new Maungapohatu shop

'Examining the proceeds of the first land sale'. Stereotype attitudes towards the land, Maoris and alcohol, as portrayed in the *Auckland Weekly News*, 24 September 1908. Cartoon by Trevor Lloyd.

with Toko, were also fined, although Toko and Maka chose to go to jail rather than pay. Rua was sent to prison for three months without choice. This, the maximum sentence possible, was imposed for the suspended charge of 1911. The 1915 charges were, in their turn, suspended. This device was intended by the magistrate, Robert Dyer, to be the means of removing him from the community at will. As Dyer said, he would then 'have a hold over him' and be able to use the law against him at any time.[7] It was on these charges that Rua was rearrested.

Early in January 1916, the Minister for Native Affairs, William Herries, took the deliberate decision to revive the old charges. No new ones were laid. The decision, which brought matters to a head, was taken in the light of two issues – that of the Tuhoe lands, and that of the recruitment of the Tuhoe for service in the war. Rua saw no need for the Tuhoe to volunteer and said so; it was decided in this context to arrest him. This action itself was the direct consequence of a meeting held at Tauranga in January, at which Rua, Dyer and Herries were all present,[8] and at which Rua and the old chief of Maungapohatu, Te Iwikino Hairuha, pressed a petition for the opening of the Tuhoe lands. Herries determined to remove the critical figure in the Tuhoe opposition in both areas of contention.

The persecution of Rua was primarily the product of war hysteria. By early 1916, rumours were spreading all over the country that Rua was arming his followers. He was said to possess a machine gun and to favour a German victory. That this was the real issue is clear from the *Rotorua Chronicle*'s report of the reopening of the charges on 22 January: Rua claimed to be the Maori 'Kaiser' and, it was said, promised 'his followers a great time when this country will be in the hands of the Germans, which event, he assures them, is soon to be accomplished.' The local constable at Whakatane, Tim Cummings, gave evidence, in a case ostensibly concerned with the illicit sale of alcohol, that it was 'practically impossible to get Maoris to enlist owing to the accused's actions amongst the Natives of the District'. 'Exit Rua', exulted the *Chronicle* at Dyer's sentence of imprisonment, pronounced in Rua's absence.[9] The *Auckland Star* was even more colourful: Rua had 'taken upon himself the title of "Kaiser," and prophesied that the other Kaiser will meet him shortly in Whakatane'.[10] This appears to be a deliberate distortion of Rua's original messianic vision. The *Star* described a bodyguard of more than three hundred men and meetings called all over the Ureweras, and anticipated 'very serious'

The Kiwi and the morality of the War. A cartoon expressing the strong fervour surrounding the First World War. Kaiser Bill replaced Aunt Sally in the coconut shies. Cartoon by Trevor Lloyd. *Auckland Weekly News, 6 July 1916*

trouble. It was at this time that the Maungapohatu community began to be popularly called a 'stronghold', and the name has survived down to the present day.

Rua's 'disloyalty' had been created by the government starting recruitment among the Tuhoe after Ngata had endorsed the plan to set up the Maori Contingent. In February, a recruiting committee for the Tuhoe was formally established, under Kereru's direction and with representatives from five of the Tuhoe sub-tribes: Ngatirongo, Te Hamua, Ngatikoura, Te Mahurehure and Ngatitawhaki. Rua opposed both registration and recruiting and few of the Iharaira came forward. They were, in fact, discouraged by Rua's teaching that the times of war were in the past: they belonged to the years of Te Turuki, the 'man killer'.[11] He drew from that prophet's teachings, and said that now his Son had come there would be no more war. As Mau Rua explains, 'War won't reach New Zealand. It is a holy land. Te Kooti said, "My Son who is coming is the man of peace, who will finish what I have started." Then he took his gun and pushed the barrel down into the ground, saying again, "War won't reach New Zealand." ' Like the Waikato tribes, the Iharaira based their pacificism on the Bible, and they called themselves the people of lasting peace, *maungarongo*. Their resistance was reinforced by that of the Waikato and the vision of their prophet, King Tawhiao. As Te Heuheu Tukino explained, Tawhiao had said, ' "As to war, I will leave it to you – the white man" '. ' "Take war with you to your own land – England." '[12] Tawhiao, like Te Turuki, had 'banished' war from the land.★ For this reason, Rua would not commit his Tuhoe followers but, like Tana Taingakawa, said officially if some 'wished to go to the war they were free to go'.[14] Indeed, some of the Iharaira had gone.†

Rua's opposition to enlistment was distorted by popular rumour into an active support for the Germans. Probably he did use the European war as an image of the end of the world in conflagration. Early in 1915, he had told Beryl

The AA sign at the Papatotara saddle, on the road from Ruatahuna to Lake Waikaremoana. The sign has since been changed into kilometres, but the description remains unaltered. Photo by Len Shapcott, 1968.

★ The various prophecies 'banishing' war from New Zealand probably originated with Titokowaru, prophet and guerrilla leader, when he broke Major von Tempsky's sword in 1868, saying 'I will break this sword, and I will bury it, and no man can join it again. Let war be returned to the great nations of the world.'[13] This continuity shows how fundamental Maori concerns were reinforced by the prophetic tradition.
† Hori Taia had enlisted and Horo Tatu, Tatu's son, left with the second Maori Contingent in September 1915.

Portrait of Rua, 1908. Photo probably by James McDonald. *Rotorua Post Collection, Alexander Turnbull Library*

Bressey and her family that he had built thrones for all the kings of the world at Maungapohatu, where they were to congregate for the Second Coming. One throne was for the Kaiser, and her father, Ernest, fairly new to the district, took the account literally, and spread the rumour that Rua was sympathetic to the Germans. He even carried a Mauser pistol.[15] Rua's apocalyptic visions were regarded seriously, as treason, even by James Cowan. He labelled him the 'war lord's representative in New Zealand', and believed that he had prophesied the Kaiser's victory. As the Kaiser's 'representative', Rua intended 'to drive the British away and restore to the Maoris all the lands'.[16]

The sly grog charge was only a pretext. Mau Rua knows it was a pretext. He tells it this way:

They come up, 'Well, here you are, you haven't sent your soldiers up to the war, eh?' And he'd tell them, 'Well, I am training my soldiers. I've got five hundred soldiers.' He said, 'Why send my soldiers overseas? Why? There's a time. The war shall be just.' That's why they manhandled him. That's the reason.

These rumours were fruitfully – and tragically – taken up by Numia Kereru in his renewed leadership struggle with Rua, which once again involved the issue of the land. At the beginning of June 1915, Crown land purchase had resumed in the area, after a cessation of nearly four years. Tuhoe land was now sold in individual shares, in direct violation of the Urewera Act, and this action had reopened all the old divisions. In May 1915, Te Iwikino and Makarini had initiated a petition for the removal of all the restrictions on the *Rohe Potae*. (They had also asked for leniency over Rua's imprisonment.[17]) This petition, with 478 signatures including Rua's, had been presented to Parliament in July. It was the focus of the meeting with Herries at Tauranga.‡[18] It asked that the people should be able to dispose freely of their land like private individuals, by lease or by sale: one law for both peoples. This view was opposed by Kereru. In February 1916, he wrote to Herries to protest against these efforts by Rua to reopen the land question. Kereru said, 'At the present time [Rua] is working for his people – the German people and says that Germany would win the war. . . . Perhaps he is doing this to deter the police from arresting him. If he is not arrested, his people would consider that he is "the God".' Herries drafted his answer:

Reply that sooner or later Rua will be arrested we want to do it by ordinary means without resorting to force if we can but Numia can rely on it that we will not let him go free. The mana of the law must be maintained.[19]

In a further letter, he assured Kereru that Rua's petition, which he was intending to press with a visit to Wellington, would not succeed. 'I will keep to my word not to allow the restrictions to be taken off the Urewera Country. There is not much chance of Rua coming to Wellington except as a prisoner'.[20]

When Rua had been jailed in 1915, there had been those who hoped that the subjection of his tapu person to *mahi taumaha*, hard labour, would destroy his mana. Instead, in the rituals of late 1915, all his followers cut their hair and a new era began. But Rua had foreseen that the persecution of the Messiah, as prophesied in the Scriptures, would not cease. A lament, which he is said to have composed in Mount Eden jail, foreshadowed the day when the shackles, *mekameka*, would again be placed on his wrists, but this time at Maungapohatu.

‡Here is the origin of Rua's 'more than three hundred' (and his five hundred) 'soldiers'.

84

> He Tangi
> *A Lament*
> Na Tai Hepeti
> *By Tai Hepeti* [Rua Hepetipa]
>
> Ei taukuri, te mamae i ahau ki te ao rere mai,
> *Alas, the approaching cloud brings anguish,*
> E komingo i roto ra ki taku whaiaipo;
> *Stirring memories within me of my beloved;*
> I ra rongo e au he karauna kingi ka u ki Maungapohatu:
> *The news comes that a King's crown has settled on Maungapohatu:*
> Mekameka i aku ringa.
> *Chains upon my hands.*
> Ka pai e te iwi ka rite nga karaipiture:
> *That is good my people for the Scriptures are confirmed:*
> Nuku mai e te tikanga hai hoa moe ake,
> *Move closer o righteousness my sleeping companion,*
> I waiho ai au hai maungarongo.
> *I have been left as peacemaker.*
> E tatari atu ana te ope i nga anahera
> *The company are waiting for the angels*
> Kia au iho ai taku moe ki te whare –i –ii!
> *That my sleep may be sound in the house.*[21]

Portrait of Whatu with the long hair of a Nazarite. *Te Huinga O Te Kura, Matahi.* Photographed, by courtesy of Heta Rua, by Gillian Chaplin, 1978.

In this lament, Tai (as he is known affectionately) foresaw the coming of the police – the 'King's crown' – to Maungapohatu. Te Puhi Tatu, who sang us this lament composed in the style of the love song of the deserted, explained that the tangi tells of the 'government's legal persecution of him' – 'Ko te tangi tenei a Tai Hepeti i te patu a te ture a te Kawana i a ia'.

On 19 January 1916, the Maori constable at Opotiki, Te Kepa Tawhio, brought the new summons to Rua. Rua dictated a reply, which Te Kepa wrote down for him.

Greetings. – I am very busy with my grass these days. Kindly adjourn case until next Court, next month, when I will come over in answer to your summons.[22]

As Andy Grant, the district constable, was later to point out, once the cocksfoot harvest (upon which depended the income of the people) had started it could not be stopped without all the seed being lost. The harvest had begun in January. But Dyer was not told this; nor was he told that Te Kepa had written the letter for Rua and had informed him that there would be another session on 15 February.[23] When the court met on 22 January, Dyer judged the letter to be in contempt. In Rua's absence, he sentenced him to a total of three months' imprisonment on three charges and a fine of £100 and costs on the remaining two. These were the charges of 1915 for which Rua believed he had already served his sentence. Not only Rua but the *New Zealand Herald* and some of the local police also had understood it that way.[24]

Below
Te Puhi, daughter of Tatu. She was Whatu's second wife; they were married for four years and then parted. Photo by Gillian Chaplin, 1978.

New warrants were issued for Rua's arrest. On 11 February Grant, Te Kepa and Sergeant Denis Cummings of Rotorua (who was Tim Cummings' younger brother) arrived at Ruatahuna looking for him. Learning that he was at Te Waiiti, about three miles away, Cummings left Te Kepa at Ruatahuna, because he had heard that Rua was angry with him. Early on the morning of the 12th the two policemen found Rua at Te Waiiti, where he had come to remove the tapu on the old graves.

The accounts of what occurred at Te Waiiti are totally conflicting. The episode is critical because it was upon the words which Rua used there that the later charges of sedition were erected – charges which were not part of the original case. These charges, made under the 1908 Crimes Act, were added in an attempt to establish a major conspiracy amounting to disloyalty. The Supreme Court jury acquitted him of these charges. As Mr Justice Frederick Chapman observed, this acquittal meant that the main police account of what was said at Te Waiiti was untenable.

Grant, in his sworn deposition made in the lower court at Rotorua, described how he had read the three warrants of commitment to Rua, in Maori, in the middle of which Rua interrupted, saying, ' "That is the same thing as I have been arrested on before" '. Grant tried to explain the legal intricacies, but was able to make no impression. At this juncture, Rua invited them in to breakfast. After the meal, Grant again tried to persuade him to come with them and again Rua said, ' "No Ive already served my time for these things." ' For nearly three hours they talked and then Cummings said, ' "Well we arrest you." ' According to Grant, Rua replied,

'You try and arrest me, that is what I want,' and he pulled off his coat and he said 'Just fancy a dog like you trying to arrest me' and he walked out through a little gate on to the stock track and he called out in English . . . 'Come on arrest me' and he said to his two sons 'Look they are coming to arrest me, come on,' and he also called out to his tribe . . . [He] said 'If you put your hand on me you will drop down dead.' [This remark Grant said he took to be a claim to supernatural power.] Then [Rua] ordered his people to go and get the horses and that he was going back to Maungapohatu. Accused started to walk up the hill and we called him back again. . . . He said 'No I wont come, the English are no good, they wont give me a licence to sell drink'. He said that the Governor told him that we were all one race the Maori and Pakeha. . . . Accused said 'The English are no good, You have no country and no King.' He said 'I have influenced 1400 men not to enlist' 'Any money that I have I will give to the Germans, the English are no good, they have two laws one for the Maori and one for the Pakeha' At the same time he said 'You have no right in this country' to Sergeant Cummings. 'This country belongs to us the Maoris'.[25]

Finally, he made to ride away, 'in a "huff" ', as Grant put it, but he turned back and shook hands with both men and talked to them for a further half hour. He said to send a 'big man', the 'Governor' or a Minister, if they wished to pursue the matter.

Andy Grant, district constable stationed at Te Whaiti from 1900 until his death in 1923. This photograph was taken in April 1916. He was married to a Maori from Rotoiti, Te Wehi Paerangi, and was a well-liked figure in the Ureweras. Photo by A. N. Breckon. *Blue Album, Alexander Turnbull Library*

In Cummings' version Rua's attitudes are more provocative. When Rua 'refused' to accompany them he said,

'No, I No go with you, I die first. I'll die on my land before the Government will take me' I said 'Come on now Rua dont be foolish. You come quietly because you will have to come' He said 'No you put your hand on me and you start the big fight, the fight I want with the English Government, the Government No good he wont give me the licence for the liquor.'[26]

Rua offered any sum to purchase such a licence saying, ' "The pakeha get the licence, why not the Maori" '? When the horses were saddled up, he asked for the 'big man' to settle this, because, as he said, ' "I the big fellow in the Maori," ' and told them that he had sent a petition, signed by 480 men, and that he had 1400 men and would not let any of them go to the war. Cummings asserted, moreover, that Rua said he had no intention of sending them, because ' "You got no king now", "You got no land" and I said "Oh yes, we have got a King in England Rua" "Oh," he said "He no good he beat" "The Germans win" "When the German win, I'm going to be the King here" "I be the King of the pakeha and the Maori" '.[27] Cummings, and also the road inspector, William Snodgrass, who had come with them from Rotorua, were later to say that Rua's manner was like a 'raving lunatic': he was 'foaming at the mouth'.[28] But Grant said that, during the entire three hours, the 'utmost good humour prevailed'. Cummings, who stated at first that Rua gathered 100 of 'his tribe' around him in a bellicose manner, later admitted that there were only about twenty men at Te Waiiti at the time, as indeed Rua had said.[29] Cummings also admitted that he had taken 'notes', as he had been instructed to do by John Cullen, the Commissioner of Police, 'in case' Rua made use of seditious language, and that he had sent Snodgrass back to Ruatahuna to fetch Te Kepa so that he too could be a witness, although in fact he was too late. The obvious distortion in Cummings' account was that the land petition was made to seem a statement about the war. The 1400 men, as Grant well knew but did not admit, was the total number of the people in the Tuhoe district. As Rua

Te Waiiti, 1916. The people are standing at the gateway on to the stock track. Photo by William Carter. *Lundon collection*

Pinohi, 1916. He wears the medal given to his father, Tutakangahau, by Lord Ranfurly. *Mrs E. Murphy Album, Alexander Turnbull Library*

put it, 'I did say that I have 1400 people under me (men, women, and children) and that this number of people . . . opened up the first sale in the Urewera Country. . . . [They were the] Names in the Urewera Land'.[30]

The Maoris who were present at Te Waiiti described the events very differently. Rua himself said that he had refused to go voluntarily with the policemen because he believed that he had already served for these offences. Moreover, he wanted 'to force their hands and make them prove the rumours which they had been circulating about me', that he had fortified Maungapohatu.[31] He specifically asked for a Minister to come to the community so that he could see for himself its peaceful nature. 'My great object in insisting that he should come here [was] to explode the report started by a Native school teacher at Te Whaiti.'[32] This was Ernest Bressey, who had been advocating the execution of 'the law' against the 'Maori Kaiser', before others emulated him.[33] Rua said, 'I want to draw your attention to the fact that the policemen have lied throughout. They said I had machine guns and cannons when I did not.'[34] But the Minister did not come, 'thinking I was belittling him.' As for Grant's claim that Rua had asserted that he possessed magical powers: ' "if it was true that death would ensue from touching me, why did they not drop down dead when we shook hands" '?[35]

In his Daily Diary, Grant entered an unusually lengthy description of this day's events but he mentioned nothing about the war, the 1400 men, or the Germans. The Maori witnesses consistently denied that the war had ever been discussed at Te Waiiti. Pinohi, the son of the old chief Tutakangahau, was adamant on this: 'No. That is the very thing that has brought me to Auckland. I have heard people telling such falsehoods about what Rua is supposed to have said.'[36] Pinohi, Rua said at the trial, was one of the few Maoris present whom he had permitted to remain within earshot of the discussion, for he and the police had withdrawn, as he did not allow his conversations with Pakeha to be overheard.[37]

Grant and Cummings did not arrest Rua at Te Waiiti. Rua said that finally he held out his hands to be handcuffed and invited them, ' "arrest me" '. He said he wanted them to take the initiative and remove him of their own volition.[38] But they did not – in fact, they denied that such an incident ever occurred.

Rua's arrest became a major political issue. Apirana Ngata, whose relations with Rua were already strained, was sent to Maungapohatu to try and persuade him to submit peacefully. He knew nothing of the details of the situation; Rua gave him the copy of the summons and told him that the offences were those for which he had already served. Ngata thereupon promised to investigate the case and to explain to Alexander Herdman, the Minister of Police, why he had not given himself up. They also agreed that, should the government establish satisfactorily that Rua was in the wrong, he would voluntarily submit himself; but Rua was emphatic that the police should have no part of it. He stressed that he was having great difficulty with some of his followers who were outraged that he was being repeatedly persecuted for the same offence. Indeed, a meeting had been held at Matahi and a petition, dated 24 January, was drawn up by the old chiefs Paora Kingi and Te Iwikino, together with Makarini, Rua's secretary, for the 'whole of Israel', and sent to the Prime Minister. This was the origin of the *Star*'s report of the formation of a 'bodyguard' in a series of Urewera meetings. The petition warned that if a force came to seize Rua for offences which had already been dealt with, then a 'gun will be fired' ('Ka paku te pu'), in traditional challenge. 'Although I be small, if needs be, I will face you.'[39] Altogether twenty-nine of the Iharaira signed, including Whatu and Toko, although others, including Pinohi, refused, seeing it as unduly provocative. Rua himself told them that he did not wish them to interfere, because he did not

want his authority undercut.[40] Instead, Rua had reiterated to Ngata that he wanted personally to see a 'big man' in the government.[41]

Ngata returned immediately to Wellington and on 11 March called on Herdman. Ngata's message created for Herries the opportunity for which he had been waiting, and to which he had certainly been alerted. For Cullen had already initiated the preparations for an armed expedition to Maungapohatu, which he viewed as a 'probability'.[42] The arrangements for the arms had been started, even before Cullen had permission from Herdman,[43] who was, in fact, a close friend and had appointed Cullen as Commissioner. Similarly, plans to swear in special constables, if needed, were already under way with the New Zealand Legion of Frontiersmen at Opotiki.[44] Herdman and Ngata now agreed that Rua should be told to come to Ruatahuna to meet Herdman and that this action, it was to be understood, amounted 'practically' to giving himself up. If Rua were to submit in this manner, Ngata would try to use his influence to obtain a partial remittance of the sentence. A man known to both Ngata and Rua, Tai Mitchell, a Maori surveyor from Rotorua, was sent to Maungapohatu with letters containing this advice. In actuality, Mitchell forwarded the letters from Ngata and Herdman from Ruatahuna, and then carrying a second letter from Herdman, went to Maungapohatu on 17 March. Herdman was at this time at Ruatahuna, accompanied by policemen, contrary to Rua's understanding with Ngata. Rua had sent an answer to the first letters: ' "I desire you to come here, as you are in the light, and I am in the darkness." '[45] At Maungapohatu, Mitchell added his own warning to Herdman's demand that he come immediately to Ruatahuna, and so to Auckland. If he did not submit, the Urewera country 'would be filled with soldiers'. To this ultimatum, Rua replied only, 'Well, if the soldiers are coming, let me know.'[46] And to his people he said, if the soldiers came, 'the trees will become soldiers and protect us'. Some took him literally.[47]

Mitchell returned from Maungapohatu with the overwhelming impression that Rua was convinced that he was being persecuted by being punished twice for the same offence—an impression which he did not correct, nor did he let Herdman know that Rua still believed this.[48] Herdman's second letter had warned that the government would 'take immediate steps to have the law enforced'. Herdman remained fixed in the belief that he was dealing with a belligerent rebel, who had 'defied the authorities. . . . Clearly the Crown was bound to see that the law was obeyed'.[49] This supposition Herries had reinforced. Such stereotyped misunderstandings would, in turn, underlie all

John Cullen, Commissioner of Police, 1916. Cullen retired from the force on 23 November, aged sixty-five. It was rumoured that he had planned this expedition as his last glorification. *Mrs E. Murphy Album, Alexander Turnbull Library*

the subsequent newspaper accounts of events and become standard public opinion. The gap between the government preconceptions and the Maori understanding was total; the tragedy was that the government acted on its assumptions. Had they not believed fixedly in Rua's bellicosity they might have seen that every doubtful event up to now could have been otherwise explained. But in 1916, the Coalition government looked for conspiracy. The men who actually planned the police expedition into Maungapohatu were those who believed most strongly that armed resistance would be awaiting them. It must be added, however, that Paora Kingi's petition might seem to have given them cause to think so.

John Cullen was responsible for the military-style expedition which was organized. He justified himself, 'I was entitled to go armed to a man whom I knew to be a desperado'.[50] But Cullen already had a reputation for making events conform to his expectations: at Waihi, in the strike of 1912, he set in motion the violence which he, unlike the local police, predicted. He also misrepresented those events subsequently.[51] For Maungapohatu, Cullen assembled a large police party, including some of the mounted police whom he had used at Waihi against the strikers. He anticipated conflict and ordered a 'capable surgeon' for 'any of our men [wounded] in conflict with Rua and his followers'.[52] Herdman agreed to an expedition on this scale because, he said, 'the only course left open was to send in a force to seize him. . . . It was quite evident that drastic action ought to be taken immediately'.[53]

Three police contingents were organized to converge on Maungapohatu. The smallest came from Whakatane: three men, Te Kepa and James Blakeley, with Tim Cummings in charge. They came up the Waimana valley, guided, partly out of friendship, by Hauwaho Tamaikoha, a follower of Rua, and

accompanied, for some of the journey, by Tori Biddle, Rua's son-in-law. They reached Maungapohatu on the evening of Saturday 1 April, the first of the three groups to arrive. The second came from Gisborne: seven men under Sub-Inspector Jimmy Johnston, setting out on 31 March and riding up the Hangaroa river track. Under orders to conceal their destination, Johnston, new from Auckland, had hired a buggy for an 'outing'. They soon had to abandon it on the rough track, and, instead, mount the hacks with which they had been fobbed off. After changing horses at a settler's farm, they reached Maungapohatu on the mid-morning of 2 April, exhausted.

The third and largest contingent assembled secretly at Rotorua on the evening of the 29th. There were fifty-seven constables from Auckland, Hamilton, Wellington, Tauranga, Napier and Wanganui, all instructed to travel in plain clothes to disguise their purpose.§ They were accompanied from Rotorua by John Cullen, Dr Rex Brewster from New Plymouth, and the reporter from the *New Zealand Herald*, John Birch, to whom a hint of the expedition had been leaked deliberately by the Auckland police.[54] With him went the *Auckland Weekly News* photographer, Arthur Breckon. It was rumoured in the force that Cullen sought a fully publicized account, with photographs. They all set out on the 30th, the police still in their ordinary clothes, and squeezed into six brakes. Two baggage waggons carried their arms and stores. Cullen rode in front, in the motor car. They camped that night at Murupara, most of the men sleeping on straw in the open. The next day a picnic lunch was arranged at Te Whaiti. With Andy Grant now as their guide, and various others who had joined them as packhorse men or mere itinerants, like James Craig, a chemist, who came simply for the ' "joy ride" ', they set out on the last section of the road to Ruatahuna. At Te Whaiti they had been told that Rua was preparing a feast of welcome for them, as he had always planned to do when 'the soldiers' came. Pinohi's remark, ' "If your enemy hunger, feed him" ', explains Rua's request to be informed when they were coming.[55] At Te Whaiti they were also told that if any attempt was made to seize Rua, he would simply rise up to heaven.[56] But on the road they met with a rather less credulous Maori workman who, when asked where Rua was, said ' "I don't know, but I've got a slash-hook ready for him. He no good." '[57] Overnight at Ruatahuna, they camped in a paddock and sang the old songs before they turned in, including, inevitably, 'We're here because we're here'.

§The *New Zealand Herald*, 7 April 1916, lists all the police by name.

Above
Issuing the arms, Ruatahuna. Photo by A. N. Breckon. *Blue Album, Alexander Turnbull Library*

Packing the horses, Ruatahuna. Bob Baillie, the storekeeper, stands in the centre, beside the first–aid box. His store and accommodation house were at Omakoi, where the road ended; the whole district is known as Ruatahuna. Photo by A. N. Breckon. *Auckland Weekly News, 13 April 1916*

The police on the road, Ruatahuna. Photo by A. N. Breckon. *Sergeant John Taylor, Auckland*

The next morning, 1 April, at Ruatahuna, the disguises were removed. Uniforms were donned and arms and ammunition issued. The twenty .303 carbines which the police possessed were given to those with army experience, and the rest received revolvers. Then the march began on the tracks to Te Waiiti, and from there into Maungapohatu. The path deteriorated rapidly and at Te Waiiti two of the horses fell. Thereafter, so it is said, the progress of the police party was marked by a trail of ship's biscuits leaking from the inexpertly loaded packhorses.[58] That night they camped at Mahakirua, about sixteen miles (twenty-six kilometres) from Ruatahuna, sleeping on bracken beneath the trees. On the morning of 2 April, Sunday, the party was up at dawn to begin the last nine miles (fourteen kilometres) of the mountain track, pitted with mud holes and cut by streams. At several places along the way, they passed clearings where Rua and his followers had created

Bob Baillie and Andy Grant, April 1916. Grant was in partnership with Baillie in the Ruatahuna store and accommodation house, as well as running the store and post office at Te Whaiti himself. Rua had complained about the low prices the two offered for the cocksfoot seed. In this photograph Grant is the messenger for the police expedition to Maungapohatu, while Baillie supplied much of the food. Photo by A. N. Breckon. *C. C. Webb Collection, Alexander Turnbull Library*

The expedition begins on foot with all formality. Photo by A. N. Breckon. *P. E. Murphy, Auckland*

93

The police, early morning, 2 April 1916. In the centre, one of the constables holds Bob Baillie's fox terrier, who came all the way with them. John Neil, later wounded, stands to his left. William Cobeldick, the ranger, is on the far left, wearing a broad white hat. Next to him, in Inspector's uniform, is Bartholomew Sheehan. Photo by A. N. Breckon. *Blue Album, Alexander Turnbull Library*

Below
Police in the bush, probably at Kakewahine. Photo by A. N. Breckon. *C. C. Webb Collection, Alexander Turnbull Library*

Opposite (both photos)
Crossing the river. In front (top) are Mounted Constable Thomas Wolfendale; Inspector William Phair of Hamilton, on foot; and Mounted Constable Arthur Skinner. These photographs were taken on the morning of Sunday, 2 April 1916. Photos by A. N. Breckon. *Sergeant John Taylor, Auckland; C. C. Webb Collection, Alexander Turnbull Library*

open spaces, putting in grass and establishing small settlements. Finally they climbed the high ridge, Te Kakari, from where, below in the valley, Maungapohatu could be seen three miles (about five kilometres) away. From this ridge, the police would claim they saw a small white flag flying at Maai, Rua's little settlement at the bottom of the valley and about half way to the main community. As the column wound down the narrow track to the

Waikare riverbed, they were watched through binoculars by Rua and the two small police contingents who were together waiting on the marae at Maungapohatu. When the main force reached Maai, the little white flag was gone, they said; the Maungapohatu people maintained that it never existed. It was at Maai that Cullen passed back the order to load up. This was the only order given.[59]

P. 96 (top)
The police at Te Kakari from where they claimed they saw the white flag at Maai, near, as the *Weekly News* put it, 'the outlaw's pa'. 'The flying of a white flag', it continued, 'led to the belief that Rua meant to give himself up peacefully, but as the police advanced towards the stronghold the flag disappeared.'
On the extreme left, on horseback and wearing plain clothes, is John Cullen. Grant is to his left, standing beside his horse and wearing a cloth cap. In the foreground, centre, are Constables Adam Murray and 'Curly', John Neil.
Behind them are: Constable Matt Brady, with a watch chain; Constable Bill Neil, seated one remove from him, wearing an open waistcoat and a large moustache. Behind them are: Mounted Constable Harry Maisey, with his chin on his hand; Sergeant Con Murphy, seated one remove in the same row and wearing a dark scarf tucked under his shoulder holster. Inspector Phair, who was unwell, can be identified in his cloth cap, further to the right. Photo by A. N. Breckon. *Auckland Weekly News, 13 April 1916*

(Top) see p. 95

(Top) see p. 95

Centre

Maungapohatu, Easter 1916. This photograph was taken by Percy Wilkinson, a surveyor, who was sent into Maungapohatu by the police to gather evidence for them, on 22–3 April. The two figures standing together on the marae were said to be where Rua and his sons stood, as the police approached. 'The deep gully into which Rua tried to escape is situated to the left', commented the *Auckland Star*, which reproduced this photograph on 9 June. The mountain looms behind the community, its summit about 450 metres above the settlement.

The photograph on p. 80 gives a sharper view of the community in April 1916. The steepness of the gully is more apparent and the location of the kitchens on the edge of the marae more distinct. One item of evidence which seems to be missing from all the records is the extensive plan of the settlement made by Wilkinson—and also that made by David Lundon for the defence—upon which various numbered locations were marked. Constant reference to both plans was made in the trial evidence and certain problems of location could be more readily resolved if these had not been destroyed.

The photographs collected in the Murphy Album, of which this is one, may have been taken by Wilkinson. Another collection of the same photographs, also mounted as an album, was given by Wilkinson to one of the Crown witnesses, Henry Stowell (Hare Hongi). Both are in the Alexander Turnbull Library.

Tom Collins, who came with the Auckland police, remembers wondering just what they were going to do, for they had received word, two days before, from the Whakatane police, that Rua had no intention of resisting arrest. 'We should know what we are doing', Constable Jim McIntyre said to him as they walked.[60] From Maai, which was deserted of people, they began the climb up to the pa. They were forced into single file by the 'trenchlike' nature of the track. Some feared an ambush, but there was none, for no preparations for resistance had been made. After the event, the *Evening Post* snorted with impunity, 'Bad generalship', so deeply rooted was the conviction that resistance had been planned and that Rua was a military leader. Neither armed defence nor armed attack was part of Rua's intentions.

Waiting on the marae were Rua and his two eldest sons, Whatu and Toko. The Whakatane police, who had been invited to stay at the marae but who declined and camped in the valley, climbed up to the settlement early in the morning. Rua came down from his house to greet them, accompanied by his two sons, all three dressed identically in white shirts with stand-up linen collars and flaming red ties. Rua carried the huge Covenant in his hands.

He welcomed them and James Blakeley thought he said, ' "This is the Bible, I'm the Holy Ghost. I am finished with you" '. Tim Cummings thought he had said, ' "This is the finish for you" '.[61] Rua denied any such conversation, or that he had brought the heavy Bible, but he did give Cummings the red ribbon marker taken from it for him to read. (Cummings kept it.) Written on the ribbon in gold letters and in English was a Scriptural message of peace and a text, the 'good shepherd' of Israel.[62] Rua also gave Cummings as a gift a collar bearing the impress of King George V, as an indication of his loyalty.[63] Then Rua returned the Bible to his house, according to the police, whose evidence is probably correct on the point. Rua then showed the three men around Hiona, the little dance hall, and the meeting-house. Blakeley and Cummings both thought that he seemed very excited. He kept watching the Ruatahuna track for the main body to appear, but the Gisborne police came first, all but two dressed in plain clothes, and their arms concealed, like the Whakatane police. Rua invited them to have a cup of tea. He inquired of Jimmy Johnston if ten sheep would be sufficient to feed all the police who were coming. To Gerald Maloney, whom he knew, he said, ' "You come too soon for the Kai, Kai not on till 1 o'clock." He said "you're like the first Christ, you come too soon. . . . I am the proper Christ, Father son and the Holy Ghost, that's me" '.[64] He counted the ten police who were now there and added, ' "A lot more men coming over the hill." ' To Myles Doyle, whom he also knew, he said, ' "It's all right, 100 men here" and he waved towards his people sitting on the bank. He said "There is plenty of Kai, all going to have tea, I'm Rua the Holy Ghost, that's me" '.[65]

Bottom
Whatu, Rua and Toko on the porch of Tane Nui A Rangi, 2 April 1916. All three are dressed identically in breeches and puttees, much in vogue before the war. Constable Bill Sleeth of the Gisborne police took this photograph and it was reproduced with Gerald Maloney's account of the expedition, written for the *Police Journal* in November 1937. *R. A. Creswell, Palmerston North*

Above
A view of the main buildings of the settlement, taken on 2 April 1916: Tane Nui A Rangi; Hiruharama Hou; Hiona; the *whare kanikani*, or hall for traditional dancing.

Opposite (top)
The marae, as the police approached. Some of the Maoris are sitting on the bank to the left. Photos by Constable Bill Sleeth. *R. A. Creswell, Palmerston North*

Opposite
This caricature illustration by Harry Rountree accompanied an article written in 1916 by James Cowan, entitled 'Rua the Prophet'. The drawing was captioned 'Several policemen dashed off in pursuit', and suggested that Rua was urging his savage followers to fight from 'the temple': such an image is directly denied by the photographs which follow. *Wide World Magazine,* XXXVIII, 1916, 234. *National Library of Australia*

When the main party reached the stream at Maai, Rua asked Tim Cummings to go down to Cullen. He said, ' "I want the soldiers kept back, [and] a korero with the rangatira." '[66] But when Cummings encountered Cullen, the Commissioner said that they had come to arrest Rua, and that he should be handcuffed because he had already 'got away' once before.[67] The police party continued to wind its way up from the bottom of the valley, with Cullen and two mounted constables, Arthur Skinner and Thomas Wolfendale at their head, their rifles visible through the glasses. Then the party went out of view from the marae. Rua went over to those of his followers sitting on the bank to the left of the marae and spoke with them. 'He was stooping down with his hands on his knees talking to them, and they were paying great attention to him.'[68] What he said none of the police knew. The Maoris were clear that he told them that, should he be arrested, they were to offer no opposition: ' "Well, if you will not go inside you must not interfere, and even if I am dragged through the dust and my face is spat upon, don't interfere." '[69] Rua returned to stand on the marae, near the flagpole on which he had hoisted, as a 'sign of peace', his flag *Kotahi Te Ture*.[70]

The following reconstruction of what happened is based on the evidence given at Rua's trial, evidence which is itself riddled with contradictions. The actual trial documents were destroyed, along with all the early criminal records of the Auckland Supreme Court, in 1949. The newspaper reports are, therefore, necessarily the only public sources, along with the depositions made by the police in the preliminary hearings in Rotorua. However, in the course of writing this chapter we were generously given access to the voluminous private papers of Rua's defence counsel, Jerry Lundon.‖ From these three major sources, we found that the least reliable witnesses are those on the Crown's side who presented views which appear to be structured. But it is also clear that manipulation of evidence occurred on both sides. In this mire, from which complete truth is probably irrecoverable, we can point out

‖ A detailed study of the trial evidence, deriving from this source, will be published by Judith Binney. The amount of material is such that it could not be assimilated into the limited scale of the present work. It is to be expected that the complete assessment of the Lundon papers will result in some degree of reinterpretation of the material presented here.

'KOTAHI TE TURE MO NGA IWI E RUA MAUNGAPOHATU', 'ONE LAW FOR BOTH PEOPLES MAUNGAPOHATU': Rua's flag confiscated by the police as evidence for 'sedition'. It is 4.67 metres long and 1.80 metres deep. The letters were first cut out and then stitched over in contrasting colours. The flag was deposited at the Auckland Institute and Museum by Cullen in 1930; it properly belongs to the people of Maungapohatu. It is an indication of the duration of prejudice that the *New Zealand Herald* could still describe it, in 1957, as Rua's 'insolent' inscription. *Auckland Institute and Museum*

the implications of some of the contradictions.

Cullen cut up the bank and rode straight onto the marae towards Johnston, who was standing near the meeting-house. Gerald Maloney, who was watching, was convinced that 'Rua never thought the police would march right up on to the marae and arrest him out of hand. He would expect the police leader (Commissioner Cullen) to come up first with one or two of his officers, as was the usual old Maori custom, and have a long "korero" over the matter first.'[71] Traditional courtesy demanded some ritual of welcome and Rua undoubtedly expected that the armed police would remain below, as he had requested. But Cullen merely asked which man was Rua, and, still on horseback, beckoned to him. Rua walked a couple of paces away, and stood still. Cullen, perhaps attempting to counteract the impression of force he had created, then called out awkwardly 'Haeremai', and walked his horse towards him. Johnston began to move; Rua took a step or two towards Cullen and then, according to the police evidence, turned to run. The two mounted constables had at this moment appeared over the edge of the marae, their carbines glinting in the sun. Both Grant and Maloney observed this

The police party riding up to the marae, 2 April 1916. Cullen said that he halted the force, about three hundred yards from the pa, and arranged them 'so that all would be in a handy position if any trouble arose.' Here, Cullen rides in front with Tim Cummings immediately behind him. He is followed by Sergeant John O'Hara and Grant, who is wearing a soft cap and light riding breeches. Dr Brewster follows, then Cobeldick in the large white hat. Skinner appears at the edge of the frame. This sequence was described precisely by the Senior Sergeant, John Cassells, in his Deposition, and he seems to have had this photograph in mind. Although Wolfendale rode alongside Skinner, it remains a curious fact that he, like some others, never gave evidence. He came onto the marae with Skinner and was involved in the wounding of Paora Kingi.
Hiruharama Hou and the *whare kanikani* are on the horizon. Photo by Bill Sleeth. *Mrs Mary McKenzie, Paraparaumu*

Right
'View of front of house showing flagstaff and persons in about same position as Rua stood when Commissioner arrived.' This photograph with this caption was among the defence counsel's evidence. Photo by William Carter. *Lundon Collection*

coincidence, and Grant was quite explicit that it was the abrupt appearance of the horsemen which caused Rua to panic and attempt to take flight.[72] He waved his hand to his people sitting on the embankment to go back, and called out, 'He pu era. He kino'. The implication of the words was disputed in the subsequent trials, but the weight of the evidence was towards the simplest interpretation: 'They have guns. That's bad'. Johnston grabbed at Rua as he turned toward the embankment. As he seized Rua, Rua's left sleeve was ripped off; Johnston kept it as a 'memento'.[73] Cullen called, 'The man's bolting; collar him', in some versions;[74] in others, Bill Neil from Rotorua, who had walked near the head of the main column with an axe to clear the track, simply leapt on Rua, struck him, and attempted to handcuff him. In the ensuing struggle, the men rolled down the bank on the south-east side of the marae. As Neil rushed at Rua, he apparently dropped the axe; Whatu seized it and came to defend his father, the axe raised. Sergeant John O'Hara snatched the axe from Whatu, who was immediately arrested. As Judge Hosking was to observe at Whatu's trial, six constables gave such varying accounts of Whatu's actions that no reliance could be placed upon them. All that could be said was that Whatu had hold of the axe and ran in the direction of his father.[75]

At the same moment, Awa Horomona, who had been with Rua on the marae since early morning, also rushed into the melee around Rua. Michael Fahy, from the Wellington police, tackled Awa, but he was a strong man and he knocked Fahy's rifle from his hand. Pukepuke Kanara, who had been sitting on the bank, picked it up. Harry Maisey, who arrested Pukepuke, saw him with the gun. The moment Pukepuke realised that he had been observed, he threw it away under one of the nearby huts. He would, however, be charged with pointing the gun at Skinner.[76] Awa was struck heavily by Skinner from his horse with a newly-cut riding stick, batoned by the Senior Sergeant in charge of the column, John Cassells, and frog-marched back to the centre of the marae.

Rua had fallen down the bank between two of the kitchens, struggling with Johnston, Neil and a third constable who had joined in, James Williamson. This man, Rua said, struck him heavily. Cullen, standing up in his stirrups, gave the order to frog-march Rua up onto the marae. Face down, held only by the wrists and feet, he was lifted from the ground. It was at this moment that

Whatu, Rua and Toko waiting for John Cullen as he rode onto the marae. Rua's arms are outstretched and Cullen seems to be turning to look back at the police behind him. Is this the moment when Rua put up his hands and said, 'Taihoa', as the Maori witnesses described? In Rua's words, 'I told him "Taihoa" until I should get my people to withdraw and I could have a quiet talk with him. I made three steps forward and saw the policemen with guns. He should have kept his people back until he had time to talk to me. I was in the act of going up to Cullen when his police behind forced matters, they rushed up.' This account is supported in William Cobeldick's evidence. He said that Brewster took a photograph of Rua, his arms outstretched towards Cullen, the moment before Johnston seized his arm. This, then, is probably Brewster's photo. As Tom Collins puts it plainly, 'Rua didn't resist at all, but the proper evidence wasn't given.' *Lundon collection*

Awa Horomona and Tioke, arrested. The blood on Awa's temple from the baton wound is clearly visible. Awa's daughter, Tawhaki, was Toko's wife. *Bernard Teague, Wairoa*

Portrait of Bill Neil in the uniform of the mounted police, 1916. *Len Shapcott, Cambridge*

the first shot was fired. The effect was cataclysmic: the crack echoed from the hills, the dogs barked, the women, some of whom were still on the bank, screamed and ran, and the police scattered in all directions.[77]

The police, in giving their evidence in the lower court, were adamant that it was a Maori shot, although they disagreed on where it came from. Some, like Andy Grant, thought it was fired from the far side of the gully; others, including the *Herald* reporter, said that it came from behind one of the huts at the edge of the marae. Birch was very specific: it came from behind the nearest hut on the left of the marae, which he later identified as 'the cook house'. But many of the police at the Supreme Court trial stated that the shot came from the far side of the gully, where there were no police. Those like Tim Cummings and James Blakeley, who maintained it came from the edge of the marae, were also 'certain' that no police were there either. But Cummings also said that by the time Toko was in the gully and was called upon to halt (a time others considered virtually simultaneous with the first shot) there were police in the gully.[78] George Rushton said the same.[79]

It is impossible, now, to establish who fired that shot. The Maori witnesses, in collusion, accused Skinner of firing it directly at Rua, lying on the ground. This was a concoction, later exposed at the perjury trials of 1917. It is, however, still believed by a number of the Iharaira. Arthur Skinner, a well-known wrestler, had acquired notoriety for his free use of his baton and riding crop during the Waihi strike of 1912. Cullen and Skinner had been specifically associated together in one incident there¶ and Cullen kept Skinner close to the head of the column, as they rode up to Maungapohatu. Cullen named the old man Paora Kingi as the man who had fired the first shot, although none of the other police were prepared to. Paora may have been singled out because he had initiated the petition to the Prime Minister, warning that a 'gun would be fired'. Certainly Cullen's original cable to Herdman suggests this association: 'Paora Kingi came in yesterday . . . . This man who wrote Prime Minister in January threatening to shoot if Rua arrested. I think it was Kingi who fired the first shot as he was in vicinity where it was fired.'[81] Paora was also seriously wounded by

¶The unionist, Oliver Noakes, swore that he had been set upon in a narrow alleyway and batoned by Cullen and Skinner together. This incident was widely known.[80]

police fire – shot in the back when, according to all the Maoris, he was unarmed. But as an old warrior for Te Turuki he had a reputation; among the Maoris, at least, it was known that he possessed Te Turuki's sword.

It is indeed possible, as the storekeeper's daughter at Murupara said, that the first shot was fired by a rifle which went off accidentally.[82] If so, it must have been one of the police rifles, because, as the police admitted, none of the Maoris visible on the marae were armed.★

Arthur Skinner was singled out as having fired this shot by Rua's defence counsel, Jerry Lundon and William Carter, because of his reputation.[85] They concurred in naming Skinner because they wanted to break down the police account that a planned ambush awaited them and that the shot was part of such an ambush. Lundon decided to name Skinner, although he did not know who fired the shot.[86] He did so because he believed that Cullen had been seeking a confrontation at Maungapohatu. The two men were themselves old adversaries from the Waihi hearings, when Lundon had acted for the miners at the inquest on a man who had been batoned to death. His decision to name Skinner was an error of great magnitude.

Cullen gained one supporter in naming Paora. William Cobeldick, the ranger who joined the main force about ten miles from Maungapohatu, finally also named him, although at first, in 1916, he was careful to state that he did not know. He had, however, consistently refused to accept Lundon's version and in the perjury trials of 1917 said that he had proved to his 'own satisfaction' that Paora had fired the first shot. Carter was convinced that the police had pressured Cobeldick because of an old offence. Cobeldick had lost his job in 1896 for sheep stealing. Certainly Cullen dug up this record in 1916,[87] and Cobeldick had tried to avoid giving defence evidence in Rua's trial. Cobeldick stated that he had been warned by a policeman, 'Watch that old man! He is the

Henry Matthew Stowell and Arthur Skinner, outside the Auckland Supreme Court, 1916. Stowell, who was a half-caste, gave linguistic evidence for the Crown at Rua's trial. *Mrs E. Murphy Album, Alexander Turnbull Library*

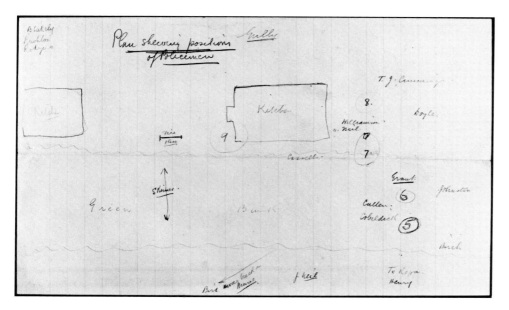

★ There was much dispute over what kind of gun had been fired. Both Andy Grant and William Cobeldick, the Rotorua ranger who had met up with the main police contingent, thought that it might have been a .22 rifle. But Cobeldick was cautious: 'No man could say what that shot was fired from.'[83] The Maoris said that Skinner had fired with a revolver. The police then brought evidence that Skinner had exchanged his police revolver for Cassells' rifle about an hour before they reached Maungapohatu, although Skinner kept his revolver holster. But, as Lundon noted, Cassells originally stated that he was unarmed when he first reached the marae and therefore grabbed a rifle: it could not have been an 'exchange'. Lundon received two anonymous letters alleging that Skinner was carrying, as he was said to have done in the strikes, his own automatic pistol.[84] This charge, put to Skinner by Lundon, was of course denied. If all this evidence is accepted, Skinner appears to be rather over-equipped: one rifle, two hand guns, and a riding crop!

Andy Grant and William Cobeldick, outside the Supreme Court in Auckland. *Mrs E. Murphy Album, Alexander Turnbull Library*

man who fired the first shot.' Paora was then running in the gully; he was fired at by Skinner and Wolfendale. As Lundon pointed out, it was curious that the constable who made this identification of Paora was himself never identified. Moreover, as Skinner said, the old man running in the gully did not appear to be armed, so he ceased his fire.[88] David Lundon, the surveyor, who drew a detailed map of the Maungapohatu community for the defence, also stressed, '*Natives had no guns. All the way up the hill Poura was visible to the police*'.[89]

Cullen had named Paora also because of what Tori Biddle had originally told him at Maungapohatu on 3 April: 'Tori Biddle told me that Paora Kingi fired *the first shot* – next day Monday'.[90] Biddle also said that Kingi had fired four or five shots from up the hill. Cullen himself was not prepared to name Paora publicly until the Supreme Court hearings, and Biddle denied that they had had such a conversation. But by then Biddle was a central figure in the naming of Skinner, although later he would be forced by the police to admit that this identification was perjured. Old Paora simply denied all the accusations, and maintained throughout that he had been unarmed.

The police had to prove that the shot came from the far side of the gully as part of their case that it could only have been a Maori shot. But there is yet another aspect to be borne in mind. Eric Lundon, Lundon's eldest son, has stated to us that it was the Maori accounts of the death of Toko Rua which persuaded his father that the police version of events was a tissue of lies. The death of Toko lies at the heart of Lundon's calculated perjury. The two most contentious issues raised by Rua's trial – the naming of Skinner and the manner in which Toko died – are closely associated.

When Johnston seized Rua, Toko ran from the marae into the gully on the left. Still unarmed, he ran up the far side of the gully and one of the constables, Ernest Jarrold, covered him with a rifle at the ready. He did not fire† and Sergeant Hugh Cox called out not to shoot. Toko hesitated, raised his hands in surrender, and then ducked away into the scrub at the top of the gully. He reappeared some moments later inside the fence surrounding Hiruharama Hou and then began to fire down at the police. But as Andy Grant said, 'It is not possible that Toko Rua fired the first shot.'[91] From both the Maori and

† This incident occurred at the same time as the arrest of Rua and the firing of the first shot. However, it seems clear that Jarrold did not fire, although Carter was still speculating on this possibility in 1917.

Paora Kingi, 1916. He wore two rugs over his European clothes, one about his knees and the other around his shoulders in the style of a chief, when he gave evidence in Rua's trial. He was still in great pain as a result of the shoulder wound. One newspaper wrote, 'His taking of the oath was a lesson in dignity, and except that his rugs were of European manufacture, he looked like the original of a portrait of an old-time chief.' *Mrs E. Murphy Album, Alexander Turnbull Library*

police evidence it seems that Toko, who was a marksman, took his gun from his house at the top of the gully and opened fire inside the paddock. Once Toko began shooting, the police retaliated en masse.

The police had been given no instructions. On this Tom Collins and Harry Maisey are definite. As George Rushton said at the time, 'No one waited for orders everyone sailed for anyone he could get.'[92] Things happened with such abruptness, provoked by what Collins and Maisey both consider ill-judged actions on the part of Johnston and Neil, that there was no time for coherent orders. But in Collins' view, the decisive error was the fact that the police column, still winding its way up the track below the meeting-house, broke ranks and poured over the bank onto the marae and into the paddock where Hiruharama Hou stood, which brought some of the men straight into Toko's line of fire. The cause was the 'stupidity' of the sergeant in charge of the column, whose anonymity Collins has been scrupulous in preserving.[93] This man, it can be established, was John Cassells, who ordered the force to break their formation; the consequence was, in Collins' view, the unnecessary deaths of Toko and his close friend, Te Maipi Te Whiu.

Collins, who had walked near the head of the column, reached the marae as the first police were struggling with Rua and he, with John Neil, who was subsequently seriously wounded, took off in chase of Toko. Collins states that he was prevented from giving evidence at Rua's trial by Cassells, because he had made known his opposition to the large number of arrests (more than thirty) made on that day. He gives an account which is quite at variance with the main police depositions and shows that some of the police concealed not only evidence but also a concern among their colleagues as to what actually happened.

As Collins reveals, there existed a sharp conflict within the police between those who had adopted a 'conspiracy' theory to explain the events at Maungapohatu – in particular Cassells and Cullen – and those who remembered certain facts observed on that day: that all the Maoris visible on the marae were unarmed, that a feast of welcome was being prepared, and that in the end two (or perhaps three or four) Maoris grabbed weapons. As Collins put it, 'There was not a smell of a revolution out there, that day. . . . It was they who wanted to make a conspiracy where none existed.'

The account of Arnold Butterworth supports Collins by showing that the police actions on the marae were themselves illegal. It was essential to the police argument to establish not only that a conspiracy to attack existed, but

The police column marching in single file, after the first of the mounted men. Photo by Constable Bill Sleeth. *R. A. Creswell, Palmerston North*

also that Rua had resisted arrest; otherwise, Cullen and the police were criminally responsible, under the very Crimes Act they were to use against Rua, for their own excess of force. This use of unnecessary violence resulted in the deaths of the two men. Butterworth, who came with the Gisborne contingent, states explicitly that there were attempts to distort evidence, initiated by Cassells to conceal what he knew had occurred; that is, a police assault. Butterworth says positively, 'Rua didn't resist at all. It was an illegal arrest, and he didn't resist either. He was attacked.'

Cullen and Cassells were both seriously implicated if it were established successfully that no resistance had been offered at Maungapohatu before Rua was tackled. Cullen, as the Commissioner, was responsible and Cassells had

Right
Tom Collins and (opposite) Arnold Butterworth. Photos by Gillian Chaplin, 1978.

lost control of the column. The gravamen of the Maori accounts of Rua's behaviour on the marae was precisely this: he had merely held up his hands and said 'Taihoa', when Johnston, and then Neil, grabbed him. It is the nub of Tom Collins' remark, previously quoted, 'Rua didn't resist at all, but the proper evidence wasn't given.' Butterworth adds, 'In some way, it was hushed up. I don't think the facts ever properly came out. If they did, there was a miscarriage of justice.'

Moreover, Cassells attempted to dictate the statements to be made by some of the police officers, which was in itself an illegal action. Butterworth, who did not give evidence at any of the trials, refused to sign his prepared statement at Maungapohatu, 'and tore it up in front of Cassells and others and threw it on the ground. There wasn't a bit of truth in the statement, in the part I read.' The heart of the police account was to insist that Rua had taken flight, forcing Johnston and Neil to act, and Cullen to command them to act. Butterworth is certain that Cullen shouted to Johnston to arrest Rua as he turned towards the other Gisborne police standing near the eastern track. He believes that Rua was looking to them for guidance, because he was sweating with fear at the display of rifles.

The problem had another dimension, which some of the police, at least, soon became aware of. Rua's arrest, under the warrants which the police carried, was illegal on a Sunday. This fact was brought out in the subsequent Supreme Court trial. Butterworth, who remembers that the Gisborne police discussed this very issue as they came in with Johnston, is very clear about the implications of the assault which Cullen launched.

The arrest was illegal. We worked out that Cullen would be guilty of eleven charges from murder or manslaughter down to common assault. The death of those two men were murder; another was causing bodily harm to those that were wounded. There was assault, with intent to kill. There's so many. There were eleven charges there, with capital punishment or very long terms of imprisonment. We worked it out when we were coming home. We wondered where we stood . . . .

'Boys' Own Paper'-style cartoon of the fight. This illustration, by Harry Rountree, accompanied Cowan's article on Rua, published in 1916. It was captioned, 'He was in the act of delivering a blow at a constable with an axe when he was felled.' Heroic police struggle with savages. It was this particular episode upon which the Supreme Court Judge was to decide that the police evidence was unreliable. Parallel to this propaganda, was a fictionalized account – supposedly an eye witness account – published by the *Poverty Bay Herald* on 5 April 1916. One of the civilians, who had travelled ' "to see the fun" ', told the paper how Cullen had divided the force into four sections, of 25 men each, and had closed secretly in the morning fog(!) in a four-pronged movement upon the pa. Then a signal from a gun was given and the four sections rushed to within three hundred yards before the 'natives' patrol' was even aware of their presence. Cullen then told Rua to surrender. ' "I'll fight for ever and ever and ever," replied Rua. "Stand back," he cried, "for we are going to fire now." ' Then the battle broke out, 100 of Rua's followers coming to the defence of their leader with shotguns and rifles. Rua fought fiercely 'armed with a breech-loading fowling piece, and when he discharged both barrels he was rushed by five men', etc., etc. The description of the informant suggests James Craig, from Manaia, Taranaki, who later gave rebuttal evidence for the Crown. *National Library of Australia*

Portrait of Te Maipi. He is with his wife, Puti Hikihiki. Photographed, by courtesy of Rata Takao, Piripari, by Gillian Chaplin, 1977.

This gun is said to be Toko's Mauser. It is an automatic .30 calibre pistol, with a 900 metres measured range. Inscribed on the chamber is the manufacturing name:
Waffenfabrik Mauser
Oberndorf A. Neckar.
It is the 'Standard Prewar Commercial' model, 1896. It came originally to the storekeeper at Ruatahuna, wrapped in fragments of a flag and with the associated legend that it had been hidden after Toko was shot. Toko's Mauser was certainly known to have existed: Hillman Rua can remember it. It could be turned into a shotgun by having a wooden stock attached, and Doyle reported finding the stock for a Mauser at Maai, when the police searched the houses. It is presumably the same Mauser upon which Ernest Bressey built his rumours.
Anonymous private collection. Photo by Gillian Chaplin, 1978.

Opposite (top)
Rua and Whatu under arrest. In the left background, wearing a soft hat, is Gerald Maloney, who is holding Te Maipi's gun, with which, it was said, Te Maipi had wounded Constable 'Darkie' Wright.
This was the Browning automatic shotgun. Jimmy Johnston, bearded, stands in the foreground, left; James Williamson stands behind Rua's torn sleeve; Sergeant James Henry is on the right.
Photo by Bill Sleeth. *Mrs Mary McKenzie, Paraparaumu*

The main police claim had to extend, therefore, even beyond the assertion that Rua had bolted. It had to include an account of a prepared ambush, for which he had given a signal. But as Cobeldick explicitly said in evidence, 'I could not say there was an ambush.'[94]

Two young men were in fact armed. They were Toko and Te Maipi. From the evidence we have gathered, and despite Maori statements at the time, we must conclude that both were armed and that Tom Collins and other police were right in saying so.

Te Maipi was found with a jammed shotgun (a Browning automatic single-barrelled 12 gauge) under his body. According to the police, Toko originally fired with this gun, which he got from his own house, but he passed it to Te Maipi when he was wounded in the right arm. The Maori witnesses also said that Toko passed this gun to Te Maipi, but that Te Maipi was killed immediately, because he did not know how to use it. The Maori witnesses, and all our Maori informants, were adamant that Te Maipi had no gun of his own. But the police said that Toko had another gun, which he took from Te Maipi. It was a large single-barrelled Mauser pistol. With this, Toko fired again, using his left hand. In his account, written to the Crown Prosecutor on 18 April, Cullen said that after Toko's right forearm was smashed, 'he then had to drop the shot gun, which was picked up by Te Maipi, who had been using a large Mauser pistol. Toko Rua then took the pistol and commenced firing at the police'. In a slightly fuller version, written two days later to Herdman, Cullen added that a third man, wearing a red shirt, who was with the two youths in the upper paddock, escaped with the Mauser.[95] This man

108

was seen by other police, but his presence was denied by the Maoris. He was never identified. The existence of Toko's pistol, with the associated legend that it had been hidden, seems to give credence to the police account. The Mauser was Toko's favourite gun, which he usually kept in Hiruharama Hou.[96]

Toko and Te Maipi were killed in the paddock behind Hiruharama Hou; Tom Collins describes the events as follows. He and John Neil went after the 'two boys', Collins calling to Neil, who was just ahead of him, to take the 'one on the left'. But Neil was shot through the abdomen and, it was discovered later, emasculated. Collins threw himself behind a large tree stump, about seventy-five yards (sixty-eight metres) from the marae. Here he was joined, he says, by John Reilly, a former Imperial serviceman who had one of the .303 carbines. (Reilly did not give evidence.) The two young men were running for a large building on the horizon, Hiruharama Hou. At this moment the police burst through, out of formation, armed only with revolvers and running recklessly into the line of fire from the shotgun. It was for this reason, argues Collins, that Reilly had to shoot to kill. Te Maipi died instantly, shot through the head. Toko fell to the ground. The shooting was all over in a matter of minutes; Collins emphasizes that if the whole incident had lasted the twenty or thirty minutes, as in the official version, there would have been as many police dead. At the trial, he claims there was a consistent effort to 'camouflage' the basic fact that the police had broken formation and thereby made unavoidable the deaths of Toko and Te Maipi. 'Everything that was done was done to cover that up.' 'If the police had kept to their formation there would have been no more casualties [than John Neil]. They opened up on the Maoris.'[97]

The police depositions concerning the deaths diverge from this account. Toko began firing from the paddock near the head of the gully, down the track at the police running up from the marae. John Neil was shot by him. Neil said he was hit when he was at the junction of the Gisborne track, by the stump.[98]

Opposite (bottom)
The tree stump. This photograph was found among the Lundon papers; the marked inner portion was reproduced in the *Auckland Weekly News*. Tom Collins, who has had a copy of the inner portion since the event, comments that the photograph was a reconstruction, posed after the shooting had stopped. The three men at the base of the stump Collins has identified as John Garvey, himself (both armed with revolvers), and the third man, armed with a rifle which cannot be seen, as John Reilly.
The photograph looks towards the hills to the south-west of the Maungapohatu settlement. The large building in the background is probably the guest house; it cannot be Hiruharama Hou because of its damaged roof. Tree stump '17' was at the junction of the Gisborne track, and the fence at this point was on a high bank, but as the upper part of the settlement was littered with tree stumps, the precise location of this photograph remains somewhat uncertain. Photo by A. N. Breckon.

Toko was first wounded in the paddock, near the fence, his right forearm smashed by a bullet. A trail of blood was found across the paddock leading towards Hiruharama Hou.[99] He was seen again, with Te Maipi and an older man wearing a red shirt, in the long grass of the paddock, behind and to the west of the house. All three were armed, according to the testimony of George Rushton and William Rogers; Gerald Maloney, who was with them, noticed only that Te Maipi was armed.[100] Rushton called out, in English, to surrender. Te Maipi began to put his hands up, and then both Toko and Te Maipi fired at the three policemen, said Rushton. They retaliated, and Te Maipi died instantly, shot in the head. Toko fell near the corner of the little building, the House of the Covenant. The man in the red shirt fled, carrying, said Rogers, Toko's large pistol.[101]

Pinepine, Toko's mother, witnessed some of these events, as she hid inside her house at the south-west end of the paddock. She saw Toko with a gun in the paddock. Te Maipi followed him, she said, but had no gun. Then she saw Toko running back with his arm bleeding. At the rear of her own house, she hurriedly bandaged his wrist. Gerald Maloney, alone of the police, remembered that, when Toko's body was found, the wrist had been freshly bandaged.[102] Pinepine then fled into her house again. When she tried to come out (carrying, as it now seems, the Covenant) she saw Toko crawling, wounded, under the table on which the wash-tubs stood behind the house.[103] She fled, and the police saw her go. Toko died near the House of the Covenant. He died with three wounds in his body.[104] The people of Maungapohatu are convinced, without any shade of doubt, that Toko crawled, badly hurt, under Pinepine's house. The third wound was made by a policeman who hauled him out by his boots and shot him in the back, 'like a bloody dog'.[105] As Harimate Roberts said to us, Pinepine did not see the third shot fired, but she saw the wound and knew that he had been shot again after she had left him by the house. If this is so, Toko's death was murder.

The one who said she had witnessed this shooting was Waereti. She, with several of the other women, had hidden inside Hiruharama Hou. She changed some of the details in her evidence, apparently under persuasion from Carter, in an attempt to strengthen her account,[106] but remained unshaken that she had seen Toko dragged out by his feet and shot. Although the medical evidence seems to contradict her account, it is not without its own problems. Toko had received two chest wounds. Dr Brewster stated, in his original report, that the one on the left, below the heart, was from the front. He also said that neither bullet had gone right through. Cullen also said that there was no mark on Toko's back and that the bullets had not passed through.[107] Nor was there any mark on his clothing or skin consistent with having been shot at close range.[108] But Dr Brewster's evidence was simply read, in his absence at the War, and he could not be cross-examined; nor had there been a proper inquest, because the bodies had been interred at Maungapohatu. Dyer, acting as coroner, had decided not to ask for an exhumation, as it would be 'very harassing to the feelings of the natives',[109] although he was worried about the dubious legality of holding an inquest without seeing the bodies. It was Cullen who originally decided that an inquest would be 'unnecessary', indeed 'impossible', if the bodies had to be brought out. He therefore had them buried at Maungapohatu.[110]

Waereti's description of Toko's death is firmly believed by all the people of Rua. It is also said that Te Kepa, just before he died, told the Waimana elders that their understanding of Toko's death was substantially true.[111] John Cassells certified that he thought that he had been the first to find Toko's body. It was lying at the rear of Pinepine's house, on its back with the head up against the building. He turned it slightly to see if Toko was dead. He also admitted that he had fired his rifle from the fence at the back of Pinepine's house, and he contradicted himself directly as to when and at whom he fired.[112] George Rushton also found Toko's body at the rear and to the left of Pinepine's house, lying 'on his stomach, with his head towards the whare and his legs upwards.'[113] He found it after the police had searched Hiruharama Hou and driven the women out of the house. He did not think it had been dragged and he considered Waereti's description of the manner of his death inconceivable. Tori Biddle revealed in his later confessions, which are themselves uncertainly motivated, that Waereti had altered her account, and that other women, who had not witnessed Toko's death, decided to give her story as their own. But the Maungapohatu people rejected Tori Biddle's confessions and have sustained an unwavering commitment to the original, and appalling, explanation.

The bodies of the two young men were placed inside Te Whare Kawenata by the police. On Monday afternoon 3 April, they were interred while most of the men from Maungapohatu were still held captive. Six of 'the most harmless' were released to help with the burial, but there were no coffins, due to the 'great haste displayed' by the Commissioner.[114] The police formed a guard of honour for them, but there was no tangi.

When the first shot was heard, Rua was being lifted from the ground. As he was forcibly carried towards the marae, he called out. The words the police said he used were 'Patua, Patua!' They argued it was a command to strike or to kill. On this word, which by itself is meaningless, they rested much of their case that they had faced a planned attack, for which Rua had given the signal. The defence marshalled evidence from Maori speakers that the words could only have been part of the cry of despair, 'Kill me, kill me' – 'Patua au', 'Patua

Opposite (top)
Pinepine, and (below) Wairimu and Waereti, 1916. Waereti had left Rua by this date. *Mrs E. Murphy Album, Alexander Turnbull Library*

Below
The House of the Covenant, beyond Pinepine's house, at the south-west end of Rua's enclosure. The buckets of water, to wash from, are to protect the tapu of the house. The women, said to be some of Rua's wives, are mourning the young men, whose bodies have been placed inside. Notice the flowers to the right, always associated with Pinepine. The *Weekly News* published this photo on 13 April and marked, to left, with 'X' 'X' the spots where Toko's and Te Maipi's bodies were said to have been found. There was some confusion between Pinepine's house and Te Whare Kawenata. Photo by A. N. Breckon. *C. C. Webb Collection, Alexander Turnbull Library*

Tawhaki, widow of Toko, 1978. Photo by Gillian Chaplin.

Whatu, Rua his head wounded from being struck, and, behind him, Maka Kanuehi, arrested. Photo by A. N. Breckon. *Auckland Weekly News, 13 April 1916*

Opposite (bottom)
'Darkie', William George Wright, being assisted. He had been shot in the lungs, at stump '17'. According to Collins, Wright had been at the head of the column when it broke formation; Wright himself said that he 'rushed' up to the Gisborne track when he heard the firing. Constable Andy McHugh walks behind carrying Wright's knapsack, which took much of the shot and saved him from probable death; Myles Doyle is on the left, in riding breeches. Photo by A. N. Breckon. *Auckland Weekly News, 13 April 1916*

au kia mate', which, he said, he called out to Neil. Put down before the meeting-house, Rua was ordered by Cullen to shout to Toko to cease shooting. Grant, acting as interpreter, said that Rua replied, ' "You sing out yourself, you can sing as loud as I can" '. Grant reminded him that Toko would recognize his voice, and Rua then called; but Toko was out of earshot and the police firing was by now general. Rua and Whatu were then bundled down out of sight on the western side of the meeting-house, but Cullen ordered them to be brought back to the open space of the marae. It was the women who brought the firing to a halt. Sent out by Rua, they began to walk slowly from the marae, calling, 'Children of Israel, hokimai, hokimai'. As they walked up the track beside the gully, the firing died away.[115]

Four constables had been wounded, two seriously. Two Maoris had also been badly hurt and some others, wounded, ran away and did not return to the pa. One of those seriously hurt was old Paora Kingi, who was shot from behind in the shoulder. Paora, Collins said explicitly, 'was just an old man running away, who got caught in the cross fire.' Paora said the same, that he was shot as he fled towards the gully on the east of the marae. He hid for two nights in the bush, in fear, and only returned when he was found by one of the women and taken to Brewster for examination. When he told Cullen that he had been unarmed, Cullen replied, ' "If you had not been shot, I would have taken you in charge, on account of signing that petition." '[116]

Heripo Kaata, a youth, was also seriously hurt. He too denied that he had been armed and said that he had been hit as he tried to hide in the scrub at the top of the gully. No gun was found near Heripo.[117] But the police said that a regular fuselage from 'hidden marksmen' had opened up from the whares at the head of the gully, a 'veritable ambush'. Grant, who admitted it was rather 'hard to tell', thought eight or ten Maoris might have fired from the scrub;[118] Butterworth estimated at the time 'eight or less'; Birch guessed twenty or thirty.[119] A planned ambush was central to Cullen's justification of their

This photograph was part of the defence collection. It was described as depicting the locality where some of the people ran to hide. It was taken from stump '18', where the 'Policemen were firing at fugitive natives men and women.' The white spot, above the central hut, was 'about where Herepo was wounded.' Photo by William Carter. *Lundon collection*

Centre
Constable Alexander McCowan (left) and
Constable John Neil (right). *Auckland Weekly News, 13 April 1916*

actions. As the Crown Prosecutor, Joseph Tole, had advised him urgently, it was 'Important [to] show that in running away Rua designed [to] draw main body police within gunshot of natives posted in bush'.[120] Consequently, Cullen stated firmly, 'The opinion I formed was that accused intended to bolt across the gully . . . and the police would naturally follow up on the open track and then . . . would come under close range of a deadly fire.'[121] But as Gerald Maloney observed, 'I did not see the slightest signs of preparation for shooting. Everybody there were friendly until the arrival of the Commissioner and armed force.'[122]

The four policemen who were wounded were all hit with shotgun pellets and, as Cullen himself said, all four were probably shot by Toko, although

Above
The women being brought from
Hiruharama Hou under police guard.
The houses are those scattered at the
top of the gully.

Opposite (top)
The women bundled together on the
ground. The *Weekly News'* caption to
this photograph stated that the
women and children were sitting
behind cover while the firing was
still in progress. But, as the next
photograph reveals, they are, in fact,
being held under police guard after
the firing was over. The woman
wearing the head scarf is Kumeroa
Te Rika, Pinepine's sister and wife of
Teka. Left centre sits Wairimu, her
hair plaited and wearing a dark
blouse. The little girl with plaits is
Tangi, daughter of Rua and
Pinepine. Beside her, in the
foreground, is Whakaataata. The
woman to the right, wearing a large
neck scarf, is Te Arani, wife of Rua.
Opposite (bottom)
Under guard. Some hours have
passed since the women were
brought out from the houses. Two
police stand on guard, one with a
drawn revolver visible in his hand.
That this photograph was taken after
Continued, p. 116

others were certain that Te Maipi had hit Wright.[123] But McCowan also
received a .22 bullet in the right arm.[124] This is, however, little evidence on
which to construct an 'ambuscade'.

One of the policemen is still remembered, albeit anonymously, in the
folk-lore of the Tuhoe. 'One of the policemen was sorry for the people. He
saw a man passing in the trees, above the meeting-house. The one he was with
was a sniper, so the other said, "Give the rifle to me, I'll shoot him." So the
policeman gave him the rifle and instead of shooting the man, he shot a pig. He
was sorry for the Maoris.'[125] The 'accidental' shooting of a pig is remembered
in the police annals, too: it angered Cullen at the time.[126]

After the firing had ceased, the police began to search the houses. The
women were brought down from Hiruharama Hou. The police called out,
saying, ' "If you don't come quickly we will shoot you." '[127] They took the
women down to the marae at gun-point, four officers walking in front, some
beside, and some behind them, as Rua's wife, Te Akakura, said. They held
them prisoner, bundled together.

Both the police and the Crown Prosecutor stated that the women were
never held prisoner. In one of the accompanying photographs, which was not
reproduced in the newspapers, a revolver is clearly visible in the hand of one of
the constables on duty. The length of the shadows reveals that several hours
have passed since the women were first brought out of the houses. That night,
the women refused to re-enter Hiruharama Hou, with its smashed front door,
and throughout the night they sat on the grass, outside the fence, 'silent and
desolate',[128] occasionally moving in a dance to keep warm. They were not
allowed back into their own houses, they said, even to get blankets. The police
denied that the women were restricted in any way and, to discredit them, had
to conceal the fact that some of the houses were used to imprison the men.

Thirty-one men were arrested, of the forty-eight who were said to be there

The men, handcuffed. Maka Kanuehi, Pukepuke Kanara, Rua, Whatu, Awa Horomona and Tioke Hakaipare. The policeman at the back left is Bill Neil. Standing behind Rua, is James Williamson. Andy McHugh, helmeted, is beside Awa. Notice Rua's torn left sleeve. Photo by A. N. Breckon. *C. C. Webb Collection, Alexander Turnbull Library*

Continued from p. 114
the shooting was over is also evidenced by the fact that the woman in the front of those being escorted from Rua's house can be seen in this group, sitting on the right. Wairimu sits in the centre of the group looking across her right shoulder. Next to her, on her left and looking in the same direction, her hair parted in the centre, is Te Puhi. Beside her, half obscured, sits Mihiroa, with a child on her knee. Pehirangi stands at the back, left, her hand to her mouth. Photos by A. N. Breckon. *Len Shapcott, Cambridge; Auckland Weekly News, 13 April 1916; John B. Turner, Auckland*

that day.‡ Not one of the men arrested had been armed.[129] Most of them were held for twenty-four hours, imprisoned in kitchen '9', in some of the houses, and in the meeting-house. A few, like Makarini, were kept prisoner for three days.[130] The people of Maungapohatu called it, understandably, the 'occupation' of their *kainga*. Finally, four men were taken out under arrest, in addition to Rua and Whatu. The four, Awa, Pukepuke, Maka and Tioke, were variously charged with assault on the police. Nine men were kept in the meeting-house on the first night, handcuffed together, alongside the wounded. Against one wall of Tane Nui A Rangi were also piled the arms and ammunition taken from the houses. Many of the guns, which were for hunting, were not loaded and came from Maai, where they had been placed on Rua's instructions.[131]

Few in the meeting-house slept. The constant changing of the guard and the steady pacing of the sentries outside added to the unease. Every once in a while, one of Rua's wives was seen to peep in through the back windows. Candles, placed down the centre of the floor on wooden battens, threw huge flickering shadows across the prone bodies of the wounded. Most of the police slept outside beside an open fire, made 'near the whare, from the rear of which the first shot had been fired.'[132]

‡ Makarini compiled a list of 48 men present at Maungapohatu on 2 April: two were killed, two badly wounded, and thirty-one were locked up. The others ran away, except for old Ru (Te Akakura's father) and the two who came with the police from Waimana, Tori Biddle and Hauwaho.

NEW ZEALAND POLICE.

~~Plimmerton~~ Wellington

Date: 13th October , 1936.

REPORT of G.G.Kelly, Senior-Sergeant , No._____

relative to Firearms taken by Police from Rua in 1916.

150,000/2 31—15607

I respectfully report having examined the collection above referred to and make the following recommendations:-

No.							
No.1	Shot Gun	D.B.B.L.	Hammer Type.				Useless.
2	"	"	"	"	"	"	Suitable Police Museum.
3	"	"	"	"	"	"	Useless.
4	"	"	"	"	"	"	Useless.
5	"	"	"	"	"	"	Suitable Arms Bureau.
6	"	"	"	"	"	"	Suitable Police Museum.
7	"	"	"	"	"	"	Useless.
8	"	"	"	"	"	"	Useless.
9	"	"	"	"	"	"	Useless.
10	"	"	"	"	"	"	Useless.
11	Shot Gun	D.B.Muzzle Loader 20 Gauge.					Suitable Arms Bureau.
12	Shot Gun	S.B.B.L.12 Hammer					Useless.
13	"	"	S.B.M.L.				Suitable Police Museum.
14	"		S.B.B.L.				Suitable Arms Bureau.
15	"		S.B.B.L.				Useless.
16	"	"	S.B.B.L.				Useless.
17	"	"	Browning Automatic				Suitable Arms Bureau.
18	"	"	S.B.M.L.				Useless.
19	Rifle		Repeater M.1890				Suitable Arms Bureau.
20	"		Single Shot '04				Suitable Arms Bureau.
21	"		Repeater				Suitable Police Museum.
22	"		Single Shot				Suitable Police Museum.
23	"		Single Shot				Suitable Police Museum.
24	"		Single Shot				Suitable Police Museum.
25	"		Repeater				Suitable Arms Bureau.
26	"		Single Shot				Suitable Police Museum.
27	"		Snider				Suitable Police Museum.
28	"		Snider				Suitable Police Museum.
29	"		Snider				Suitable Arms Bureau.
30	Revolver						Suitable Police Museum.
31	"						Suitable Police Museum.
32	"						Suitable Police Museum.

Of the weapons recommended for destruction I recommend that the locks only be sent to the Arms Bureau for experimental work.

Gregory G Kelly
Senior-Sergeant.

he Commissioner of Police, Wellington.

The Supt
Auckland

ing these firearms is that the owner of each may claim it at any time - Is there anything attached to each firearm to identify to whom it belongs?

12.10.36

Te Hauwaho Tamaikoha. He would give evidence that Cullen, impatient, shouted '"Get out you dirty bloody Maori"' to Tori Biddle, as he stood uncertainly on the marae when the firing started. Cullen later apologized for thinking, as Biddle put it, he was 'a common Maori'. This episode revealed the racism that was usually hidden, and the dilemma of the half-caste like Biddle. *Hine Nui Te Po, Te Waikotikoti marae, Te Whaiti.* Reproduced by kind permission of Professor S. M. Mead, Victoria University of Wellington.

Left
List of the thirty-two guns collected from Maungapohatu in 1916. The police refused to return them, but accepted that they still belonged to their original owners who, they said, could always come and claim them. By 1936, most were, indeed, 'Useless'; in 1916, many were already obsolete. Butterworth found two of the old Snider carbines, which he said, 'I'd rather be in front of than behind if anybody fired them.' *P1, 1916/233, National Archives*

While the police were searching the houses for weapons, several groups went off without an officer in charge, an action which caused comment later.[133] Hiruharama Hou was found to be bare of furniture and 'not at all like its imposing exterior', but there were valuable rugs and mats on the floors, and on the walls prints from illustrated papers, 'depicting religious subjects'.[134] All went well, Collins remembers, until the theft. With five or six others, he was searching a small whare when he accidentally tipped over a sewing-machine and all its contents spilled to the floor. One of the police pocketed a note – a tenner as Collins remembers it – and a greenstone mere. Jim McIntyre saw the theft and reported it to Inspector Bartholomew

Sheehan. The constable involved, William Joyce, confessed and was suspended; the money was put 'where it could be found again'.[135] Five days after the police returned to Auckland, Joyce 'resigned' from the force.[136] But Sheehan, who was called only to give rebuttal evidence on the charges of theft which had been made, said that he had been unable to substantiate the one complaint of stolen money reported to him.§[137] There were, in fact, other complaints, although the police, at first, tried to conceal them. A list was made and given to Te Kepa and Inspector Phair at Maungapohatu. Pinepine said that she had lost £100, taken from her iron cash box. Cobeldick remembered seeing this with its lid open. Te Iwikino lost his greenstone mere, and Akakura a greenstone tiki and a greenstone heart, taken from Hiruharama Hou. Among the Lundon papers there is a copy of this list, a full page detailing jewellery, money, confiscated guns, and the Covenant – all missing, they said, from Maungapohatu. Lundon received an anonymous letter telling him of Sheehan's investigations and naming a second constable as guilty.[138] Te Kepa had, in fact, made some inquiries at Maungapohatu. In his rebuttal evidence, he stressed the considerable confusion which undoubtedly had occurred.‖ As a consequence, the complaints were stifled and no admission of any theft made. Instead, the very complaints were used to question the credibility of the Maori witnesses. Justice Chapman said that they gave the impression that the police had acted like the German soldiers in Belgium. Because such a notion was unthinkable to him, he concluded that no evidence was sustainable against the police;[139] instead, it was all a Maori conspiracy.

The bitterness left by the assault on Maungapohatu is the source of many of the beliefs which are now entrenched in the Tuhoe communities. We have been told many things as our informants came to trust us. As historians, we know that some are not 'true' in a factual sense. But another truth exists in the very retention of these beliefs. The Maungapohatu people were invaded by an

§ Sheehan had been one of the police who had questioned the need for so many arrests. Although he had compiled a report on some aspects of the police conduct at Maungapohatu, he was not initially called to give evidence. His rebuttal evidence concerned the charges of theft, and the question of the arms which Skinner was carrying.

‖ It is now accepted by the Maungapohatu people that Pinepine hid the Covenant and, in her distress, forgot where.

Te Moana I Kauia, wife of Hurinui Apanui, and Te Akakura, outside the Auckland Supreme Court, 1916. Hurinui Apanui handled much of the financial detail of Rua's trial expenses. *Mrs E. Murphy Album, Alexander Turnbull Library*

The police surrounding Hiruharama Hou; this photograph was another reconstruction, posed after the event. In actuality, the police went in doubled up, and in short runs, because they believed there were men in the house. The *Weekly News'* caption stated boldly 'They advanced in open order, like well-trained infantry, surrounded the house, broke the door in, and called upon all within to come out. Only Rua's nine wives and several children appeared to answer the summons. They squatted down under cover, within sound of the firing.' Photo by A. N. Breckon. *Auckland Weekly News, 13 April 1916*

armed force of seventy men, who acted, for the most part, on the assumption that an ambush had been laid for them. The police force 'remained in occupation and control of Maungapohatu for some three days'.[140] The shock suffered by the community is evident in the explanations which they have developed for themselves. Many of the police, they believe, were really prisoners from the Auckland jail; they were 'not even police'. Opposite the marae, the police dug a huge pit with vents in its sides, to burn the corpse of the dead constable shot by Toko. This legend of the dead policeman is a persistent one and dates at least from May 1916. In the earliest known version, the policeman was said to have been cremated by the Maoris.[141] One of our informants said he 'saw him shot' and thrown into the police pit: 'I saw it with my own eyes. I remember everything'. This man was at Maungapohatu as a young boy, watching the events from behind a tree stump near the marae. He saw the man who 'died' shot in the abdomen. This was John Neil. He also saw Rua 'shot' that day, in the back of the neck as he lay on the ground. He 'saw' Rua shot by the man on the black horse – Skinner. To this day he knows that he saw this happen.¶ He knows, too, that Rua had that wound for the rest of his life. 'The bullet went in the back of his neck and came out through his ribs. . . . That's the place where the spear went in Christ. But no bones broken, nothing. Just like Christ.' The figurative wound which Rua would carry all his life after 2 April 1916 had become the reality, around which further beliefs would grow. In this way, the living mythology of the Messiah was reinforced

The police triumphant, parading before Hiona as a conquered 'citadel'. Photo by A. N. Breckon. *P. E. Murphy, Auckland*

¶ Makarini's description of what he saw reveals the basis for this belief. Makarini heard the shot, saw the black horse jump, and Rua lifted from the ground: 'I thought Rua had been killed when I saw him being carried back'.[142]

and strengthened, so that the people could endure the memory of the events.

They made Rua and his son dig their own holes, three holes. The pits were to bury them, alive. They stand there, and Rua told the policemen, 'Well if you are going to put me to death, I want you people to shoot me, once. One shot. If you don't kill me with one shot, that to let you people know that I am the Son of the living God.' So they shoot him all right. That's why we believe all those things will happen in days to come. That's why he's in that tomb there.* I myself have been bathing that wound ever since. From 1928 I bathed that wound. You can see for yourself, being shot, it got his lung. Missed his heart. Well, he lived from that day, from 1916 right up to 1937. And no medical treatment; he only had the Maori way.

One woman told us:

Rua put the flag up that day because he didn't want war, you know, guns. But the Pakeha went straight up and fired the first shot. Straight up and pulls the handle and bang. Sunday, mind you.

*Rua's tomb at Tuapou. The people are waiting for his resurrection.

Rua, his head still bandaged from the blow he received. Whatu stands beside him; Sergeant Henry is on the right. Photo by A. N. Breckon. *P. E. Murphy, Auckland*

This photograph was captioned in the *Weekly News*, 'The restoration of law and order in the Urewera Country'. Cullen, on horseback, leads the prisoners out from Maungapohatu. Rua, in his torn shirt, is beside the horse. Tioke follows. Whatu and Awa are behind and largely obscured, but recognizable by their hats, are Maka and Pukepuke. Bill Neil brings up the rear of the police, carrying the axe over his shoulder. Photo by A. N. Breckon. *Auckland Weekly News, 13 April 1916*

And her husband continued:

Rua said to the one who wanted to get him to jail, 'I won't go'. And he said he would send the seventy police to Maungapohatu. And Rua said, 'Oh well, if you've got that much of soldiers, I got that much too. I fight you'. That's what he said. 'If I die in the first shot, I'm the son of man. If I don't I'm the Son of God. Well, then the Pakeha people go back to England, where they came from.' That's what he said. That's why he got shot, to see how he's getting on. . . . The only one who saw that wound was Tangiwaka, Pita Te Taite's wife. That was the gift given to her. She was the one who attended that wound. She knew all the cures from the forest, leaves, plants. For each wound, she knew the tree to get. Because she was gifted with that.

One woman still remembers the blood which would sometimes pour from the wound in his side; for a younger woman, the cut on Rua's forehead, where he fell to the ground (or was struck), 'represents the Crown of thorns'. For another, who was a child in 1916, he would sometimes bear visibly the stigmata, the nail holes of Christ's passion, in his hands.

After that day, when Toko and Te Maipi died, Hiruharama Hou and its paddock was the place where blood had been shed. Some say no grass will grow where Toko fell. One woman, who was there in 1916, explained her feelings this way:

Well, nobody would stay then in the pa. But at night we saw the lights. We heard the music and saw the lights, different lights, lovely blue lights, in that house, in Rua's house. We saw the shadows of the *kehua* [spirits] dancing inside, passing through the windows. That's how we know there's a holy place at Maungapohatu. A holy land. A place for the people. And Rua said to us, 'Go back to Maungapohatu. Don't sell Maungapohatu. Because it is the holy land.'

On Wednesday 5 April the police and their six prisoners began the journey out. Rua and Whatu were handcuffed together in what they remembered as a nightmare of pain: the handcuffs had no swivel and they were forced to walk in single file behind the horses. (Six had been taken from Maungapohatu but they were not for the prisoners.) At Ruatahuna, the arrested men and the wounded police were all transferred to brakes and driven through to Rotorua, where a great crowd gathered to witness their arrival. Rua was on the verge of tears as he entered the jail. From Rotorua he was transferred to Auckland. The police party and their prisoners arrived at Newmarket railway station on the 10th. Here, 'under strong guard', the six prisoners were transferred again into a brake, before a large crowd of onlookers, and taken to Mount Eden prison.

The police leaving Maungapohatu in the early morning. The *Weekly News*, publishing this photograph on 13 April, took the opportunity to comment again on this land which 'should be opened up to civilisation by means of roads and railways'; a land 'which has been dominated by the Maori outlaw, Rua, until his arrest'. In the background is Hihitauheka, the left hand summit of the twin peaks, and below lies the Kakewahine valley, virtually unchanged today. Photo by A. N. Breckon. *C. C. Webb Collection, Alexander Turnbull Library*

Hepetini rere-rangi.
Hepetini in flight.
He kukupa heri-reta,
A carrier pigeon,
Haere ra te kukupa,
Farewell pigeon,
Heria te reta, me te aroha hoki
Carry the letter, and the love
Ki oku hoa aroha.
To my beloved friends.
Mo te wa i wehe-wehe ai matau. . . .
For the time we are apart. . . .

7 Noe 1916, Maai
7 November 1916, Maai[143]

The long and bitter legal process began. Rua was held, at first, on a nine months' sentence, imposed for the 1915 charges and now increased by his default of the fines. Tioke, Maka, Pukepuke, Awa, and Whatu were all refused bail, on the grounds that it would be 'highly undesirable' that they should 'go back to their stronghold at Maungapohatu.'[144] Herries seized the moment to build on the mood of triumph clamant in the newspapers, and gave a speech at Ruatoki, on 14 April. He told the Tuhoe that he would not, in reprisal, confiscate their lands. He was not, he said, 'going to be a murderer of land, as Rua had been a murderer of people, but he would ask them to assist him in his desire to show . . . that there was a way of settling this country without resorting to confiscation. He therefore asked them to assist him in purchasing, at a fair price, the interests of those natives who wanted to sell land.'[145] In the views of men like Herries, long an advocate of individual tenure, the 'pacification' of the Ureweras depended on breaking up the land block. The sharpest irony was that Rua himself had long supported partial European settlement and the opening of the country by roads, but the image of him as 'disloyal', 'seditious', a 'baneful' leader of his people, would now be

Rua, handcuffed to Whatu, who is climbing down from the brake on their arrival at Rotorua, 7 April 1916. Photo by Stewart and Bennett. *Auckland Star, 8 April 1916*

'Shorn of his hair and his "mana," Rua reaches Auckland in custody': so captioned by the *Auckland Star*, 12 April 1916. The picture shows Rua and Whatu crossing the bridge at Newmarket station, Auckland, 10 April. The *Star* commented that 'Well-fitting navy blue coat and trousers, cap and light street boots transformed the "prophet" into merely a big [sic] well-dressed Maori.' A 'red necktie was the only splash of colour in his dress.' Handcuffed together and with 'downcast eyes he and his son . . . walked along the platform to Remuera Road, escorted by Sergt. Cox and Constable [Thomas] Trotter. They were followed by four other Maori prisoners in charge of Constables McHugh and [Alexander] Hamilton, and the whole party, without any fuss, boarded a waiting brake and were driven to Mt. Eden gaol' (11 April 1916). Trotter gave Rua a pair of binoculars, which are now in the Urewera National Park Museum.

systematically propagated. Yet none of the trial juries accepted these stereotypes. Not one of the charges against Rua relating to 2 April 1916 could be sustained. Similarly, the charges against the five other men either failed or were abandoned. Only on one charge was Rua found guilty – that of offering 'moral' resistance to the police at Te Waiiti on 12 February. And on that issue, eight of the jury subsequently protested formally against the savagery with which their verdict was interpreted by Mr Justice Chapman.

Mr Justice, later Chief Justice, Frederick Chapman, 1916. *Mrs E. Murphy Album, Alexander Turnbull Library*

Rua was tried on charges of sedition, of counselling Toko, Te Maipi and others to murder or disable the police at Maungapohatu, and of resisting arrest at Te Waiiti. All the charges relating to resisting arrest at Maungapohatu were dismissed by Chapman, who accepted the submission of the defence that warrants for commitment to prison could not be served on a Sunday, except for certain specified crimes with none of which Rua was charged.† As a consequence, Rua's arrest was declared unlawful. The question of the illegal Sunday arrest was in a sense, a technicality; it obscured the issue of the excess of force employed by the police. The decision, however, was vital, legally, for it followed that it was legitimate for Rua to resist arrest, and for others to help him, even to the extent of inflicting serious wounds, so long as he did not

† Only warrants in cases of treason, felony or breach of the peace could be served on a Sunday, under the Lord's Day Observance Act. Chapman commented that confusion had arisen in police practice, and it had become assumed that a warrant for imprisonment without the option of a fine, as in the case of Rua, could be served on a Sunday. However, Butterworth is clear that the Gisborne police had discussed the warrants, which Johnston subsequently executed, and knew them to be improper for the planned arrest on Sunday. But they assumed that Cullen, as a J.P., must have a correct warrant. He did not.

Letter written from Mt Eden prison, signed by Rua, appointing Jerry Lundon as his barrister. On 8 June Lundon's fee was fixed at five hundred guineas. Whatu's signature is also appended to this earlier letter, sent to Wiremu Hunui of Te Waimana. *Lundon collection*

order an attack upon the police. Four of the original eight charges laid by the police were invalidated by Chapman's ruling.[146]

The trial was the longest in New Zealand history, until 1977. The Crown summoned thirty-four witnesses and sixteen new witnesses in rebuttal; the defence called forty-one.[147] The hearings occupied forty-seven days; Rua himself was five days in the witness box. There are Aucklanders who can still remember him, travelling every day in a horse-drawn carriage from Mount Eden jail down Symonds Street to the Supreme Court. Every day he came up through the trap-door from the cells below the court, dressed in his brown overcoat, white shirt and bright red tie. Every day, he listened with his interpreter to the conflicting evidence.

Mr Justice Chapman, in his summing up for the jury, pointed to problems inherent in the police evidence. Their case rested, he said, on their assumption that an ambush awaited them, for which Rua gave the signal with the words, 'Patua, Patua!' The 'hidden marksmen' at the head of the gully constituted this ambush; the removal of the 'little white flag' was part of the scheme. Against this comprehensive interpretation were the Maori statements that only Toko

Jerry Lundon and Rua, 1916. *Mrs E. Murphy Album, Alexander Turnbull Library*

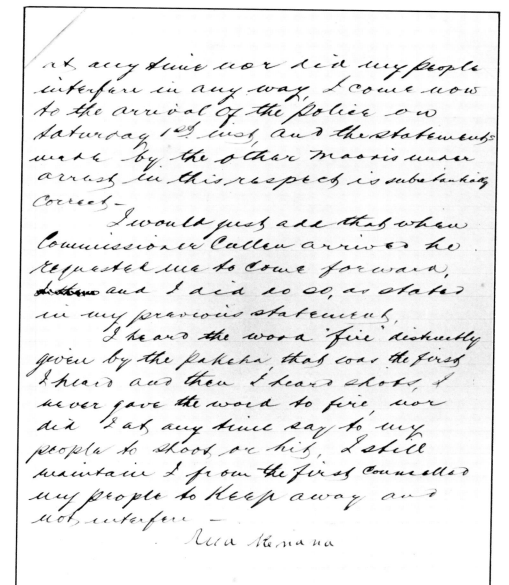

Last page of a statement made in prison on 22 April 1916, signed by Rua. *Lundon collection*

John Birch. *Auckland Weekly News,*
22 June 1905

Selwyn Mays, counsel for the
prosecution in the lower court
hearings at Rotorua; Parekura Anania
from Ruatahuna; Te Moana I Kauia;
James Craig, Auckland, 1916. *Mrs E.*
Murphy Album, Alexander Turnbull
Library

was armed – despite the fact that McCowan was hit with a bullet from a pea
rifle. But Chapman also specifically observed that if there was no planned
design and no prearranged defence lines, then there could be no signal. He
decided to rely on John Birch, the *New Zealand Herald* reporter, as a neutral
witness. But Birch's accounts, written for the *Herald*, were based on his
accepting the view that there had been a plan of resistance, that Rua had run
from the police to draw them after him, and that the firing from the gully had
been a 'veritable ambush'.[148] He did not change his opinion. Birch's account
throughout bore the stamp of Cullen.

Mr Justice Chapman himself failed to remain impartial. When the jury
returned, declaring Rua 'morally guilty' on only one of the charges on events
at Te Waiiti, and apparently unable to make up its mind on the Maungapohatu
charges, he took the opportunity to pronounce at length upon Rua's ' "long
history of defiance of the law" '. He sentenced him, as a member of a race
whom he considered to be 'still in tutelage', with severity, in order to show
that the arm of the law was long and reached ' "every corner of the great
Empire to which we belong . . . . That is the lesson that your people should
learn from this trial" '.[149]

Chapman committed Rua to one year's hard labour, followed by eighteen
months' imprisonment for 'reformative purposes'. The *Auckland Star*'s
headline proclaimed, 'LAW TRIUMPHS', while the editor of the *New Zealand*
Herald wrote sanctimoniously: 'The conviction of Rua upon a comparatively
minor charge will be generally acceptable to the public, and should satisfy the
ends of justice.'[150]

Yet it would appear that a number of the jurymen were outraged at
Chapman's interpretation of their intentions in finding Rua guilty of offering
'moral' resistance to the police at Te Waiiti. On 4 August, eight of the jury sent
a letter of protest to the *Auckland Star* against the 'severity of the sentence
inflicted'. Simultaneously, they sent a petition to the House, stating that they
felt 'that our decision was entirely misunderstood and that Rua Kenana is
paying a penalty for the error and that it should be rectified either by a Pardon
or by his *Prompt release*'.[151] The text of the letter to the *Star* read:

In giving our verdict . . . 'Guilty of moral resistance' in respect of the charge of resisting the Police at Wai-iti, we meant to convey that we were agreed that Rua had no intention of resisting the Police in any physical manner but that he would not go with them voluntarily and until the position was satisfactorily explained to him.

We considered Rua wished to be formally arrested as a matter of protest for we believed he was of opinion that he was being persecuted and in that respect we shared his opinion.

We were surprised at being discharged as we had not definitely concluded that agreement upon the Maungapohatu charges was impossible. We were also anxious to bring a rider in regard to the Maungapohatu charges recommending the exhumation of the bodies of Te Maipi and Toko Rua – the natives killed – as we think there should be some investigation made.

The direction of His Honor the learned Judge, that the verdict was one of guilty, conveys the impression that we were agreed that Rua was guilty of resistance. This is not so, for we think that Rua had no intention in that way, and we did not consider the Police evidence reliable of the Wai-iti affair, and based our verdict upon the evidence of Rua and his witnesses.

We are astounded at the severity of the sentence inflicted under the circumstances, and absolutely amazed at His Honor's statement that our verdict meant that we believed the Police statements as to Wai-iti, and felt that the evidence of Rua and his witnesses was perjured. We had not any such belief and we state explicitly that ten of the jury were in favour of an absolute acquittal preferring to believe the native version of both Wai-iti and the Maungapohatu incidents. Our sympathies were and are entirely with Rua, both as to his treatment by the Magistrate and by the Police. We voice a deep and sincere regret that the proposed amendment in the Juries Act enabling acceptance of a three-fourths verdict of innocence is not the law of our land, for if it were Rua would have been honourably acquitted upon all the eight charges.[152]

In their petition to Parliament, they went over the same ground, adding that 'in sentencing Rua to imprisonment and detention upon our verdict a grave miscarriage of Justice has resulted.' Furthermore, they recommended that a 'full investigation into the alleged occurrences at Maungapohatu on the second day of April 1916 be made'.[153]

The foreman of the jury, Arthur Graham, did not sign. When interviewed by the *Star*, he asserted that Chapman had asked them if they meant their verdict to be interpreted as 'guilty', and that they had assented. There had been time for other members of the jury to have raised an objection, he argued, and he denied that the question of exhumation had ever been discussed. Two others of the jury supported Graham.[154] It seems certain that Carter had prepared the letter and taken it around members of the jury,[155] but it is improbable that the eight would have signed against their own feelings. Indeed Carter wrote to Lundon, informing him that the jury 'are anxious to

Pukepuke's trial: drawings from the *New Zealand Observer*, which ran a series covering the trials with singular crudity. The black horse with the cropped tail was Skinner's horse, which jumped when the first shot was fired. The Crown Prosecutor was Tole; 'Just Jerry' was Lundon; the Senior Sergeant was Cassells; Rua's 'right hand' was, probably, Wi Hape, his interpreter, who played a large part in gathering witnesses – and, also, helping to conceal one voluntary witness, who gave contradictory evidence, at Pukepuke's trial. Cartoon by 'BLO' (William Blomfield). *New Zealand Observer*, 7 October 1916

get letter inserted in paper at once.' Graham, he added, was not prepared to sign without 'discussion with the rest of the Jury'.[156] This division in the jury undoubtedly helped to render their protests ineffectual, although in December the Crown abandoned the proposed retrial on the Maungapohatu charges.

However, yet another tortuous chapter of the saga began to unfold, that of the trials of the other men arrested at Maungapohatu. The first case to be heard was Pukepuke's, which resulted in an acquittal on the charge of attempting 'grievous bodily harm' against Skinner. The charges against Whatu collapsed entirely because of contradictions in the police evidence; the judge directed that it was not a satisfactory case to put to a jury. The dubious and even trivial nature of the police accusations against those who had come, legitimately, to Rua's aid was becoming apparent. As a result, the Crown abandoned the remaining cases.

As Lundon observed at Whatu's trial, the Supreme Court hearing of Rua's case had established that the police had committed an assault which had led to the loss of two lives. 'It was', he said, 'a peculiar state of affairs that the whole of the weight of the Crown and its legions should be used for the purpose of crushing these people, and trying to put them in gaol.'[157] But the legal torture did not end here. On 8 November Tori Biddle was arrested for perjury, on Cullen's orders. An excited telegram, in code, announced that he had signed a statement admitting his offence. Two days later, Makarini, Tioke and Tahu Hirawano were also arrested; Mahia Hakeke and Tutara Kauika would also be added to the list of those charged with perjury. But of these men only Tori Biddle and Mahia were prepared to admit the concoction of perjured testimony. In so doing, as Makarini commented in his statement of 11 December, Biddle was setting up the defence lawyers as responsible. Makarini remained adamant: 'It was not Mr Carter that pointed Skinner out. It was me.'[158]

As Biddle described it, Carter and the surveyor, David Lundon, had come to Maungapohatu in May to gather evidence. Lundon drew a diagram of the positions where everyone had been when the first shot was heard. Biddle acted as spokesman for the community and Carter took down notes as he talked, with others chipping in. Biddle said that it was here that it was first agreed to name Skinner as responsible for the first shot; at a later meeting, held at the Waipapa Maori hostel in Auckland, where most of the witnesses stayed, Jerry Lundon agreed to this collusive fiction.[159] He also said that it was at Maungapohatu that Carter got Waereti to modify the details in her story of Toko's death, and in particular to change her account of where she had been standing beside the fence, so as to make it physically possible for her to have seen a policeman dragging him from under Pinepine's house.

Tori (Benjamin) Biddle, 1916. He wore a portrait of Rua attached to the pendant on his watch chain, during Rua's trial. Tori was married to Whakaataata. *Mrs E. Murphy Album, Alexander Turnbull Library*

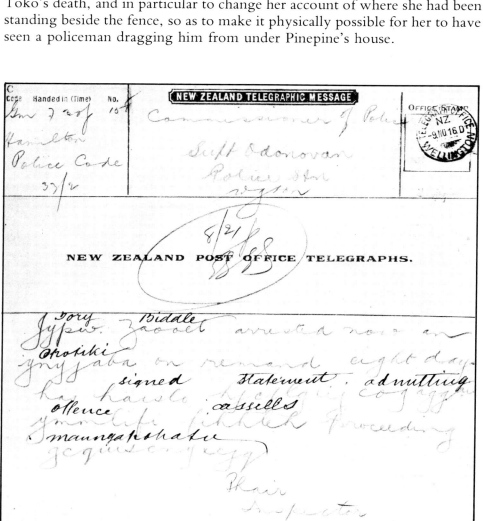

Telegram in code from Inspector Phair announcing that Biddle's confession had been obtained. *P1, 1916/233, National Archives*

Hokimate, wife of Kirihi, 1916. *Mrs E. Murphy Album, Alexander Turnbull Library*

Biddle's account seemed to receive support from two other Maori witnesses: Wi Hape, Rua's interpreter, who was himself arrested on the charge of secreting a witness, and Hauwaho, who had acted as guide for the Whakatane police. Wi Hape described the rehearsing of details by Hokimate and Wairimu, to support Waereti's statement. He added, '*Mr J. R. Lundon did not credit this story, he thought it was too barefaced and cold blooded. I only acted as interpreter in this matter. This statement is true.*'[160] Hauwaho, in his statement, described how, at Waipapa, Lundon had tried to get him to concur in the naming of Skinner: '*Lundon said "Some of your friends say that Skinner fired the first shot. I said "Oh no I wont say that Skinner fired the first shot". Lundon then turned round to Tori and Makarini and other natives and said in English, "He's no good he wont say that Skinner fired the first shot". Lundon was angry and left me.*'[161]

Hauwaho's statement reveals at least the indirect intrusion of the police, in the phrasing, '*and other natives*'. Moreover, Hauwaho himself accused the police not only of using Te Kepa to put pressure on him, but also to translate his statement incorrectly in a manner which seemed to corroborate Biddle. He 'would not', for Tori had 'turned over to the side of the Police.'[162] Carter stated explicitly that police pressure had created these linked confessions. Writing after the trials, he said, in a letter of protest to the Minister of Justice, that the statements had been extracted by 'pressure and bribery and other corrupt means by . . . police officials'. The statements were false and 'were known to [police] officials to be false.'[163] Carter named Cassells and Kepa as the two men most actively involved. As Makarini said, in a supplementary statement, 'After Cassells and Kepa had been to see Hauwaho he, Hauwaho, came to see me. He said to me "By golly it is very hard – they are tempting me in every possible way – I expect I will fall into their trap." '[164] Tahu, in his statement, made it clear that Biddle was being influenced by Cassells to persuade them to concur, with offers of release from prison. It was Biddle who persuaded Mahia to make his statement, and who told Tutara not to 'mind about Carter or Lundon they are not much good.' But Tutara refused to change his original opinion: 'I saw it with my own eyes. I still think Skinner fired the first shot.'[165] Even Tioke, who had only just been released from prison on the previous charges, which were never heard, would not budge. 'I realised . . . that Tori had jumped on to the other side and was going to act as a . . . Kohuru' – one who deals treacherously.[166]

There is little doubt that Biddle had been bullied by the police, whether by threats of violence and by jeering, as both Tahu and Tioke reported, or simply by the suggestion that he might save his own skin. There is also evidence that Biddle had acted earlier as a police informer on the sly grog charges. 'Biddle, the double-dealer, the pimp', Tole described him. Biddle himself said in the Rotorua Court, that he was 'heartily sick of lawyers and others, and of the whole thing.'[167] Equally, it is clear that once the police broke Biddle they mounted a major campaign against others. As Wi Hape cabled Lundon in panic, on 28 November, 'Hawaho sold the whole bush Mahia arrested yesterday by Keepa.'[168]

Biddle was sentenced to nine months' imprisonment for the perjury to which he had pleaded guilty. According to Carter he tried to change his plea at the last minute; according to Cassells he did not.[169] Mahia, who also pleaded guilty, was not allowed to change his plea and he, too, was sentenced to nine months.[170] The others fought the charges, and finally won their freedom. Tioke was acquitted, on a retrial; faced with this decision and the prospects of two further retrials, the Crown abandoned the cases. Makarini was never brought to court.‡ Herdman had become embarrassed by what had at last come to be seen as a needless persecution of the Maungapohatu people.

When finding Tioke not guilty of perjury, the jury also expressly cleared Skinner of the accusation of having fired the first shot. They stressed that Tioke had made his allegation because of the 'excitement' which was rampant at the time among both Europeans and Maoris involved.[171] The Crown had made it clear, also, that it was not implying that Rua's defence counsel, Jerry Lundon, had concocted the story.[172] Yet Biddle's version carried this implication, and it stuck. Carter, who was also directly affected, denied much of Biddle's reconstruction of their conversations. He wrote to Lundon in great concern, after he had obtained a transcript of Biddle's first statement to the

‡ The juries had disagreed in the trials of both Tutara and Tahu. Wi Hape, who had been sentenced for secreting Mahia when a voluntary witness at Pukepuke's trial and so preventing him from being recalled for questions, was released immediately, when the Crown sought a stay of proceedings in the perjury trials on 24 April 1917.

The records from these trials have survived but they were not available at the time of writing, because of the conditions of storage at the Hamilton Supreme Court. The material is also in the Lundon collection.

Huhana Tutakangahau, sister to Pinohi; Tahu Hirawano, father of Kiha, Rua's wife; Waereti, 1916. *Mrs E. Murphy Album, Alexander Turnbull Library*

Rotorua Magistrate's Court, and said, 'The fact, if it be the fact that Skinner fired the first shot, was not impressed upon me until I saw the prisoners in the Gaol at Auckland when both Biddle and Tioke stated that he was the man. It may be that Makarini had said that Skinner was the man prior to this but, he had not at that time to my knowledge, identified him.' He added, 'You must bear in mind that at the time we were at Maungapohatu it was not said nor was it certain although indications pointed that way that Skinner fired that first shot but the Natives were positively certain of that when they either saw the photo or, saw the man himself in the precincts of the Court.'[173] He shifted the burden of responsibility on to the Maoris, as Makarini had already accepted, or to Lundon, who knew Skinner's reputation.

The human cost of these bitterly contested legal battles was tragic for everyone. For Jerry Lundon, it brought about the marshalling of evidence against him by the Auckland Law Society with a view to his disbarment. If another case of alleged professional misconduct had not ended his career as Auckland's leading and most outspoken criminal lawyer, he would have had to face this accusation. There is little doubt that he acquired powerful enemies in his dogged determination to get a reopening of investigations into the behaviour of the police at Maungapohatu. At Tutara's trial he had called for 'a public inquiry, untrammelled by legal procedure . . . into the whole affair.' The police story was simply 'not reliable.'[174] He had drafted a petition to Parliament on 1 May 1917 on behalf of the Maungapohatu people, calling for a full public inquiry not only into the events of 2 April 1916, but also into the manner in which police officers had tried to persuade some of the community to change their testimony. He mentioned the great losses that the people had suffered, being forced to sell off their stock and some of their lands, to raise funds for the defence costs, 'upon charges which should never have been brought against them'.[175] But Lundon himself was brought down: his suspension (on 2 May), like his subsequent disbarment, was made on a technicality which the family believe was used deliberately to destroy him.§

For the people of Maungapohatu the trials brought economic ruin. On Cullen's insistence,[176] they were saddled with the cost of the police expedition itself – over £900 – and they also had to find the money for the defence costs. Rua himself 'fixed' his fee to Lundon at five hundred guineas.[177] In addition there were Carter's costs, David Lundon's costs, and the costs of the interpreters. There were the costs of all the other trials. Denis Cummings, in a report written in defence of the police against Carter's complaints, stated that the Maoris imprisoned for perjury had nothing but bitterness against the defence lawyers: they had paid Lundon £1850 and then Rua had got two and a half years, ' "No good that fellow" '.[178] The people were forced to sell their stock and to sell their land. The entire herd of sheep from Maungapohatu – 357 – were sold off in June 1916. Rua's five steers were sold. Whatu sold his shares in several blocks of land. Te Amoroa sold his shares in two blocks and raised thereby £10 to pay his expenses to come to Auckland to give evidence. A list would be almost endless. As Awa, Pukepuke, Maka, Tioke, and Whatu wrote sadly to Lundon, 'We have suffered great loss through having to sacrifice lands for the purpose of raising money for our defence'.[179]

§ This is not the place to discuss the issues of Lundon's disbarment, except to say that he was dismissed for over-charging. He took £100 from a client for the release of the client's own money (£500) from a fixed deposit account. The man was an alcoholic, placed on Rotoroa Island and Lundon looked after his money for him, to prevent his family from getting access to it. The £100 had been a sort of bet or 'bargain', payable only if Lundon succeeded – as he did – in breaking the deposit. The interest on the remainder, kept in a trust account by Lundon, was paid regularly to the client's wife, until the man reclaimed his money. There was no question of embezzlement, but if it was seen as taking a contingency fee, it could have been regarded as unethical practice.

Above
This photograph was taken at Maungapohatu in 1916 and includes some of the elders, although identifications are difficult. The three men on the far right are: ? Tahu; behind him, ? Miki; and Te Iriwhiro Te Wiremu, the old chief of Te Waiiti. *Mrs E. Murphy Album, Alexander Turnbull Library*

...penses incurred in connection with arrest of Rua.

		£	s.	d.	
Sergeant Cummings	Travelling expenses	1	15		*Feb. 10/13*
Dist. Const Grant	" "	2	18		
R. M. Company	Motor car hire	7	2	6	
H. B. Motor Coy.	Motor hire	25	5		*Mar 14/20*
J. Cullen	Travelling expenses	6	12	6	
H. T. Mitchell	Services and expenses	27	8		
H. L. Transport Coy	Motor for Mitchell	26	–		
R. M. Company	Transport of police	157	2	6	*Mar 13 -*
" " "	Motors for ambulance	30			*Apl 6.*
" " "	" " Minister	15			
" " "	" " Magistrate	6	10		
" " "	Motor for messages, etc.	45			
Inspector Phair, Amounts	Accommodation of police				
paid for	at Rotorua	67	13	3	
" "	Meals and beds, etc at				
	Ruatahuna and Muripara	86	9		
" " "	Hire of horses, saddles,				
	guides	169	4	6	
" " "	Meat	3	2	6	
" " "	Bread	2	13	2	
" " "	Medical comforts	5	3		
" " "	Sundries	1	12	6	
Baillie, R. C.	Food and stores	56	6	3	
Dr Brewster	Medical services	26	5		
Gisborne police	Travelling expenses	21	9		
Dist.Const.Grant	" "	8	10		
J. Cullen	" "	10	12		
Hon. A. T. Ngata	" " ,etc.	92	19		
Defence Department	Missing equipment	3	8	7	
Police Store	Blankets and sheets lost	5	3	6	
	£	911	4	9	

The police expenses for mounting the expedition, collated 15 June 1916. These were charged to the Maungapohatu community. Additional medical expenses for the treatment of the four wounded policemen came to £115.19.0; these were also considered 'payable', but it is not known if they were added to the bill. *P1, 1916/233, National Archives*

In August 1916, the people themselves had petitioned Massey, as their 'father and guide', to help them in their suffering. The trial of Rua, they said, had utterly ruined them, and they felt that they had been 'very badly . . . treated'. The Supreme Court had declared Rua's arrest illegal; it had 'resulted in the deaths of two of our number and the wounding of two others in our hapu and in the suffering and substantial losses by many of us.' They sought a 'thorough investigation . . . into the whole conduct of the police at Maungapohatu', and also clemency for Rua and for those still imprisoned, awaiting trial. For their pains they received an abrupt note from Herries to say that 'in view of the lawless acts of Rua and his followers towards the Police . . . it has been decided that the law must take its course.'[180] Like all the other petitions and complaints, it was stifled. A request from Maui Pomare for the release of Whatu and the others as an act of grace was also rejected. Instead Cullen concentrated on the jury: the 'Red Feds and other undesirables' who had packed Rua's jury, in his view, should not be allowed again, and he asked for double the usual number on the panel, in the next sequence.[181]

The indifference, bordering on brutality, shown in the government's treatment of Rua's people is revealed starkly in the letter written by Captain Herbert Macdonald, sent to investigate their situation on behalf of the Waiariki Maori Land Board:

The Natives were very reserved in speaking about Rua, and view with suspicion every European who asks questions. It is true there are no sheep and cattle on the land, which, the Natives informed me, the area was about 3,000 acres, the cattle and sheep having been sold to defray the expenses of Rua's trial. One native, Tauru, is very anxious that the land should be leased, after cutting out sufficient land for their own use, while Paitene Tapeka, who said he owned 20 shares, is anxious to sell, and there are others living at Ruatahuna, who are willing to sell, and I would suggest that the Crown should buy all the shares at once that are offering. Rua's sympathisers are anxious that the land should remain as it is till his release. This is bad policy.. . . .
I do not think it would be good policy to give Rua's wives any assistance. If assistance is given it is an admission on the part of the Government that they are helping Rua to keep his wives together till his release.
No anxiety need be felt as to Rua's wives or children starving. Natives always help one another and if ever they become short of food they will either go back to their own people, or get married to other Natives.[182]

Judge Browne of the Board whole-heartedly endorsed this report. He confirmed to Herries that there was no need for government assistance. 'The offer of help too might possibly be misunderstood. It would probably be considered by most of the Natives as an indication of weakness on the part of the Government, and an acknowledgement that Rua had been badly used. The best way to assist them and to help European settlement at the same time will be to send the Land Purchase Officer into the district to continue the purchase of their surplus lands.'[183]

In April 1918, Rua was finally released from jail. He returned to a community which had been torn apart by its experiences. Many had left Maungapohatu, and the land was already becoming overgrown. Facing him, and apparently in his place, was a new figure – the Reverend John Laughton of the Presbyterian mission. To these challenges, Rua responded with considerable skill.

4 If Canaan Is Destroyed Can the New Canaan Arise?

Immediately on his return from prison, Rua encountered the continuing controversy over the recruitment of the Tuhoe. Only a week before he first reported to Andy Grant at Te Whaiti, Grant was writing that resistance would strengthen the moment Rua arrived; only Rua's followers, he said, were hanging back from registration:

It shows the feeling of Rua towards the Govt; he could if he was loyal send word to his people to enrol. Rua in Mount Eden Gaol, is a different man to Rua in the bush. Rua's nice talk in Gaol is all humbug, and I am almost certain as soon as he comes out, there will be trouble . . . over conscription. His followers are counting the days . . . and they will follow him more than ever. The petition to get his sentence shortened shows that they still believe in him, all his wives are still waiting for him.[1]

The 'conscription' of the Maoris, gazetted in 1917, was in actuality applied only to the Waikato people, in reprisal for their sustained resistance. Yet Cassells was arguing on the same lines when he commented on the problems of 'conscription or enrolment' in the Urewera district, which suggests, at the very least, the common attitudes. He, however, found less resistance among Rua's followers. Nevertheless, he deemed it advisable to discuss with Dyer the propriety of liberating Rua 'at the present time', for his ' "Mana" ' was 'just as strong as ever', and warned against it. Dyer also thought he knew what

Maungapohatu, early 1919, not long after Rua returned from jail. Hiruharama Hou still stands, though soon it, too, will be demolished. Hiona has already gone, its timber being re-used to build Rua's separate meeting-house at Maai, below in the valley on the Waikare river. After the shedding of blood at Maungapohatu, a new community had to be created. *Auckland Weekly News, 6 March 1919*

Rua's attitude would be. 'Rua's control over his followers has not in any way decreased, and . . . they still look upon him as Wairua Tapu (The Holy Ghost)'.[2]

Rua took them all by surprise. He encouraged registration – especially among the very young, the very old and the crippled. James Cowan came to believe that a notable 'unofficial' recruiting agent was none other than 'Ruatapu-nui', now a 'staunch supporter' of the King; he brought in, he said, about fifty volunteers by the end of the war.[3] But the Tuhoe know better. Rua sent Te Wairama, the hunchback, and Pukepuke, who suffered severely from asthma, but Pukepuke's sons, 'three big healthy boys', failed to pass the medical examination. Kino Hughes tells the story this way:

Everybody in Taneatua saw the black clouds. They ask Rua, 'Rua, what do they mean?' He says to his people, 'The war finish.' He says, 'The government want the people to go to the war. Well, we'll send them to the war. Everybody's signing, even the old men. They just take you to Auckland.' The government said everyone had to go, so he sent all his people, even Te Wairama. But the government won't take them, because they're too old. And he said to the others, 'It won't be long. No more war; all the people will come back.' And the people at Taneatua start laughing. 'They won't take us to the war?'

Or as Hillman Rua tells it:

Rua was at Ruatoki at the unveiling of Kereru's headstone. Apirana was there, at the hui. Apirana asks Rua, 'Rua, if you were God, as you say you are, well, why don't you stop the war?' I thought, oh well, that's a hard one to my uncle. And he stood up and he told Apirana, 'As a man, as a Parliament, you are trying to run the whole show of the Maori. Why don't you stop the war yourself? And now you want me to stop the war. I will.' That's what Rua said. 'With these boys of mine, the war will end. They will come back from Auckland.' It came true. It wasn't two months after, when his boys came to Auckland, to the tents there, and within a week the war was over. And he said, 'These boys ended the war.'

His ingenuity probably derived from knowledge he had acquired in Auckland, or from Ngata himself, as to the course of the war and the actual length of time taken to train men at Narrow Neck. In this way, Rua shielded the Tuhoe from the imposition of the ballot, which the Waikato had to endure from May 1918. He also removed the stigma of disloyalty and re-established himself as the prophet with vision.

The other challenge to him came in the form of a remarkable man, Hoani Laughton. When Rua returned to Maungapohatu he discovered that, a month before, two Presbyterian missionaries had visited the community and that, after lengthy discussion, the elders had offered the little dance hall as a school. The community had wanted a school for a very long time; it was a Trojan horse which presented Rua with a formidable opponent.

In 1913, Te Iwikino and Pinohi had first petitioned the Education Department and had offered ten acres of land at Maungapohatu as a site. (Rua himself also offered 3000 acres in the Whakatane valley, north of Ruatahuna, for a 'college'. This move came to nothing, because the government wanted land nearer the coast.) In March 1914, William Bird, the Inspector of Native Schools, came to Maungapohatu and accepted their gift of land, with the particular purpose 'of making the first attempt to open up the district to the European.'[4] Rua, Te Iwikino, Pinohi and others signed the deed of transfer. But these plans too were shelved. The reasons given were the difficulty of access, and also the war; but the real issue was the Department's conviction that while Rua remained influential it was pointless to start. Accordingly, Herdman was encouraged to remove Rua from the Ureweras. He was told, on 29 March 1916, that the school was to be suspended 'Until . . . [Rua] is disposed of in some way, and the results on the people can be gauged'.[5] This was the stereotyped reaction; it reinforced the assumptions which lay behind

The mission house built for Laughton and his father. When Laughton left, it became the home of the new state schoolteachers, Irene Paulger and her assistant, Ethel Roseveare. Ethel Roseveare sits on the verandah; she taught at Maungapohatu from 1925 until 1931. On the right is the little chapel for the manse, the only 'church' Laughton was permitted to build at Maungapohatu. *Ethel Roseveare Collection, Mrs I. McHaffie, Dunedin*

Rua and the Reverend John Laughton, on the steps of Rua's new home at Maai, 1920. Rua is wearing the clothes which Laughton bought for him in Rotorua.
Many of the good early photographs from the mission days were taken by Sister Annie Henry, an enthusiastic photographer. *Laughton Album, National Museum*

the police raid, and ignored not only the fact that he had given the land but that Ngata had persuaded him, in 1909, to withdraw his opposition to Native schools.[6] When Bird urged Pinohi, 'do not let Rua take from your children the blessing of Education',[7] Pinohi reacted with justifiable anger:

Te Akakura and her son Henare, who died when a youth. *Sister Annie Henry Collection, Alexander Turnbull Library*

'Daddy' Laughton, John Laughton senior, who helped with the first school and who remained at Maungapohatu until 1926. The photograph, taken at a mission conference, probably in 1922, is from Sister Dorothy Keen's collection; she was stationed at Maungapohatu from 1921 until early 1924, when ill-health forced her to leave. *Mrs Olwyn Rudd, Christchurch*

I felt hurt when it was suggested that it was owing to Rua that no progress was being made . . . .
I wish to put this matter as forcibly as I can, that I want you to bear with us and to hold fast to the movement for establishing the schools . . . .
It is rather a peculiar thing that Rua has got into difficulties owing to this question of fire arms and 'patua,' while at the same time he was striving his utmost to get the Maoris amenable to the European law in conformity with the provisions set out in the Treaty of Waitangi. . . .
And in reply to the suggestions of the Education Department expressing repugnance of Rua and his proceedings, I say that it is I who suffer and I who should express my repugnance of these [police] actions directed against our people and our community. . . .
I hope it will be agreed that from what I have stated, I look at the matter from both points of view, that of the Pakeha and that of the Maori, and I say that as we Maoris do not intend to allow that episode to interfere with our progress in the matter of these schools, so I ask the Educational authorities to meet us in the same spirit in the matter.
I want to specially ask you to send along Mr. Bird [Te Manu] to us during Christmas when we shall have a very large meeting at Maungapohatu. We want, in fact, to 'bury the hatchet.' We want this arranged so that Te Manu be recognized as a chief of the 'Marae' at Maungapohatu.[8]

Instead, expense became the excuse. Bird thought that the Department might get away with it at Maungapohatu because the people would think that the government was 'taking *Muru*' – by which he meant reprisal for 2 April 1916.[9] But Pinohi offered the *whare kanikani*, and a young woman teacher who visited it in March 1917 reported enthusiastically, 'It is a splendid building, excellently built, & quite weather proof . . . . For ventilation there are two large doors opposite to each other & windows above them which the Maoris have promised to hinge so that they will open.'[10] When Bird investigated, he formed a different opinion. The dancing hall was too dark and unsuitable as a school; he urged that they build themselves a paling school. Bird, who was locally born, decided to secure the interest of Te Akakura, whom he had known from their school-days at Ruatoki. If she became interested, the teachers would 'thus have a good friend', and Rua would also give his support. He suggested to her that she write to Rua; Akakura said that 'I should write myself – *she added that I knew his address*.'[11] On 25 May 1917 Bird sent this letter to Mount Eden jail:

To Rua
Greetings to you in these troublous times I am writing to say that I have been again to Maungapohatu to carry to the people the school for their children.
I have asked them to help me in this matter so that the school may come forth as the messenger of spring.
I spoke to Patu . . . and at her instruction I am speaking to you to ask you to support my request.
Your family at Maungapohatu are very well and they want the school to begin for the children so that they shall learn what they should know.
Therefore, I hope that you will advise your people to listen.[12]

But by February 1918, Bird had changed his mind again. The costs of the trials had torn the community apart. The stock was gone and the people, unable to support themselves and with nothing to keep them there, had migrated in such numbers that he thought the school was now 'unnecessary'. To do him justice, he was unhappy about breaking faith with those who had tried so hard for a school.★

The initiative was seized by the Presbyterian mission, and the arrangements were made by the time Rua returned. Only the desire for a school persuaded the Iharaira to accept Pakeha in their midst. As Bird had observed, 'no ordinary pakeha would get a welcome of any kind there at present.'[13] Indeed, Rua was extremely displeased with the decision and refused to allow the Presbyterians the promised use of the *whare kanikani*. When John Laughton

★ In 1974, the ten acres given to the Education Department, and never used, were finally returned to the owners.

arrived he was greeted by a haka of enmity and his first task was to persuade Rua to cooperate in the school. The encounter was remembered by both men: it was 'a mutual sizing up', recollected Laughton. 'Rua knew his people had agreed to accept the Christian missionary teaching. Naturally, he had a good look at me and I at him. It was not a promising alliance.'[14] From this strained beginning sprang a remarkable working relationship. Harimate Roberts describes the understanding finally reached by the two men in this story:

All the old people were working with the timber to make a house for Mr Laughton. But then Mr Laughton asked the old people to build a church, a church house. The old people don't like that and that's the time when Mr Laughton got angry with the people. Rua went up to Mr Laughton, as he came down from the meeting-house, one Sunday, back to his own house. I'd been to look at the pigs and I met my father [Rua] and I stayed to listen. That's how I heard Rua telling Mr Laughton, 'Never mind making a church at Maungapohatu, that's your church, the school. You can have the children. But leave the old ones to me.' That's how they came close together.

Indeed, this became the basis of their understanding. Rua gave Laughton the children. He 'decreed', said Laughton, 'that all the children of his people were to be brought up in the instruction of the Presbyterian Church.'[15] From this commitment sprang the close association of the Presbyterian Church with the Tuhoe which still exists.[16] Not only did Rua withdraw his ban on the gift of the dance hall, but he ordered timber to be sawn at the pit to make the first school benches. More, as Laughton said, 'Rua went afield and gathered in the children of his now scattered followers and filled the school to overflowing.'[17] When it opened in July 1918, there were eleven pupils, but before the year was out Laughton and his father, who came to help, were struggling with a class of forty-two. They had neither slates nor blackboards. Instead, the children brought sticks of charcoal from their homes and drew on the floor. At the end of each day, the floor had to be scrubbed and cleaned, ready for the next onslaught. As numbers grew, bags of grass were hauled in as extra seats.

The *whare kanikani* as the school, about 1921. It was described as being thirty feet in diameter, with walls eleven and a half feet high. It stood about two and a half feet off the ground. In front is the muddy slide made by the children, and a play house. The cleared hill to the right, across the river, and down which the track winds, is Tukutoromiro. *Sister Dorothy Keen Collection, Mrs O. Rudd, Christchurch*

139

Above
John Laughton (centre), with his assistant, John Currie, and their class outside the *whare kanikani*, 1920. Laughton was born in 1891 and died in 1965. Currie was appointed as his assistant, for a year, in 1920 and later returned as the missionary to Maungapohatu. *Laughton Album, National Museum*

Girls who attended Laughton's first school at Maungapohatu:
Back: Pare Mahia; Maggie Tautau (Korekore); Rangi, daughter of Rua and Pinepine.
Middle: Puhata Teka; Te Ao Mihia; Te Hina Teka (Tuhiwai).
Front: Hine Miki; Te Hirata Whitu (Te Aaraka). *Sister Annie Henry Collection, Alexander Turnbull Library*

Opposite (top)
Boys from Laughton's school:
Back: Hena Tuwairua; Paetawa Miki; Mautini Wiki; Paro Miki (Tata).
Front: Te Rewa Te Amoroa; Henare, son of Rua and Te Akakura; Wi Whitu. *Laughton Album, National Museum*

Opposite (bottom)
Bringing in the school blackboard – Sister Annie Henry on the track between Ruatahuna and Maungapohatu. Because Laughton was not a trained teacher, and she was, she came to help in the early years. She was stationed at Ruatahuna. *Sister Annie Henry Collection, Alexander Turnbull Library*

The little *whare kanikani* remained the school for four and a half years. It was then demolished and the timber used to build a new two-roomed schoolhouse near Toreatai, the old pa site lying about half-way between the Maungapohatu settlement and Rua's separate community, Maai. The site was given to Laughton by Huhana, sister of Pinohi, who had recently died. Laughton had

The new schoolhouse, built in 1922, of pit-sawn timber and a split paling roof. That year, there were thirty-two children on the roll, including nine of Rua's. *Sister Dorothy Keen Collection, Mrs O. Rudd, Christchurch*

Huhana Tutakangahau (right), with Hurike, wife of Pinohi, and baby Kume Tapui Ohlsen, and their cats, outside Huhana's home at Toreatai. *Sister Annie Henry Collection, Alexander Turnbull Library*

Six of Rua's children as pupils at the new school, 1922 or 1923.
Back: Horomona; Rangi; Ripeka; Mei.
Front: the twins, Te Mata and Hira. *Sister Dorothy Keen Collection, Mrs O. Rudd, Christchurch*

142

The new school (extreme left, rear), and the teachers' original house (extreme right), at Toreatai. In 1921, Dorothy Keen and Jessie Grieve were appointed as the mission's schoolteachers, and this two-roomed cottage was lent to them as their home. In the foreground is their *whata* or raised storehouse, and to the left is Huhana's kitchen. She gave this land to the mission for the school. *Sister Dorothy Keen Collection, Mrs O. Rudd, Christchurch*

The *waapu*, the timber 'wharf' or sawpit. Mangere Teka is cutting timber for alterations to the school. The woman on the right is unidentified. *Whakatane Museum*

built his own house nearby and some of the timber from the council building, Hiona, which was demolished on Rua's return to Maungapohatu, was similarly used for it. Laughton was fond of remarking that 'even out in Maungapohatu, we dwelt within the walls of Zion.'[18]

The construction of the new mission community was not the only physical change at Maungapohatu. When Hiona was demolished, its timber was used haphazardly to build the new meeting-house at Maai, Te Kawa A Maui, the house for those who dwelt under the mountain, called the backbone of Maui's fish. This was opened on 20 February 1919. Subsequently, when Hiruharama Hou was pulled down its timber was used in the construction of Rua's new house, also built at Maai. The old name, Hiruharama Hou, was transferred with the timbers to the new house. This was smaller than the old Hiruharama Hou, with eight numbered bedrooms, one for Rua and each of his wives then living with him. Seven kitchens were also built, one for each wife and her family. Pinepine remained apart, as before, living in a separate house at the main community.

Maungapohatu, Easter 1933. This photograph shows the three centres of settlement. In the foreground is Maai: Rua's house, the kitchens and storehouses, and the tennis courts dug into the hill behind. In the middle distance are the mission and the school. The schoolhouse is on the right; the mission's 'lower cottage' is at the left and, in the rear centre the 'manse', the house built for Laughton. Above is the main settlement, grouped around the old Mapou pa. The meeting-house, Tane Nui A Rangi, is the most conspicuous building there. Photo by Rex Norman, Rotorua.

Another view, looking down from the main settlement. In the foreground is the manse. The buildings at its rear (left) are the post office and clinic. Mail was delivered every second Friday in the early 1920s, brought in by packhorse from Te Whaiti. Below, left, is the school, with the porch which was added in 1931, and the school shelter shed. Below, right, is the 'lower cottage', built for the mission when the Education Department leased the manse. Behind this complex is Toreatai, the site of the original pa of that name. In the far distance, across the Waiawa stream, is Maai. Photo by John Laughton. *Whakatane Museum*

Behind these physical changes lay human changes. These can be traced before 1916. Already, that year Hiona seemed to be much neglected. Rua said that, when not used as a 'Court of Justice', it was used as a store for the grass crop and wool clippings, but Hokimate was more direct: 'We don't go to the round house, that is the hay house.'[19] The entrance to the upper storey had been removed, probably when the tapu was lifted, and Birch observed its derelict appearance:

The interior was dusty, and the floor covered with particles of wool . . . what used to be a revolving table, at which . . . 'the 12 apostles' [sat] . . . would revolve no more, nor could it

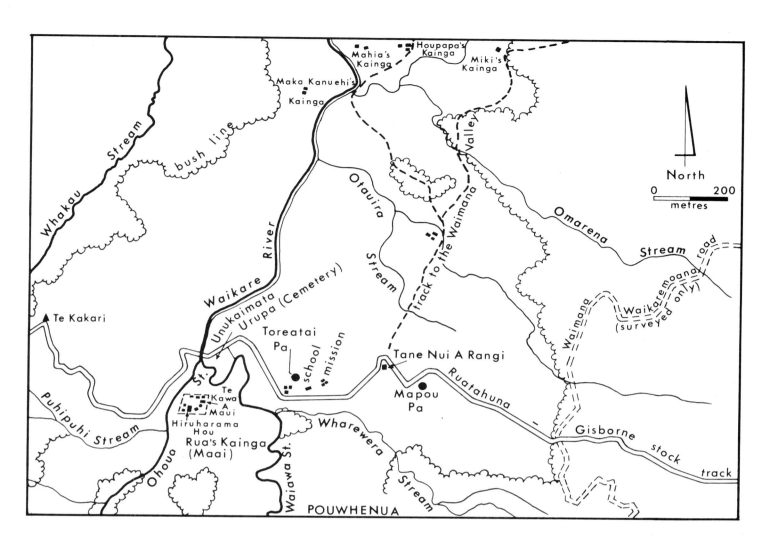

A diagram of the settlement at Maungapohatu, about July 1924 (derived from the survey map of July 1924 [Thomson and Farrer, ML 13642, Department of Lands and Survey, Hamilton] and a map drawn for the authors by R. A. Creswell). The position of the main buildings at Maai has been deduced from photographs. Scattered family *kainga* had again become the characteristic pattern of settlement, before Rua regathered the people, in 1927.

Maai, probably May 1927. Rua's house, Hiruharama Hou, surrounded by the seven kitchens of his wives. In the foreground, the large whitewashed building is Te Kawa A Maui. Largely obscured by it, is the additional *wharepuni*, sleeping house. The track to Ruatahuna (down which the police came) is clearly visible on the hillside to the right, across the Ohoua river. Maai is on a promontory lying between the Ohoua and the Waiawa, both headwaters of the Waikare river.
Whakatane Museum

Waereti and Mihiroa, about 1918.
With them are Waereti's two
children, Rangipaea, daughter of Rua
(at the back); and John Ru Tahuri.
Waereti no longer lived with Rua as
his wife. *Sister Annie Henry
Collection, Alexander Turnbull Library*

Below
Te Arani or Meri, Rua's eleventh
wife, as an older woman. Te Arani
left Rua and remarried. Piripari
marae, photographed by courtesy of
Rata Takao. *Whakatane Museum*

have done for months past from the look of it. Its edges and the surrounding benches were linked by many cobwebs. The wooden 'pulpit,' with its huge, four-barrel, base was turned with its face to the wall, and everywhere was the mark of disuse and neglect.[20]

There is little doubt that the community had shrunk substantially before 1916. In December 1913, when Pinohi drew up a list of the children who would attend the hoped-for school, he cited the names of twenty-nine families, including Rua's, who were then at Maungapohatu.[21] In 1916, many of the men who came to Maungapohatu to be present when the police arrived were no longer living there: for example, Tioke, Makarini, Awa, Tahu. The physical neglect was the consequence of the fact that many of the Iharaira had scattered to seek employment, most particularly after they ended their 'separation unto God'. But the actual destruction of the original buildings of New Jerusalem was the result of the events of 2 April 1916, for the violation of Rua's tapu house and the deaths of Toko and Te Maipi demanded the demolition of the old buildings. As Te Puhi explained, 'It was because blood had been shed that he made his move. He separated the Iharaira and he and his wives went down to Maai to live. He separated his people . . . so he could observe how stout-hearted they were, to live and organize the belief well. It would not be fitting for him to live there any more.' The coloured emblems of Hiona were white-washed over when the timber was re-used. It would be half a century before the designs reappeared through their concealing coat.

Maai now became the new Iharaira centre. While Rua was still in prison, Te Akakura and the other wives who stayed at Maungapohatu lived there 'in seclusion'.[22] When Rua returned, he built a little *wharepuni*, or sleeping-house for visitors, alongside the new meeting-house. The Saturday services of the Iharaira were held at Maai.

These Saturdays were the focus of the community's activities. During the week, each family held its own services. Every family had its own particular prayer, a passage or text from the Scriptures,[23] but on Saturdays they gathered together and the Riwaiti led them in their worship. The people sat in the open, crowded on to the flat below Rua's house. He, with others of the Riwaiti, remained seated on the verandah above.

Then the Presbyterian service followed. John Laughton came to understand the principle that worshippers in different faiths could share their services and come together in the 'one house'. He knew that the community believed that Rua was the Messiah, but there was no purpose in seeking directly to challenge that faith. The respect which Laughton gained among the Iharaira, and the Ringatu at large, stemmed from his capacity to accept their legitimacy, for they shared one God. We would suggest that this fundamental principle of Laughton's life derived from his early missionary experience of working alongside Rua Tapunui and grew with their mutual respect, for both men were visionaries.

After the services, Rua talked to the people – about everything. He talked about the need to ration food carefully and instructed them how to conserve their supplies. He watched over the distribution of the meat. He warned of worse times, when food would be rationed and when even cups and saucers would be taxed. It would be the sign of the imminence of the new world. He spoke of going out to work and how to manage; he organized groups to capture the wild horses which roamed near Te Whaiti; he sent men to see if there were enough pigeon to open the season, or whether it should be delayed; he told the parables and sang the prophecies of the days to come. He talked of Wainui, the 'lost' land on the Ohiwa harbour, which Te Turuki had prophesied would become a source of contention. It was one of the old grievances of the Iharaira: 600 acres of confiscated Tuhoe land given by the government to Te Turuki in 1891. He had set it aside for the Ringatu church, but Rua claimed it as the Messiah of the Tuhoe and the 'son' of Te Turuki.

Rua's claim to it (as well as other challengers) led Ngata, in 1921, to set up a trust for the block, to prevent its partition. But the claim remained until Rua's death as a major source of conflict within the Ringatu, [24] while the Iharaira mourned its loss to them, 'Te Morehu Tangata', the Remnants of the Lord's People. On one special occasion, a Saturday just after Rua's Christmas at Maai, he sent out the women and the girls (and a few of the men) each to pluck a flower of their choice and to bring it to him. From the flower he foretold their futures. 'Bringing in the flowers' was an event everyone still remembers; his

Above
Rua teaching from the verandah of Hiruharama Hou, at Maai, January 1927. Photo by E. T. Pleasants, Auckland.
(Top) see p. 148

'Bringing in the flowers'. Whakaataata, Rua's daughter; Matatu Mahia; Te Aue; Pinepine, at Maungapohatu. The first three are wearing kiwi cloaks; the white feathers are kereru. This photograph was taken on the same occasion as the portrait of Pinepine on p. 19. *Sister Annie Henry Collection, Alexander Turnbull Library*

words for their future they carry with them.[25] In such ways, he interwove the pragmatic with the prophetic and set the discipline by which 'our father's word was law'.[26]

Following the prayers and the services, at about three in the afternoon, the ovens were opened and the people had their first food since the previous day.

Rua also restored discipline to the community with specific laws and regulations. On Fridays, the ovens had to be cleaned and scrubbed, and a committee of women inspected every one for dust and stains. The earth floors had to be damped and swept with manuka brooms. He saw to it that everyone bathed in the river. Smoking remained prohibited and had to be indulged in most secretly by the disobedient.

P. 147 (top)
Saturday at Maai (top photo). The people are dispersing after the Saturday services in front of Hiruharama Hou and are heading towards the ovens, from which the steam rises. *Ethel Roseveare Collection, Mrs I. McHaffie*

The manse in winter. The front verandah of the house has been enclosed. This photo was taken in July 1940. *Meri Taka, Auckland*

Mihiroa; Teiria, first wife of Hillman Rua; and Te Akakura at Matahi. Teiria died in February 1923 and the photo was probably taken not long before. Akakura holds one of the fine lacebark kits made by the women. Her lacebark hat is at her feet. *Phem Doull Collection, Mrs N. Bracey, Christchurch*

Life was hard at Maungapohatu. The winters were always severe; worse, epidemics struck. During the early part of 1916, the people suffered terribly from measles; then the 1918 influenza pandemic took its heavy toll, killing Kiha, and also Whirimako (who had by then left Rua).[27] The 'black Flu' swept through the Ureweras in December, having been brought back by those who had been in the last training camp at Narrow Neck. The Health Department, in a vain attempt to contain its spread, isolated the whole region. Rua's own death was mistakenly reported on 16 January 1919.[28] He had, in fact, urged his followers to retreat to Maungapohatu as a refuge or to stay in isolation in their own settlements, at Tawhana or at Matahi, and to avoid contact with each other.[29] The epidemic was at its very worst in the Gisborne area,[30] where many of the Tuhoe sought casual work during the summer months. Maori deaths, proportionately much higher than European deaths throughout the country, were heaviest in these regions. The severity of the influenza (whose actual toll is not known), can be judged simply by the fact that the old people who survived still date events as 'before' or 'after' 'The Flu'.

At the end of February 1919, when the worst was over, Rua moved with his

149

Piimia, who married Rua at Matahi; Winiati, usually called Ti (also Ti Whakaawe, or Margaret), the daughter of Piimia and Rua; Rua; Te Ariki, son of Pehirangi and Rua. About 1928. *New Zealand Herald, file*

family to the Waimana valley. Here the winters were kinder and the land more suitable for maize, the new cash crop which would largely replace cocksfoot as their staple source of income. He went first to Tawhana, the land dedicated by Te Turuki, and then came to Matahi to live.

Matahi was, like Te Waimana, founded as a deliberate decision of the Iharaira. Its construction was decided upon in 1910, at a meeting held in February at Te Waimana, when the rules for the settlement were drawn up. Rua was 'appointed' ('Me whakatu Hepetipa') for the new community at 'Matahi' ('Opening the Eyes at the Beauty of the Place'), and a council was set up.[31] Many of the families who were driven from Te Waimana with Rua two years later resettled there. It now became the focal point of the Iharaira in the valley. By 1921 there was sufficient population (about two hundred) for the Presbyterian mission to decide to open a school. It was the first Maori school in the valley since the closure of the old Te Waimana school in 1907. Hori Hiakita, a staunch follower of Rua, gave the meeting-house to the mission as a temporary schoolroom. Indeed, it had been the success of the Maungapohatu school and Rua's support of it which had encouraged the Matahi community to petition for their own mission school.[32]

In October 1921, Phem Doull began teaching the children, accompanied by a large and 'interested audience of parents and friends.'[33] In 1922 three of Rua's children were attending and by the following year nine were regular members of a class of twenty-six children.[34] When the new schoolhouse was built in 1922, the meeting-house was released from its perpetual clutter of benches and desks, but soon proved to be too small for the burgeoning settlement. Late in 1924 Rua ordered the little meeting-house to be replaced by a larger one, which was erected in a week. Everybody in the community took part, the children carrying pieces of timber, according to their size, down from the bush to the timber wharf, where it was pit sawn. Twenty men worked on one side of the house and twenty on the other, and there was a tohunga for each side, when 'they put him up'.[35] People came from as far as Taranaki for the opening, on 1 January 1925, the sacred first day of the Ringatu year. They sang for the Tuhoe one of Te Turuki's songs of the years of fear, when the echoes of the Pakeha rifles and the beat of the horses' hooves could still be heard.[36] The house was named, after much thought, Te Huinga O Te Kura, The Coming Together of the Fine People.[37] It was built as a house to bring together the Ringatu, the Iharaira, and the Presbyterians; to 'make there a peace'.[38] It was a house of unity, in whose conception Laughton was involved.

We are all in the one house, Presbyterian, Ringatu. The Twelfths is the time when every people is welcome, just to have a chat. We give you your part. You have your part, I have mine. After my turn is finished, it is your turn. One turn, then another. That's why Rua built that house for Mr Laughton and the Twelfths. That's why he named that house.[39]

It was in these years at Matahi that Rua married his twelfth and youngest wife, Piimia. With him still were Te Akakura, Mihiroa, Te Aue, Pehirangi and Pinepine; Te Arani and Wairimu had left. A new home was built for him at Matahi, the house with the rainbow room. This was an ornamental living-room, with a high central arch representing the rainbow. It was the rainbow down which he had returned from Maungapohatu mountain, after

Opening day of the new school at Matahi, 1922. On the left: —; —; Kaka Sam; Kirihi; Taiepa; —; Takao; Mrs A. Gorrie, the teacher. On the right, the adults are: Te Ra Hui; Hami Taupo, father of Kaka Sam; Hori Hiakita (Hori Tokoahu; Piki Hori); Paora Kingi. The building was made of pit-sawn timber, cut for the mission by the community. *Phem Doull Collection, Mrs N. Bracey, Christchurch*

Te Huinga O Te Kura, at its opening on 1 January 1925. On the right is the mission marquee. *Grace Johnston Collection, Mrs G. A. Fowler, Wellington*

The house with the rainbow room, derelict, 1963. It had stained glass in the front verandah. Parnell Titoko, who went with Rua to Gisborne in 1906, stands alongside. Photo by Dick Scott, Auckland.

Opposite (top)
The typhoid camp at Maungapohatu, 1925. The tents were erected at Toreatai, alongside the home of the mission teachers, where John Laughton had also lived before the manse was built. Two rows of tents stretched out from the house. Daddy Laughton stands to the left.
Bottom
At the typhoid camp. Annie Miki (Matekoraha); her husband, Hemi Tawa, with the accordion; her brother, Paetawa, in the centre. *Sister Annie Henry Collection, Alexander Turnbull Library*

his first vision of Christ. It was the sign of hope, or God's promise to Noah, in the bow in the cloud, of their everlasting covenant. In the rainbow room, people gathered to talk and chat over the events of their daily lives.

In 1922 the Waimana dray road was begun to Tawhana. It made possible the planting of much of the valley in maize, barley and grass for commercial sale. Rua was the driving force behind this expansion. The money the people earned was paid into a common fund from which he bought the basic supplies for the community. Those who lived there then remember still the great festivities after the grass had been cut and the hay gathered, when polo was played on the mown fields and they feasted together. These early years at Matahi were times of joy, although even then some drifted away, seeking casual labour to earn money for themselves.

In the winter of 1924, Rua returned to Maungapohatu. Then the news came of an outbreak of typhoid fever, which had struck the children particularly severely. Three people died. Sister Annie Henry, who came from Ruatahuna to help in the camp set up by the Health Department, recollected the impressive manner in which Rua mastered the necessary medical knowledge:

Dr Hercus . . . told Rua what the disease was. With a scrap of chalk, he drew on a board a diagram of a normal stomach and the stomach of a patient suffering from typhoid, to show Rua why patients . . . must not be given any solid food, however much they plead for it – because, in typhoid, the wall of the stomach becomes thin, so that a piece of solid food can puncture it, killing the patient. When two Health Department nurses arrived, we left. As soon as Rua met them, he produced a piece of chalk, sketched on a board exact reproductions of Dr Hercus' diagrams, and used them to explain to the nurses. . . . Yes, Rua was an intelligent man, willing to learn and quick to grasp knowledge. I liked him. He did a lot for his people while he was alive.[40]

Long before this, Rua had understood that bad sanitation causes bad health.

The new schoolhouse was a centre for the community's activities. Here, adults and children are gathered. *Sister Annie Henry Collection, Alexander Turnbull Library*

Irene Paulger, 1926. She taught at Maungapohatu from 1925 until ill-health forced her resignation, in 1947. *New Zealand Herald, file*

Rules of hygiene had been a first principle of the Maungapohatu community. At Matahi it is said that he hunted people out into the river every morning with his stick. As a faith-healer he had always accepted the practical elements of medicine, whether drawn from Maori herbal knowledge or Pakeha techniques. Both had their place, as the Waimana schoolteacher learnt to his surprise, when a child, taken to Rua for him to heal a broken arm, returned with the bandages undisturbed. Rua had simply prayed for the child's health.[41] Laughton, in his turn, acquired considerable respect for the Tuhoe knowledge, not only of herbal curatives but also of the setting of broken bones.[42] Rua's intelligence and pragmatism can be recognized in his cooperation with the Presbyterian missionaries, who by the early 1920s had become significant figures in the Tuhoe communities.

The typhoid epidemic at Maungapohatu meant that the school, which had temporarily closed because of staffing problems, remained closed. But the determination of the community to get the school open finally forced the Education Department to accept a responsibility for what they described as probably the most inaccessible school in the country. In May 1925 it was reopened under the care of a woman who would become almost as influential as Laughton: Irene Paulger. She was renamed by the people, Huhana, after the old woman who had given the land. The school became a focal point of the community's life, because of her dedication. She found staunch supporters in Miki, the *rangatira* of the community in the 1920s, and his eldest son, Te Heuheu, who succeeded him on his death in 1928. When a new blackboard for the school was needed, years later, Te Heuheu carried it all the way on his back from the Papatotara junction. (For his labour he was paid 5/- by the Education Department.) Many of Rua's children attended the Maungapohatu school and Rua, at least in the 1920s, made certain that they did attend. Irene Paulger's school started with a roll of forty-five children, seven of them Rua's. The desks arrived a year later, brought on packhorses in pieces and patiently reassembled by Laughton: twenty-five double desks, in four different sizes, which would serve the school until it closed.

Although Rua had announced that his return to Maungapohatu in 1924 was to be for good,[43] in fact he soon returned to Matahi. Then, at the beginning of 1927, he revived the millenarian element in his teachings. The place of refuge

Lena Ruka and her husband, Te Heuheu Miki, at Maungapohatu. *Sister Annie Henry Collection, Alexander Turnbull Library*

Top
Inside the abandoned schoolhouse. The Department of Education closed the school in 1950.
Bottom
The schoolhouse, derelict. Photos by Gillian Chaplin, May 1977.

Rua and some of his household and visitors, at the back of the house at Maai, May 1927.
Back: Te Urikore from Ruatoki, famous for her songs; Te Aue; Te Akakura; Hikihiki (Ngahiwi), also from Ruatoki; Pehirangi, with her baby, Te Ariki; Piimia, with her daughter Ti.
Front: Harata, from Ruatoki, who was on the women's committee; Rua. Harata is making one of the lacebark kits. *Alexander Turnbull Library*

from the wrath to come was again to be Maungapohatu, the City of God on earth. The regathering of the people commenced, for Rua warned that two weeks' total darkness would descend on earth before the end of May. Following the darkness, lightning would tear the heavens open and a deluge would flood the land and 'every living thing at Waimana, Ruatoki, Whakatane and Opotiki'[44] would be drowned. (Rua, it is remembered, sent one of his followers, Heahea Onekawa, down to the sea at Waiotahi to call up the waves. He was observed by a sceptic hitting the water with a stick, to make it move.[45]) But others believed and by March about two hundred people had trekked to Maungapohatu. Many had sold their stock and property, as before, to buy the galvanized iron which Rua decreed they must have to protect them from the fiery storms to come. He ordered them not to live in tents, for the lightning and the hot stones falling would destroy everything that could burn. As in 1907, reports abounded of the losses of the credulous: the man who sold his house for £4 and another who got rid of his horse and dray for half its real value.

In this manner Maungapohatu was rebuilt. The existing houses were repaired and given iron roofs. The village was carefully laid out with two main streets and the houses grouped geometrically along them. Irene Paulger was quite clear that Rua had an underlying purpose in his actions. The Health Department doctors who had lived at Maungapohatu during the typhoid epidemic, had talked to him about the poor houses and the general lack of sanitation. They had recommended that new homes should be built, with two rooms and outside lavatories. Rua, she believed, had no intention of complying openly with these suggestions and instead chose a more indirect path.

At a meeting of his people, Rua prophesied that the end of the world would come . . . . First

Above
Rebuilding Maungapohatu – Tane Nui A Rangi and the community, probably in early 1927, before fences and gardens were built in front of the houses. *Whakatane Museum*

The homes with the new roofs. Notice the separate cooking shelter at the rear of the house. *Auckland Weekly News, 2 June 1927*

Left
An example of the two-roomed, multiple dwellings built at Maungapohatu in 1927, here photographed ten years later. Photo by Andrew Fuller, Palmerston North.

Rua teaching at Maai, probably in 1927 during the nine months of Scriptural study to prepare for the fall of the stars in August. In the background, left, is Te Kawa A Maui and, beside it, the *wharepuni*. Back, sitting on the bench: Pukepuke; Te Amoroa. Rua is on the chair.
Front: seated: Wharepapa Hawiki; Tawa Kanuehi, Pehirangi's father. *Morris Collection, Alexander Turnbull Library*

would come a bombardment of stars, and after everything else had fallen from the heavens, then God himself would appear.

His people were told that the only way in which they could save themselves was to build houses (after the method described to Rua by the Health Department) with tin roofs, and on the night of the end of the world, the people were to remain indoors.

There was a frantic rush to build the new dwellings, the outdoor conveniences etc. before the time prophesied. This was done. . . . a new, clean, more sanitary village had been built.[46]

Such an explanation is, of course, adequate only at one level. He had indeed rebuilt the City of God, but the regeneration of faith required deep emotional foundations. Rua could draw on the old sources, revivified. In March of 1927, the government confiscations commission sat in Opotiki and Whakatane to consider the Tuhoe lands taken sixty years before. It decided that, since the Tuhoe had been in rebellion, they were to be given no compensation. As hope declined, grief grew stronger, and Rua could use it for his own purposes. Secondly, astronomers foretold that a comet (this time, the Pons-Winnecke) would come nearer to earth in the winter than had ever been known.[47] For Rua, it would usher in a rain of stars. Rua's promises had, from the beginning, been associated with portents in the sky: here again was a sign for those who could read its language.

1927 was also the year in which Wiremu Ratana was prophesying the return of God, in the form of the advent of the Holy Ghost in December.[48] The Mangai's rapid ascendancy as a prophet had been the source of a great deal of recent publicity, not the least in the *Auckland Weekly News*, which was read in Maungapohatu regularly. Ratana's new temple was opened in February and five thousand gathered to hear him speak from the upper porch of the twin-domed building, and a photograph appeared of him[49] similar to that of Rua which the *Weekly News* had carried twenty years before. The two stars were in rivalry, as Te Turuki had foreseen. But, Rua said, Ratana was wrong in his 'facts'. Jesus Christ would come to earth in the month of August; the event had been foretold in 1907, by the 'sun and moon and stars'.[50] Rua thus linked the advent of Christ to the original celestial conjunctions which had determined the founding of Maungapohatu twenty years previously. If this revival of the millenarian aspects of his faith did reflect 'professional jealousy', as the *New Zealand Herald* tartly put it, the roots were none the less deep.

It is also significant that Rua's desire to recreate Maungapohatu as the City of God was revealed the moment John Laughton left the community. At the end of 1926 he was transferred to Taupo; his assistant, Jim Black, carried on in his place. Hoani's departure tipped the delicate equilibrium of authority in Rua's favour. Once again the *poropiti* of the Tuhoe stood unchallenged on Mount Zion.

Those who returned to Maungapohatu in 1927 remember well the months during which they traversed the whole body of the Scriptures, from the Old Testament to the New, under Rua's instruction.† Sitting outside Te Kawa A Maui, they read and discussed the entire prophetic tradition which was to be fulfilled at the end of the winter, by the coming of Christ. The two Sons of God were to be reunited on earth.

Despite the dire predictions made in the newspapers that a hard winter lay ahead for the people, since the land was without stock and the potato crop had failed, everyone who went to Maungapohatu remembers it as a winter of plenty. There were both wild pig and cattle; there was preserved pigeon, and ample supplies of cabin bread and flour, which Rua purchased for them. The six-foot track from Tawhana had recently been cut and at last they could run a string of horses up from the valley. Horo Tatu was in charge at Tawhana and ran the team. Bulk supplies could be brought in, including sheets of roofing iron, although the journey was still lengthy and difficult. In these months, Rua said, they were not to work at raising cattle, or sheep, or 'money-making', but instead prepare themselves to receive Christ. The funding of the community in this period came, as in 1907, from the money which the families had

Horo Tatu, who ran the team of horses from Tawhana, just before he died. He married Rua's daughter, Rangipaea. Photo by Gillian Chaplin, December 1977.

† But the original English-language Covenant had been defiled and Rua deliberately destroyed it by using it as waste paper. The Ark of the Covenant was itself lost in the sack of the Jerusalem of the Davidic Kings, and it was expressly said that it should be neither remade nor remembered.

Waka kereru, a drinking trough to catch kereru (pigeon) near Maungapohatu, 1935. It was built one year before. Photo by Rowland Dickinson, Whitianga.

Opposite (bottom)
Te Akakura and Rua during the time of 'the retreat', the return to Maungapohatu from Matahi in 1927. Akakura has an oppossum skin rug. *Hine Nui Te Po, Te Waikotikoti marae, Te Whaiti.* Reproduced by kind permission of Professor S. M. Mead, Wellington.

'Off to Waimana in Rua's dray, outside his maize shed'. So captioned by Phem Doull, the mission teacher at Matahi. Maize provided the staple income of the valley communities.
Phem Doull Collection, Mrs N. Bracey, Christchurch

brought with them, raised by the sale of their property.

The *New Zealand Herald* reporter who visited Maungapohatu early in May described the new community he found. The houses, built of slab and shingle, were lined throughout with pages and illustrations from the *Weekly News* and all the floors had been made draught-proof. Each house had its own little courtyard and nearly every one had newly-made flower beds in front. At the rear were vegetables and fruit bushes, particularly raspberry and gooseberry. Inside, the furniture was mostly home-made, often from manuka wood. The village council had posted up the bye-laws in front of Tane Nui A Rangi:

Loading the mail for Maungapohatu at Te Whaiti, May 1927. Sixty-four kilometres of track lay ahead.
Auckland Weekly News, 19 May 1927

These are the laws pertaining to our courtyard: All dogs are to be tied up. No animals are to

come within the courtyard of the big house. For a stray dog (a fine) of threepence or more; for a stray horse, one shilling or more; for a pig or cow, two shillings; for leaving refuse about the yards of homes, two shillings; for leaving unclosed the gate to the courtyard, five shillings; for cantering horses through the settlement, five shillings. If fines are not paid on demand the matter will be taken before the council.[51]

The main street (now vanished) of Maungapohatu, December 1927. It is the school sports day. Notice the fenced gardens of each of the houses. Behind the meeting-house there is a *wharepuni*, now demolished. Photo by Ernie La Roche. *A. J. La Roche, Auckland*

Not only were the council's rules strict. Rua also imposed a decree during the months of Scriptural study that none could be away from the settlement for more than a night, though he did in fact relax the ruling and gave permission for longer absences.[52] These rules achieved a discipline and a concentration of energy which are still remembered as essential characteristics of the community. Rua's underlying motivation was revealed in a remark he made to the *Herald* reporter: his people were fine people, but too 'soft' to deal with the Pakeha. If the devices Rua used were themselves manipulative, his concern was to raise the Tuhoe from their poverty and to bring about a regeneration of energy, through faith. From the beginning, he prepared for the 'failure' of the millennium. He said if it did not occur 'at the time when he was to make his "try for Jesus," it certainly would before the year 2000. If August passed without the coming, which . . . will be accompanied by the destruction of all those who are not ready and waiting, then he would restock his land'.[53]

And this, precisely, he did. When the appointed night came, the people stayed indoors and waited. The next morning, they were glad to see all their homes still standing. The world had not come to an end; but the coming of God had not occurred either. 'They went to Rua. He told them that as they had built their houses to save themselves, they did not prepare their hearts for the coming of God. Therefore, it was their own fault and not his'.[54] But, instead,

Rua and some of his followers at Matahi, early 1920s. Rua is in the foreground, wearing a hat. *Auckland Institute and Museum*

Right
Teka, one of the staunchest of the Riwaiti, who remained at Maungapohatu to the end of his days. With him, on the left, is Hemi Tawa. On the right is Teka's wife, Kumeroa. The children are theirs, with Puhata behind Teka and Te Hina in the centre, her hair drawn back. *Sister Dorothy Keen Collection, Mrs O. Rudd, Christchurch*

Opposite (bottom)
Maungapohatu, December 1932. Many of the houses were divided for two families by an internal partition. In the far distance is Maai. This view looks into the gully, up which Toko had run in 1916. The two main streets of the community can be seen; the one nearer the meeting-house has now vanished. This was the road on which horses were forbidden. Photo by Andrew Fuller, Palmerston North.

they could labour to 'declare in Zion the work of the Lord our God.'[55] When Norman Nicholls, an Auckland schoolteacher, visited the community in December, there were flourishing vegetable gardens and an abundance of fruit trees. Milch cows had been brought in. (Rua was very partial to butter.) The bright flower gardens had sprung up again in the front of every house, a cheerful memory which every visitor carried away from Maungapohatu in these years. (The seeds were ordered by mail from Laidlaw's illustrated catalogue, which one of the missionaries had brought.) Many of the men were absent for the summer shearing and the money they sent back was controlled

by Rua and spent on the community. He also paid 'those in authority', who worked at Maungapohatu, men and women. A record for 1929 has survived of the payments made 'in the presence of the lord':

1)	Te Heuheu.	Tapara. [digging in the cultivations]	2000
2)	Te Koka.	Tapara	2500
3)	Katiana	He tangata tenei i tana whare ahau, e moe ana. Tetahi wana tika, koia te kai harihari mai o aku mea. Te utu tenei mo raua. t.	2500
		[I am sleeping at this man's house, and his servant carried my belongings for me. This payment for both of them.]	
. . . 12)	Huhana	Kore Kauta [for want of a cooking shed]	500
. . . 16)		Nga riwaiti. Te utu kia ratau tenei a te atua	
		[The Levites. The lord's pay to them]	
		Teka T	7000
		Te Amor[o]a. T	7000
		Tamati [Rautao]	7000
		Pita	7000
		Wharepapa	7000
		Turei [Tuhua]	7000[56]

All in all, about £865 was paid on this day.‡

These were the good years. The community had a string band – violin, banjo, and mandolin – and there were sometimes hundreds of visitors, straining their catering to its limits. Each home would bring two plates as a way of coping.[57] They built a dance hall again, but this time it was just an open floor near the meeting-house, where they held square dances and foxtrots. Ties had to be worn and drink was forbidden. In the community, each family had its own kitchen, as it had its own house. In the summer of 1929 there were

Katiana Tawa, brother of Maka Kanuehi and Pehirangi, with Ruru Tautau on his shoulders, about 1920, at Maungapohatu. *Laughton Album, National Museum*

‡ 'Tika', in the sense of 'slave' or 'servant', was a specifically Tuhoe usage. A decimal system of counting was used, and the final total was written '£86500'. As some payments were for 1250 (apparently £12. 5. 0), there seem to be problems in the arithmetic.

The carcase of a bullock being brought up from the 'kopa Maori' on a sled for the school Christmas feast in 1927. (Norman Nicholls is taking a photograph in the centre.)
Right
Opening up the feast. Kelly Kereopa (Kereopa Timi) is on the right. Photos by Ernie La Roche. *A. J. La Roche, Auckland*

Opposite
The schoolchildren feast inside Tane Nui A Rangi. This is a most unusual photograph, for only amongst the Iharaira was the practice of eating inside a meeting-house permitted. Photo by Norman Nicholls, 1927.

thirty kitchens in the upper pa, each one listed by the family's name in the Ledger book. One was Whatu's, another belonged to old Paora. Te Mata Kiripa, one of the few Whakatohea who remained, had his. Because each family ate in their own kitchen, there was no need for a dining hall, though on festive occasions the meeting-house was used. For the school Christmas party of 1927, a great meal was prepared in the 'kopa Maori', the oven of hot stones, and hauled up to the meeting-house on a sled. Long woven mats for the food were placed along the length of the meeting-house. The children and visitors

Paora Kingi, outside Tane Nui A Rangi, probably early 1920s. *Sister Dorothy Keen Collection, Mrs O. Rudd, Christchurch*

Below
Te Mata Kiripa and his wife, Kahu, at Maungapohatu. *Whakatane Museum*

sat on the floor, the Pakeha guests being placed at the head. Grace was said and then everyone ate, using their fingers with gusto. At the end, wet cloths were passed round so that all could clean their hands.[58] Norman Nicholls, who was a guest, remembers with pleasure the ingenuity with which some of the problems of isolation were solved. For marbles, the boys chipped the river stones patiently until they were spherical. He also remembers that, when he arrived, Rua refused to appear. For Nicholls was six foot three inches tall and Rua thought that he was a policeman. When Jim Black explained and amicable

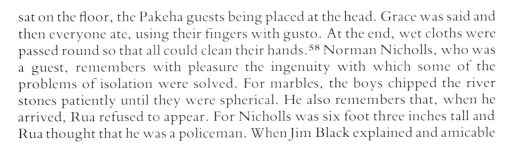

relations were established, the people lent Nicholls a horse to ride – 'Kina', or Skinner, named as an act of insult. The harsh memories were not far away.

The community at Maungapohatu stayed more or less intact until about 1931. Most of the money earned came from casual summer labour. A useful supplement was brought in by the fine *houhi* hats which the women made from sun-dried strips of the lace bark, dyed red and blue-black with natural dyes. They also sold sun-dried fungus, *pangi*, to the local storekeepers, and timber by the 'cord'. The construction of the road to Lake Waikaremoana was

Below
One of the famous *kiekie* mats made by Matekoraha, Hemi Tawa's wife. *Kiekie* does not grow naturally at Maungapohatu and is therefore much prized. This mat is one of a pair, each one taking a year to make. It carries the words of a hymn sung by the Iharaira; the second half completes the hymn.
Hemi Tawa; Paetawa Miki; Tommy Tuhua; January 1961. Photo by Andrew Fuller, Palmerston North.

Opposite (bottom)
Rua, —, and Te Aue at Otane, February 1933. Irene Paulger wrote, on 25 July 1934: 'Rua spends most of his time now at Otane, a place about twenty miles from here, and where they have commenced a dairy farm. Times are very hard with him just now, for there is not much surplus cash about. . . . A great many of the people have gone from here to outside places to work. There is nothing to do here really to bring in any money, and if it were not for the Family Allowances and the Old Age Pensions I don't know how some of them could live.' Photo by Rowland Dickinson, Whitianga.

begun at last and many of the men found work there, but it took them away from the community for days and weeks at a time. Many began to leave to live in the road-makers' camps, or at Ruatahuna, to get work. The harsh conditions of the Maungapohatu winters began to take their toll. At times, the tracks were impassable; worse, a successive failure of the potato crop brought famine. In the first bad winter of 1930, the people stayed together, somehow, but after that, family after family was forced to leave. Some found relief work at Ruatoki, on Ngata's land development scheme. Rua himself began to travel more and more frequently from Maungapohatu and the size of the community depended very much on whether he was in residence or not. Until 1932 he spent his summers in the Waimana valley and in the autumn his 'horse train' would wind its way back to Maungapohatu.[59] Finally, in the winter of 1933, he came out to the Waimana valley to live at Otane.

At Christmas time, three years earlier, he had been 'discovered' by a party of trampers, in residence with his six wives at Matahi. He entertained them on the verandah of his house with hot buttered scones and jam. He agreed to pose for a photo and disappeared inside to change. When he returned he was resplendent in a tall 'bell-topper'. In February 1933 an old friend, Rowland Dickinson, encountered him at his new settlement at Otane. Dickinson came regularly to fish for trout and remembered the first time they had met, both 'camping' in the Waimana valley. Rua was better organized than the fisherman; his wives were busy plaiting the fronds of the nikau to make a roof to shelter his double bed, which, complete with spring mattress, he always had taken round for him.[60] In the course of a long tale of which Dickinson understood very little, Rua said,

Above
Rua at Matahi, December 1930. *Mrs M.·S. Satherley, Orewa*

Opposite (top)
John Currie, 'Kari', and some of the children at Maungapohatu, December 1930. *Mrs M. S. Satherley, Orewa*

'You know, I got shot. I dead three days, then I cough and come alive all the same Jesus Christ.' He pulled his shirt up and showed me a healed wound on his back. He evidently thought I didn't believe him because he said, 'You see the bullet hole? That was when I was a dead man.'[61]

Rua's mana as prophet and Messiah in the last years of his life remained unchanged among the Waimana people. Indeed soon after Dickinson encountered him, he returned to Maai (perhaps for the last time). Many came back with him and once again he imposed a discipline prohibiting them from leaving while, for two months, they studied the Scriptures and learnt by heart the passages of the Iharaira worship.[62] As John Laughton said, they literally believed that Rua was God, and had implicit faith that he alone could save them at the end of the world.[63] After 1927, they knew it would come before or during the year 2000. 'One thing we were told every day, us people, Rua's people, when we get to 2000, it'll be at that time. . . . I don't know what or how, but it will be the change of something. Rua used to say that.'[64] They also believed that Rua himself was immortal; as he had told Dickinson, ' "Rua will never die" '.[65]

He remained their guide in all matters. Mau Rua remembers one incident, in 1934, when a hot stream of sulphur came bubbling up in the Tauranga river. They all went to have a look. Rua told them,

Just look at that and think about White Island and those mountains there, Ngauruhoe and that. We are standing on the fire. If he left that thing to sizzle, well, there'd be nothing but the destroying of the Urewera land. So he just put his hand onto it and tell him, 'You might as well go back where you came up. You're not supposed to come up', he said. 'You might blow us up.'

But after 1927, his influence remained strong only with the faithful. There

Below
Maungapohatu, December 1934. The tennis court is about where the original Hiruharama Hou stood and was put in by the mission when Rua was absent. In the centre foreground is the same multiple dwelling photographed earlier (p. 157), but by this date many families were leaving Maungapohatu. Photo by Flora Johnston, Auckland.

Opposite (top)
Piimia, Rua's youngest wife who stayed with him through the last harsh years at Matahi. Piripari marae, photographed by courtesy of Rata Takao. *Whakatane Museum*

Left
The prophet growing old: Rua, at the unveiling of the monument over the tomb of James Carroll, Gisborne. *Auckland Weekly News, 14 March 1929*

Te Akakura and Puti, Rua's daughters, at Hiruharama Hou, Maai, January 1978. Photo by Gillian Chaplin.

would be no more conversions. He was himself growing old and less active. He suffered from rheumatism and joked about his inability to heal himself.[66] Yet he still managed to found another community, at Taramaiere across the hills to the east of Tataiahape. It was a substantial little settlement of nikau and totara bark houses, all with iron roofs. About 1935 some thirty people lived here with Rua. He never stayed anywhere for very long, however, and moved freely among his several homes in traditional fashion. But Maai itself he seems to have left for good. His daughter, Puti, who looked after it for a while, remembers how they drove the truck in from Matahi to the Papatotara saddle on the new Waikaremoana road and brought out as much as they could over the badly overgrown track. The iron bedsteads they had to leave, the furniture, the *kohua* (cooking pots), and tin trunks containing their personal possessions. Because the house was tapu they knew that nothing would be touched by Maoris. In the early 1960s there were still Bibles in every room and documents and photographs in the trunks. By now they have all vanished, purloined by casual visitors and deer hunters as souvenirs. Only the beds remain, and the tin trunks, empty, mute witnesses to the looting.

In the Waimana valley, the Iharaira communities worked under Rua's discipline until the end.

He used to tell us what to do – and I don't listen. But now, when I've lost him, I think about what he used to do with us. Be hard on us. His ways – you've *got* to do it with Rua. You've got to do everything for tomorrow, today. He made the people work. He would say, 'If it's hard, go and do it. Don't stand there and look at it; go and do it.' He was a man of that sort.[67]

But the last years in the valley were harsh. When Rua was living at his last home, at Tuapou, a report was commissioned on the problems of the Tuhoe, so grim was their situation. Its findings, in 1936, revealed that they had benefitted not a jot from the 'experimental' land legislation designed to protect them.

The Tuhoe land had been brought into Ngata's consolidation schemes during 1921–2. Their individual shares had then been grouped and allocated as defined blocks. Those shares which the Crown had purchased over the years were similarly grouped and defined as specific blocks, for the first time.[68] As part of this arrangement, the Tuhoe had given £21,000 worth of land (40,000 acres) towards the cost of the construction of arterial roads, which would open up their lands to the possibility of farming and logging. The roads would provide the means to turn their lands into a source of revenue for their support. But it was not until 1930 that the tortuous road to Waikaremoana was opened. The dray road up the Waimana valley, started in 1922, was taken only as far as Tawhana. The promised arterial road up that valley, to Maungapohatu and Te Waiiti, upon which Rua had placed all his hopes, was never to be built. It was 'postponed', to Rua's great dismay, late in 1927, then gazetted in 1930, but it never eventuated. His 'millennium' had been based on the not unreasonable expectation that a road would come to Mount Zion. Instead, by 1935 the dray road, for which the local county council refused to take responsibility, had deteriorated badly. Not only had the Tuhoe been misled in this respect (and there is a sense in which the terrain defeated everybody),§ they had been badly treated in another. No government money had been funded into the consolidation scheme for economic development. The consolidation was, in practice, little more than the means by which the

§ In 1958, the Tuhoe finally received a lump sum (of $200,000 plus interest) in compensation for the lands they had given for roads that were never built.

Hiruharama Hou, derelict, May 1977. Photo by Gillian Chaplin.

Below
Maai, January 1961. Photo by Andrew Fuller, Palmerston North.

This portrait was probably taken at the time of the discussions held at Ruatoki for the land consolidation. Te Akakura, wearing a greenstone and gold brooch on which her name is set; Rua; Te Aue. *George Stephenson, Auckland*

Opposite (bottom)
Rua, on the sunny side of the house at Maai. This portrait, taken by John Laughton, was entitled 'One of the last photos of Rua', but exactly when it was taken is not known. *Whakatane Museum*

172

Crown cut out its portion. Only at Ruatoki and Ruatahuna had Ngata started land development schemes, which were operating in the early 1930s. Elsewhere, the Tuhoe remained as impoverished and as unable to develop the harsh terrain as before.

Matahi was the largest settlement in the Waimana valley and here it was reported, in 1935, that the people 'are in poor circumstances'. They were using 'their limited areas of workable land to the best of their ability', but had been given no assistance of any kind.[69] Because it was finally realized that the felling of the bush in the higher reaches of the valley would create massive soil erosion, farming had been prohibited there from 1923. In January 1936 a government decision on conservation in the Ureweras limited the Tuhoe to farming only their 'ancestral clearings'. No more bush was to be felled.[70] Such a decision condemned those Tuhoe who stayed on their lands to the position of a proletariat working for Pakeha farmers on the more fertile coastal strips. Some of these farms were on lands confiscated from them. As the subsequent report of 1936 observed, the preservation of the timber forest was of more direct value to the European community than to the Tuhoe and if conservation was to be definite government policy, then the government had an obligation to give their 'earnest attention' to the Tuhoe needs. They earned their present livelihood largely from casual work on the roads, shearing in season, relief work, and the sale of posts to Europeans, 'who very often fail to pay them'.[71]

Rua had participated fully in the original consolidation scheme and had been a strong influence in persuading the Tuhoe to accept it.[72] He had, after all, been an advocate for the Waimana road since at least 1908. He had, years ago, offered the labour of his followers to help build that road.[73] Now, in 1936, just before he died, he was still struggling with the same battles. In December he wrote to G. P. Shepherd, one of the authors of the 1936 report:

I am afraid that if no action is taken now our arrangements would become just dreams. . . . You and friend proposed when at my home that in exchange for the fringes of my bush you would give me flat land.
I therefore respectfully request you to expedite either the exchange or to let me proceed with working the fringe of the bush land. I am standing by our arrangements in consequence of which I am holding back my axe-blade from touching the bush.[74]

Wealthy in land which they could not use, poor materially and trapped in economic bondage to the European farmers: this was the reality from which Rua all his life had tried to rescue the Tuhoe.

Rua's 'millennium' was his dream that Maungapohatu, as the sacred home of the Tuhoe, could exist and flourish. His dream had withered. No roads came to Jerusalem. Instead, he had to teach the people the virtues of poverty and give them the strength to bear it. In order to endure, they had to have the hope of a time when all would be different.

To an extent he also exploited them. There is little doubt that he spent their money on himself and on his wives. When he died, over £700 was found in his house, all in small coins, gifts from the poor to the prophet. Of the many stories told of Rua, which stress the gullibility of his followers, one took our fancy: at a tangi he persuaded those who were putting money with the grave goods, to accept his cheque instead. Rua took the coins and placed his cheque (for £800 in this version) in the grave.[75] He loved luxury and is famous for the cars he owned. One of the earliest was a seven seater Mitchell Six, which he bought from Henry Bell, who had run it as a taxi. Rua had hired it often, and the taxi and Henry travelled far abroad on Rua's various visits. Because he was so taken by it, he managed to persuade its owner to sell it, paying for it in maize. A later car was one of the original six-cylinder Chevrolets made in 1929. This he bought new, on hire purchase, only to see it repossessed because he refused to pay the interest charges.[76] (It is said that this car will return, in the days to come. It is also said that it can be seen, driverless, at night, on the road to Matahi.) But if he exploited his people, he also worked beside them in the fields. He never shirked physical labour. To the end, he ran a small herd of milking cows at Tuapou, supplying cream to the dairy factory at Waimana.[77]

It can also be said that some of Rua's economic advice was dubious. He had encouraged the selling of land. All of his wives, except the headstrong Te Akakura, sold most of their land. Even now some believe it was better to sell the land than fight over it. His daughter Puti remembers that he impressed

Portrait of Rua in an old naval coat and top hat. He was fond of both these 'pieces of extravagance'. He carries his *tokotoko*, carved walking-stick, used in oratory. *W. C. Davies, Taneatua*

The 'spine of Maui's fish', Maungapohatu. Leatherwoods cover the mountain top. There are also three tarns on the top, each one a different colour. This view looks towards the pinnacles of rock at the north-west edge of the mountain; that on the right is Te Tapapatonga O Irakewa. Photo by R. A. Creswell, 1935.

upon them it would only cause them trouble. 'Better to go out to work and earn your *kai*', he would say. Rua was shaken by Te Akakura's death, on 17 December 1930,[78] and it was followed by terrible conflict with the Ruatoki people over her land and possessions. To him, the quarrel confirmed his view that he had been right in his advice. Towards the end of his life he seems to have been trying to distract his followers from their realization that they had lost much of their land without any visible benefit. The traditional saying of the Tuhoe, which states their identity – 'From Toi and Potiki, the land; from Tuhoe, the mana and the rank' – had now acquired a bitter tinge. The 'land is the Crown's and the "mana" and the "rangatira" lost.'[79] In place of an obsessive lingering on their past, he told them to study the Scriptures and prepare for what was coming. They should not get into debt, nor run up accounts. He warned them of harder times, just before the end. It would be the sign.

On 20 February 1937 Rua died at Matahi. He died of Bright's disease and tuberculosis,[80] untreated and only too common among the older people. As he lay dying, John Currie, the missionary, visited him. In the uninformative manner only too prevalent among missionaries, he hints at what must have been a fascinating conversation. Not only did Rua scorn Currie's admonitions of mortality, but told him that he would rise on the third day.[81] He then discussed at length the text of Ezekiel 37, or the promises which God made to Israel:

Behold, O my people, I will open your graves, and cause you to come up out of your graves, and bring you into the land of Israel. . . .
I will take the children of Israel . . . and will gather them on every side, and bring them into their own land:
And I will make them one nation in the land upon the mountains of Israel . . . .
And David my servant shall be king over them; and they all shall have one shepherd . . . .

174

Moreover I will make a covenant of peace with them; it shall be an everlasting covenant with them; and I . . . will set my sanctuary in the midst of them for evermore.[82]

On Sunday the 21st the guns were fired all morning in traditional manner to drive off the *kehua*, the malevolent spirits of the dead.[83] By Tuesday, trucks and buses and cars were arriving from all over the country bringing the people for the tangi. Rua had ordered that his body was not to be taken to the marae at Matahi but to be laid out before his own house. He was dressed in purple robes, like Christ before him in his suffering,[84] and placed in a glass-lidded coffin on the open verandah of his house. At the foot of the coffin was the portrait of Toko. His five living wives sat or slept beside him: Pinepine, Pehirangi, Te Aue, Mihiroa and Piimia. As the visitors arrived, old Te Pairi Tu Terangi, the famous carver from Omuriwaka, the nearby settlement, chanted the ancient songs of mourning.

The people gathered for the fulfilment of the prophecy of resurrection. As the evening of Wednesday the 24th drew near, the tension mounted outside the house. Six hundred people had assembled, despite torrential rain which had blocked the track from Maungapohatu and turned the valley road into a sea of mud. At dusk they waited in absolute silence, until long after six o'clock, the hour of his death.‖ Then the tangi broke out anew but now the wailing had a note of 'heart-break previously lacking.'[85]

‖ There is clearly a problem of the choice of the 'third' day. The first visitors did not arrive until the 23rd, because of the difficulties of getting the news out and the conditions of the road. Forty trucks arrived on Wednesday and it was then commonly said that Rua had died on the 21st. Some odd events did occur. The glass on the top of the coffin cracked, as did the concrete, inexpertly mixed for his tomb, which had to be repaired immediately. John Laughton strove to explain the incidents pragmatically.

Portrait of Rua used for his obituary. It was actually taken in 1927. *Auckland Weekly News, 3 March 1937*

Below
Greeting the body: Rua's tangi at his house at Tuapou (Matahi), February 1937. *Whakatane Museum*

Rua's body lies on the left-hand side of the verandah of his house, the traditionally tapu side. His house is in the centre of the photograph and to its left are the marquees erected for the sleeping accommodation of the guests. *Whakatane Museum*

Right
Building the tomb at the rear of the house. Heta Rua stands in the centre of the group of three men, looking out towards the camera. *Whakatane Museum*

'Aue, Rua, we thought you more than a prophet, we thought you more than mere man. You promised you would rise from the dead on the third day, but still you sleep. Come back to us, and show us that the beliefs of a lifetime were not false, nor our hopes of salvation vain, nor our devotion and faith wasted. Ah, Rua, you were our guardian and our father, and what we shall do without you we dare not think!'[86]

The construction of the tomb in which he was to be laid was begun at the back of his house. It was built entirely of concrete and set in the angle of the rear rooms. In an unprecedented manner, Rua had set aside the money for the costs. On the Sunday before he died, he called his household together and told them that the end of his life was near. He asked for his strongbox, unlocked it, and took out a bundle of notes. This was for the coffin. The second bundle was for the tangi; they were to order the food. The third was for his burial, for which he left all the instructions.[87]

On 27 February Rua Kenana Hepetipa was placed inside the concrete vault. With him were sealed his personal possessions and objects of great ancestry: finely woven cloaks and a greenstone tiki. The Waimana people, led by Tu Rakuraku, no longer a follower of Rua, gave a final haka to cheer his spirit on its journey. Then Hoani Laughton conducted the burial service, as Rua had requested. To an undertone of keening, Laughton talked of the great good that Rua had done and the loss they had suffered of a leader of so many years. 'You were a very great chief, Rua; you were the eyes and ears of your people. You were their father.' He tried as best he could to comfort them: 'Rua is gone', he said, 'but God remains.'[88]

Those who follow Rua do not believe that he has gone. They await his return. They believe that this is why he was buried alone at Matahi. He was sheltered from the ill-will of the *kehua* of the cemeteries of whom, in later life, he had become terrified. At night, he always walked in the midst of a crowd of people to protect himself from them.[89] 'He was frightened of the deads. He don't like tapu amongst the dead.'[90] But alone he would lie in peace until the time. For he said, 'I'll be dead now. I'll come back.'[91]

Above
A front view of the house, painted in the colours of Hiona, blue and yellow. The verandah, shown here, has been enclosed since Rua's death. The house is tapu.
Below
Rua's tomb. Photos by Gillian Chaplin, 1977.

177

He was not taken to Maungapohatu. This was his command and it puzzled the elders then. When we asked one of our informants why he thought Rua had chosen to remain at Matahi, he said,

I have always asked myself that question – why he wanted to be buried at Matahi. I couldn't get the right answer. But in *my* mind, I think it is this story, the story of the thing of God which Te Kooti had. Te Kooti came to old Te Whiu, of Waimana, Te Maipi's father, and said, 'I'll give you something to keep in your hand. Keep it safe.' And Te Whiu said, 'What is it?' 'Oh – the life of the whole of the Waimana people. Something to look after them.' ¶ So, he gave that thing to Te Whiu. And when Rua came, trying to be God, one day he decided to come down from Maungapohatu, out to Waimana. He sent a man ahead of him to go and fetch from Te Whiu this thing that Te Kooti gave him. This man rode down to Waimana and he came to Te Whiu for that thing. But Te Whiu would not give it to him. So the man rode back and met Rua at Tawhana and told him, 'He won't let you have it. That's his own keep.' So, the next morning Rua sent the man again. When Rua got to Matahi, the man was there and he said, 'He won't give it to you. You're not the Son of God.' So Rua says, 'Oh well, I'll go myself tonight.' And then, that very night, this old man, Te Whiu, told his daughters and his son Te Maipi, 'That thing has gone out of my hand. That's the man all right, coming. Rua.' So in the morning they all gathered up and went to Tataiahape to wait for him. . . . He had that thing when he died. He had to die where he got that thing. . . . That's my way of thinking.[92]

Rua's tangi was extraordinary in another way. He was buried by a man of a different faith who was his friend. He was buried by one who certainly did not accept his claim to be 'a divine incarnation'. But he was buried by the man to whom he had given the children. To the tangi came some hundreds of people, many of whom did believe that he would lead them from their trials. Some of them still believe it, forty years later. Some find it hard.

Rua's tangi: the *hakari* (feast).
Whakatane Museum

¶In some versions of this story of Te Whiu Maraki and Te Turuki, the object is a key.

That's what we're waiting for now. When it's going to happen. Well, he did tell us we might have a chance to see him come back. We might have not. I don't believe him. I don't believe he's ever going to come back. Well, it's a very hard thing to believe.

There are two Sons of God, we believe. Not just one but two. One is to rule the heavens, one to rule the earth. The Father, Son, and Holy Ghost are three people, but they all came from the Father. He had two Sons. This is how we believe. One would never do without the other. When Rua was flesh and blood he was born anew. He was building the earth then, and he still is today . . . . That's the thing I believe. This man. The Son of God. Right in my heart. I believe Jesus Christ. I believe the two. That's all . . . .

Rua? Everything finish for that. He's dead, over here. Ah well. Finish. No more prophets.

Rua is the Messiah. He will come again. That is what we are waiting for. When it is the time. Same image, no different, same Rua, the same person. Everybody will see him. You, the man we didn't believe. That's the right time. The diamond is hidden now. When the right time comes – when he comes back . . . .

A story repeated. That's how the clock moves. That's how you know too when it comes round again. These are the signs we have, that it's getting into a new world.

Nothing will quieten the whole world, till that time comes, the coming of the Messiah. We are all believing in our hope, to see it.

Puti; Mau; Te Akakura; Miria Rua, wife of Mau; outside Rua's house at Tuapou, January 1978. Photo by Gillian Chaplin.

The City of God on earth remains today, largely a derelict community. Only the meeting-house is cared for, and to it, every summer, some return. It was renewed in July 1940. On this important occasion, the opening of the house with its new carvings, two bodies were also brought home. One was Whatu's, who had died in a shearing accident near Gisborne in 1936. The other

Above
The traditional *hahunga* (ceremonial display of the bones) for Whatu and Miki, 1940. The bones and the coffin are placed outside Tane Nui A Rangi, along with portraits of the dead and their dead kin. The flags are *tipuna* flags, bearing ancestral names indicating the lineage of the dead. *Kurikino* is, then, the marae flag of Te Waiiti; *Te Paena* is from Uwhiarai marae, Pinepine's marae; the third is *Whitiaua* from the great meeting-house Te Whai A Te Motu at Ruatahuna.

Right
Tane Nui A Rangi, with the new carvings put up in 1940. Photo by Gillian Chaplin, 1977.

Opposite (top)
Whatu's coffin outside Te Kawa A Maui.

Opposite (centre)
Carrying the bones and the coffin for their final reburial. *Meri Taka, Auckland*

was Miki who was killed in a truck accident at Te Whaiti in January 1928.*
The two *rangatira* were brought back for their final burial. They were greeted with rounds of gunshot and blasts of dynamite as they reached the marae.[93] It was the last great occasion until the opening of the road in 1964. By 1950 the community had shrunk to only two or three families. At the end of that year,

★ This accident is an important part of the saga of Maungapohatu. It was attributed to Te Akakura's disobedience of Rua and it is said that he forewarned of a disaster. Akakura herself was seriously hurt and had to be carried back to Maungapohatu on a litter. Another elder, Houpapa, was also killed. Miki's bones were excavated from Te Whaiti, with the help of John Currie, and Whatu's body was exhumed from Otane, where it had lain and was, as everyone remembers with some discomfort, amazingly preserved. It was all done, of course, without permission from the health authorities.

the Education Department decided to close the school. The mission itself had shut down as a separate station the previous year. Then, the private timber road brought hopes of employment for a while; as John Laughton said, the work would enable some of the 'exiled children of the mountain' to return.[94] But the logging has finished and the road deteriorates. Some families return to hunt and catch the wild horses during the summer holidays. The Maungapohatu Incorporation, established on behalf of the owners who are the shareholders, farms some of the land which was first cleared in 1907. But Maungapohatu is sinking into lonely isolation. In summer it is a sunlit valley; in winter the blizzards strike and the cold tears the flesh.

Top (right)
A portrait of Whatu, with his shortened hair. *Puti Onekawa*

Paetawa Miki, younger brother of Te Heuheu and *kaitiaki*, guardian, of Maungapohatu. Photo by Gillian Chaplin, 1978.

Top
The main street of Maungapohatu, 1959. On the right, is one of the last remaining *pataka* in use. Hemi Tawa stands outside. Below is the sunken *wharepuni*, with its earth walls, built in the early 1930s. It was later used as a 'hospital', and for confinement, to protect the babies from the Urewera winter. The floor is excavated about a foot inside the building.

The *pataka*, Hemi Tawa opening up. The piles are sheathed in metal to keep out rats. Photos by Dick Scott, 1959.

Looking across the gully to the remnants of the main street, 1968. Photo by Len Shapcott, Cambridge.

Below
Maungapohatu, 1968. The first house on the left was Te Heuheu's and was built of timber from a demolished multiple dwelling of the earlier period. These houses are near where the original Hiruharama Hou once stood. Photo by Len Shapcott, Cambridge.

The community sheltered under the
mountain, 1979. Photo by H. G. D.
White, Opotiki.

Maai and the mountain, 1975. Te
Kawa A Maui still stands, at the left.
Photo by Alan Smythe, Auckland.

Above
Colin McCahon, *Urewera mural*, 1975. The references are to Maungapohatu, the mountain, and to Tuhoe the people; to their prophets Te Turuki and Rua Kenana; to the founding ancestors of Tuhoe – Toi the wood-eater, Potiki, and Hape; and to man and the land. At the bottom, McCahon inscribed: 'At the boundary can I forbear From turning back my head.' *Urewera National Park Board.* Photo by Ian MacDonald.

Left
The emblems for the King of Clubs on Te Kawa A Maui, which was opened on 20 February 1919 and which burnt down in January 1977 (top).
The side boards (bottom) taken from Hiona and re-used at random for Te Kawa A Maui. Photos by Judith Binney, 1975.

185

Heta Rua, son of Te Aue and Rua, with his wife, Te Paea. Photo by Gillian Chaplin, 1978.

Opposite (top)
Te Ao Hou. The emblems for the King of Clubs, painted red, stand at the apex of the house and at the tips of the side boards. Inside, the four suits decorate the walls, each painted its 'proper' colour. The heart has fallen: it lies on its side, beside the spade. Some say we are now living in the time of the spade, or Pakeha dominance. Grouped together on the side walls of the house are the diamond and club, Rua's emblems. It would seem, as in all living mythologies, the meaning of the iconography can shift with individual interpretation. Photo by Gillian Chaplin, 1977.

Opposite (bottom)
Inside Rua's room in the house at Tuapou. His tomb lies immediately behind it. A portrait of his young son Henare hangs on the left; a favourite hat in the centre; to the right a collage of photos relating to Rua's life. Photographed, by courtesy of Mau Rua, by Gillian Chaplin, 1978.

186

At Tuapou, Rua's children have their own meeting-house. They have called it Te Ao Hou, the New World. It was opened on 10 August 1941 as the house for Rua's people. This marae is now the *papakainga* of the Children of Israel.†　The little meeting-house stands near to Rua's grave and tapu house, where a small window is always open in the verandah for offerings. To this day, the Iharaira keep their separate Christmas, although fewer and fewer come. The people of Rua who live in this valley are mostly the old. Their poverty is real. But they retain a strong sense of who they are and they possess a means of interpreting the present harshness of their lives with their belief that, in due time, the wheel will come full circle. The belief may not mitigate the reality, but perhaps it makes them able to endure.

Rua used to say, when talking of the events of 1916, that the people were not to 'bother about it. Just put them to shame. The Pakeha people will try and get it right. It goes down the generations.'[96] The Pakeha historians of this book have tried to get it right; and we also feel that it is not for us to judge Rua and his actions. There are many tales told about him, some of which may be true and many of which reveal him in an unfavourable light. Perhaps the only valid voices of criticism are those of his own people. Old Huhana Tutakangahau, who became closely associated with the Presbyterian mission, wrote in 1923,

For many years my poor ignorant people & I have been subjected to this man's, Rua's will. He played on our old superstitions & frightened us, so that no one dared to oppose him, except my brother . . . Pinohi. Pinohi believed in the law of the pakeha . . . . For years Rua has oppressed

† A recent comprehensive listing of all meeting-houses in the North Island has confused this house with the old house at Matahi, Pare Nui O Te Ra, which was pulled down. The Matahi marae is about half a mile farther up the valley. This list has similarly confused the meeting-houses and the two marae at Maungapohatu.[95]

us & kept us under his will, claimed our homes our lands our all & we knew not that there was a stronger law than his. He did whatever he wished with us, he took whatever he fancied, he said whatever he wanted to.[97]

Other critical voices point to Rua as a divisive force within the Tuhoe, who left most of his followers landless. The heavy drinking at the Iharaira meetings, begun as an act of defiance against unequal laws, has ended as uncontrolled indulgence. Rua also failed to provide for a future without him: the 'church' of the Wairua Tapu did not, unlike the Ringatu church, evolve beyond the belief in the man who founded it. Just before he died, he appointed a council of four, including his eldest surviving son, Heta, to carry on the faith in him.[98] There is no doubt that he had hoped that Whatu would carry the mantle of leadership, but his premature death had ended that expectation. The council failed to develop a leadership. The Iharaira have been left without an institutional structure; their only centre is the belief in their Messiah. For those who were not of the generations who knew him, there is no possibility of belief.

As a political force, he was also disruptive. His contest with Kereru split the Tuhoe into rival factions. The quarrel over Tataiahape left a bitterness still remembered. 'There seems to be a curse on that generation of people. It goes back as a curse to them.'[99] But there is another sense in which he was a force for stability. He always worked with the *rangatira* of each community: Te Pou at Tataiahape, Hori Hiakita at Matahi, and Te Iwikino, Miki, and Te Heuheu at Maungapohatu. Pinohi, for the large part, had supported him. Rua claimed no chiefly role for himself. He worked within the existing leadership structure of each community. He encouraged the setting up of councils of the elders in each of the Iharaira settlements which he founded and urged them towards decision-making. But the very nature of his claims to be the Messiah, as well as some of his methods, were divisive. At Ruatahuna, one of the largest Tuhoe settlements, his support was never strong.[100] At Whakatane, his followers gained the nickname of the 'swaggering saints from Maungapohatu' and were, one day in 1909, deliberately set upon by Ngatiawa with sticks and riding crops, in the 'Battle of the Strand'.[101] His hostility to the Native schools in the early years aroused much misgiving, which he seems to have recognized by his agreement with Ngata.

He offered a charismatic leadership when the traditional communal leadership felt itself increasingly powerless in matters which touched them deeply. In the long run he failed, and it is hardly surprising that he did so. The economic problems against which he struggled were huge. The capital which

Two of Rua's grand-daughters: Taino, daughter of Heta and Te Paea; Tauwira, daughter of Te Akakura and Paora Rakuraku. *Laughton Album, National Museum*

Two of Rua's grandsons prepare the hangi, at Waimana, 1976. Tui Tuwairua; Houpapa Tuwairua (Harry). Photo by Heather Beaton.

A portrait of Rua, in his favourite naval coat, in the place of honour in the living room of his daughter's home. Photographed, by courtesy of Puti and Mac Onekawa, by Gillian Chaplin, 1978.

he had gained from the land sales of 1910–12 was largely wasted in the heavy burdens of the trials. It was not until 1931 that the last of these debts were paid.[102] From this impoverishment, the Children of Israel never really recovered. They were unable to restock the land at Maungapohatu adequately and the ragwort took over. The money they raised at Matahi plucking maize was never enough for them to do more than sustain themselves. The failure to get the roads was crippling. The very nature of the terrain, of the harsh land itself, was against them. By 1935 the economic position of the Iharaira was that of a people trapped in a closed circle of inescapable, profitless labour, from which no visionary leader could continue to protect them. Essentially, Rua's dream had been a simple one: that the Tuhoe might survive. His millennium offered them the chance to build their City of God on their own lands. To lives which were otherwise bounded by quiet despair he brought hope that might 'show the Heavens more just'. Who would deny them that?

Genealogy

A genealogy of Rua and his wives: all bore him children, but included here are only those descendants who appear in either the photographs or the text.

*Rua's descent through Ngahiwi can be found in Elsdon Best, *Tuhoe*, II, Genealogical Table 30, and through Kenana in *ibid*., I, 606. (Kenana's father, Tumoana, was also known as Kopae; Hineko was Tumoana's mother.)
†Alive at Rua's death in February 1937 and still married to him.
‡Not by Rua.

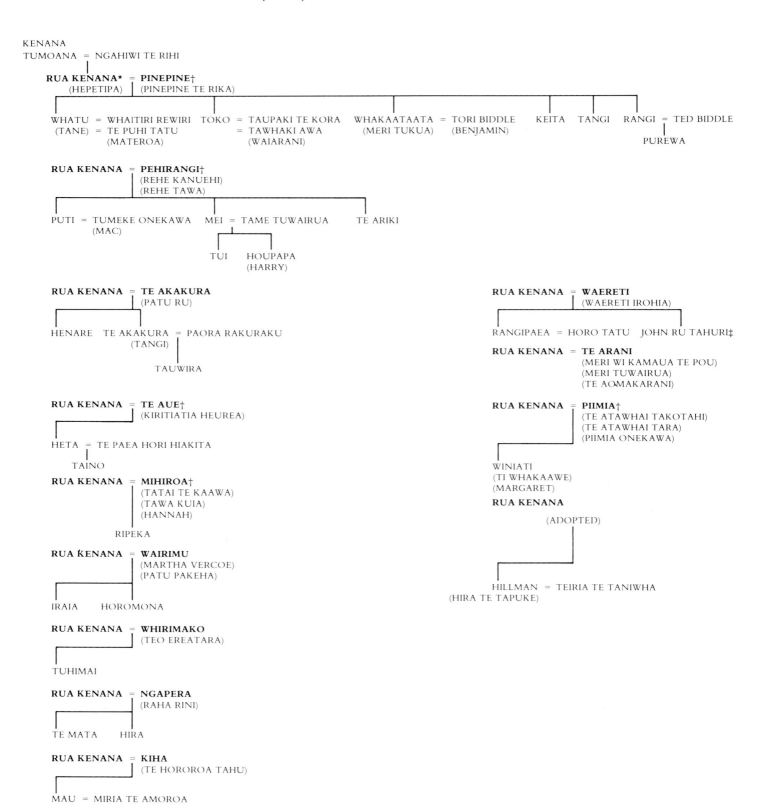

Notes

The following abbreviations are used in the notes:

AJHR *Appendices to the Journals of the House of Representatives*
APL   Auckland Public Library
AS   *Auckland Star*
ATL   Alexander Turnbull Library, Wellington
AWN   *Auckland Weekly News* (until 1934; thereafter, the title was changed to the *Weekly News*)
E   Department of Education, Auckland
MA   Maori Affairs Department, National Archives, Wellington
NA   National Archives, Wellington
NM   National Museum, Wellington
NZH   *New Zealand Herald*
O.S.: Oral source of information (followed by the name of the informant and the date of the interview)
PBH   *Poverty Bay Herald*
PD   *Parliamentary Debates*

1. THE PROPHET ASCENDANT

1 *Tuhoe: The Children of the Mist*, 2nd ed., 1972, I, 564.
2 Paul Delamere, elected leader (*Poutikanga*) of the Ringatu church, annotations to an unpublished and untitled article on the Ringatu faith by Robin Winks, p.7, mss University of Auckland.
3 AJHR, 1928, G–7, 20–21. The figure derives from the final settlements, mostly completed by 1872, when some land had been returned. There was also dispute as to what was 'Tuhoe' land, for many of their coastal claims they had conquered (or re-conquered) only in the mid-nineteenth century.
   Some Tuhoe land was also confiscated from the south-eastern shores of Lake Waikaremoana in the Hawke's Bay confiscations. The land was restored to Ngati Kahungunu, but part-ownership was established by Tuhoe claimants in the Maori Land Court; the block was then sold 'with unusual expedition' to the Crown. This portion of Tuhoe land was therefore lost, and in questionable manner, but it could no longer be called 'confiscated' land.
4 Gilda Z. Misur, 'From Prophet Cult to Established Church; the Case of the Ringatu Movement', *Conflict and Compromise*, ed. I. H. Kawharu, 1975, pp. 107–8.
5 O. S.: Robert (Boy) Biddle, Ringatu tohunga, Kutarere, and secretary of the registered Ringatu church, 5 December 1977.
6 William Greenwood, 'The Upraised Hand', *Journal of the Polynesian Society*, LI, 1 (March 1942), 69.
7 From the prophecies of the elders of the land, *Te Whetu Marama o Te Kotahitanga*, 29 August – 5 September 1931, p.9. Translation: Merimeri Penfold. This source contains different versions of the prophecies of the two stars from Greenwood, *op. cit.*, because it looks to the rise of Wiremu Ratana, the star to the west. Te Turuki's sayings now form a large body of myth and there are many different versions and interpretations according to the area and the people from whom they are recorded.
8 As told to James Cowan in 1901: 'Rua the Prophet', *Wide World Magazine*, XXXVIII (1916), 230.
9 Te Turuki's book: H. G. Davies Maori Manuscripts, III, J. C. Richmond translation, 1869, ATL. Te Turuki was quoting Mark 1, ii.

10   Te Turuki's prayer, written in the Chatham Islands and translated by the missionary William Colenso. Quoted John Caselberg, ed., *Maori is My Name*, 1975, p.110.

11   O. S.: Mrs Jessie Howden, formerly of Maungapohatu, May 1977.

12   O. S.: Boy Biddle, 5 December 1977.

13   *Hawke's Bay Herald*, 15 June 1908.

14   *loc. cit.*

15   Ruapeka, or Mangere Teka, a Ringatu tohunga who upholds the belief in Rua. Recorded in the NZBC documentary, 'Mountain of the Lord', 1970.

16   O. S.: Horo Tatu, who married Rua's daughter, Rangipaea, 27 January 1978; *Te Pipiwharauroa*, XCIX (June 1906), 3.

17   A version recorded in NZH, 19 March 1932.

18   O. S.: Boy Biddle, 5 December 1977.

19   Cowan, p.231, and a variant written by him anonymously for the *Canterbury Times*, 16 February 1916.

20   John A. Williams, *Politics of the New Zealand Maori: Protest and Cooperation, 1891–1909*, 1969, p.94.

21   Peter Webster, 'When the King Comes to Gisborne – A Maori Millennium in 1906', *Whakatane Historical Review*, XV, 1 (April 1967), 49.

22   For example, 'A Letter addressed to Tuhoe', Editor, *Te Pipiwharauroa*, CXII (July 1907), 5.

23   O. S.: Paetawa Miki, the guardian, *kaitiaki*, of Maungapohatu, 25 January 1978.

24   A reputed prophecy of Te Turuki, not kept among those held by the Ringatu church: Greenwood, p.70.

25   PBH, 14 May 1906.

26   O. S.: Paetawa Miki, 25 January 1978.

27   PBH, 14 May 1906.

28   *loc. cit.*

29   Letter from 'Ngatiawa', the anonymous and educated supporter of Rua, PBH, 4 July 1906.

30   Rua, Court transcripts, Rua trial, p.300, J. R. Lundon Collection (hereafter, Lundon mss).

31   3 August 1910: Diary, January – August 1910, typescript, NM.

32   Te Pouwhare Te Roau to Carroll, 13 September 1909, MA 13/91, NA.

33   Numbers 4, xlvii–l.

34   PBH, 4 July 1906.

35   PBH, 28 June 1906.

36   E. W. G. Craig, *Man of the Mist: A Biography of Elsdon Best*, 1964, p.121.

37   *Te Whetu Marama*, 29 August – 5 September 1931, p.9. Translation: Merimeri Penfold.

38   Greenwood, p.58; O. S.: Paetawa Miki, 25 January 1978.

39   O. S.: Tumeke (Mac) Onekawa, brother of Rua's wife Piimia and one of his close followers, 10 December 1978.

40   O. S.: Te Paea Rua, wife of Heta Rua, 18 May 1978.

41   *The Maori*, 1924, I, 127.

42   O. S.: Boy Biddle, 5 December 1977.

43   I Chronicles, 16, xviii.

44   Rangipuawhe and all Tuhourangi, 25 July 1916, Lundon mss; O. S.: Paetawa Miki, 26 January 1978.

45   Hugh Hamilton, Waimana Native school teacher, to Secretary of Education, 1, 23 June 1906, Waimana Native School File, E 37/4/187.

46   PBH, 28 June 1906.

47   Hamilton to Secretary of Education, 1 June 1906, Waimana Native School File, E 37/4/187.

48   PBH, 25 June 1906.

49   *Te Pipiwharauroa*, C (July 1906), 6. Translation: Merimeri Penfold.

50   *loc. cit.*

51   Mangere Teka, 'Mountain of the Lord'; O. S.: Kino Hughes of Ruatoki, 28 January 1978.

52   Mangere Teka, 'Mountain of the Lord'.

53   PBH, 22 August 1906.

54   Rua's message to PBH, 23 April 1907.

55   Cutting [*New Zealand Times*], n.d. [June 1906], Best Scrapbooks, M4, 19, ATL.

56   Best, *The Maori*, I, 127.

57   Cutting, n.d., Best Scrapbooks, M4, 19.

58   PBH, 10 June 1907.

59 PBH, 23 April 1907: Isaiah 62, iv, quoted by Rua.

60 AJHR, 1907, H–31, 58.

61 19 July 1907, PD, 139, 519.

62 O. S.: ——, from Ruatoki, 14 December 1977.

63 PBH, 23 April 1907.

64 PBH, 10 June 1907.

65 As told to the historian Dick Scott, 1963; PBH, 14 May 1906.

66 O. S.: Hillman Rua, adopted son of Rua, telling the same story, 21 May 1978.

67 PBH, 20 October 1906.

68 PBH, 22 April 1907.

69 PBH, 22 August 1906.

70 *loc. cit.*

71 Hamilton, letter dated 10 May 1906, *Evening Post*, 19 May 1906.

72 Hamilton to Secretary of Education, 15 June 1906, Waimana Native School File, E 37/4/187.

73 NZH, 20 April 1908.

74 H. Curran to Secretary of Education, 7 August 1907, Kokako Native School File, E 44/4, II.

75 Carroll, 19 July 1907, PD, 139, 512.

76 NZH, 20 May 1907.

77 PBH, 29 August 1907.

78 *loc. cit.*

79 Kereru, Akuhata Te Kaha, Te Pouwhare Te Roau, to Carroll, 13 December 1907, MA 23/9, NA.

80 Te Pouwhare Te Roau to Carroll, 24 February 1908, *ibid.*

81 To Carroll, 28 February 1908, *ibid.*

82 24 March 1908.

83 Rua, Court transcripts, Rua trial, p.264.

84 O. S.: Mangere Teka, 20 May 1978.

85 PBH, 7 April 1908.

86 PBH, 30 March 1908.

87 James Mackintosh Bell, *The Wilds of Maoriland*, 1914, pp.119–120.

88 PBH, 30 March 1908.

89 PBH, 7 April 1908.

90 PBH, 7 July 1908.

91 PBH, 26 November 1908; *Te Pipiwharauroa*, CXVII (December 1907), 10; Rua, statement, 11 May 1916, Lundon mss; Rua, AS, 12 July 1916.

92 Rua Hepetipa and all the Israelites, at Waimana, 15 February 1910, MA 13/91.

93 Petition presented 7 October 1909, by Tana Taingakawa and about 1250 others, MA 24/8(2), NA.

94 5 February 1910, MA 13/91.

95 Ngatikoura, Ngatitawhaki, Te Urewera, to Carroll, 13 March 1910, MA 13/91.

96 General Committee to Carroll, 4 November 1910, MA 13/91.

97 NZH, 20 April 1908.

98 PBH, 26 November 1908.

99 AJHR, 1895, G–1, 52.

100 Rua and all the Israelites, 15 February 1910, MA 13/91.

101 Cutting, n.d. [July 1908], Best Scrapbooks, M4, 33.

102 Cutting, n.d. [July 1908], *ibid.*, p.7.

103 PBH, 15 June 1908.

104 8 July 1908, p.31.

105 PBH, 27 June 1908.

106 O. S.: E. G. Armstrong, former Auckland journalist, July 1978.

107 PBH, 22 February 1915; G. J. Maloney, 'The Rua Expedition', article written for the *New Zealand Police Journal*, November 1937 and reprinted in *Whakatane Historical Review*, XI, 2 (June 1963), 62. James Cowan also reported a great *hahunga* held in the Waimana valley in 1915, to which Maoris from all over the Mataatua district came: *The Maori Yesterday and Today*, 1930, p.74.

108 O. S.: Te Huinga Karauna, Tuhoe elder, Opotiki, 8 December 1978. Rikirangi Hohepa stated, in August 1938, that he was the last survivor of the four men who knew.

109 O. S.: Arnold Butterworth, former Gisborne policeman, 9 December 1978. He did not then know the old man, whose name was given to him as 'old Elijah'.

110 PBH, 24 June 1908.

111 PBH, 22 August 1908.

112 NZH, 24 March 1908. This version – one of the earlier accounts – does not give a

location and the story is told variously as having taken place at the Whakatane Heads, Ohope beach, Ohiwa harbour, and Lake Waikaremoana. The first recorded claim to be able to walk on water is May 1906; in October 1907 Rua also stopped the government oil-launch on Lake Waikaremoana by 'casting a spell' upon it, to demonstrate his power over the waves. PBH, 26 October 1907.

2. THE NEW JERUSALEM: THE COMMUNITY AT MAUNGAPOHATU

1 O.S.: Te Puhi Tatu, former wife of Whatu Rua, 22 January 1978. Translation: Rangi Motu.
2 Numbers 1, l.
3 O.S.: Mangere Teka, 20 May 1978.
4 O.S.: Horo Tatu, 27 January 1978.
5 PBH, 23 September, 30 December 1907.
6 *New Zealand Times*, 14 August 1907; PBH, 29 August, 23 September 1907; PD, 141, September 1907, 217.
7 O.S.: Horo Tatu, 27 January 1978. (Following their ancestor, Toi the wood-eater.)
8 Bell, p.125.
9 O.S.: Tawhaki Te Kaawa, Toko Rua's widow, 28 January 1978; Heta Rua, 18 May 1978.
10 *Hawke's Bay Herald*, 15 June 1908.
11 Cowan, 'Rua', p.232.
12 Revelation 22, xvi.
13 PBH, 29 August 1907.
14 PBH, 30 December 1907, quoting the district constable, Andy Grant.
15 O.S.: Beryl Gollner, *née* Bressey, formerly of Te Whaiti, 20 May 1978.
16 PBH, 30 December 1907; NZH, 20 April 1908; O.S.: Wi Whitu of Ruatoki, 25 January 1978.
17 To A. P. Godber, 31 October 1931, Godber mss 78:12, ATL.
18 O.S.: Paetawa Miki, 26 January 1978; Webster, pp.56–7.
19 O.S.: Mac Onekawa, 16 May 1978; Mau Rua, son of Rua and Kiha and keeper of Rua's house at Tuapou, 19 May 1978; Mangere Teka, 20 May 1978.
20 O.S.: Mau Rua, 19 May 1978.
21 O.S.: Naomi Teka, wife of Mangere Teka, 20 May 1978.
22 NZH, 6 April 1916; AS, 15 July 1916.
23 O.S.: Mangere Teka, 20 May 1978.
24 O.S.: Taniko Miki, of Ruatahuna, 20 May 1978.
25 Esther 10, iii.
26 PBH, 31 December 1908.
27 O.S.: Iraia Rua, son of Rua and Wairimu, 7 December 1978.
28 PBH, 27 June 1908: see Acts 1, ii and viii.
29 O.S.: Mangere Teka, 20 May 1978.
30 William Bird, Native Schools' Inspector, to Secretary of Education, 6 September 1907, Kokako Native School File, E44/4, II.
31 O.S.: Mau Rua, 19 May 1978.
32 Rudolf Koch, *The Book of Signs*, 1930, pp.6, 97–8.
33 PBH, 4 June 1910.
34 Described by a Presbyterian missionary, *The Outlook,* 6 August 1918.
35 NZH, 20 April 1908; Laughton to Godber, 31 October 1931, Godber mss 78:12.
36 Numbers 9, xvii.
37 Ezekiel 42, xx.
38 O.S.: Te Puhi Tatu, 22 January 1978.
39 O.S.: Wi Whitu, 25 January 1978; Kino Hughes, 28 January 1978.
40 PBH, 30 December 1907.
41 O.S.: Jessie Howden, May 1977; Miria Rua, wife of Mau Rua, 20 January 1978.
42 Laws issued 28 March 1910 and signed by the Chairman, 'H. Hepiha' [sic: ? Hepetipa] and the Honourable Secretary, 'Turoa' [? Turoa Tuhua], as reported by Constable J. P. Willcocks, official member of the Mataatua Maori Council, 30 March 1910, MA 13/91.
43 20 April 1908.
44 'Taipo' (George Bourne), 'A Dusky Dowie: A Maori Prophet at Home', *Life,* Melbourne, 1 December 1908, p.498.
45 O.S.: Harimate Roberts, formerly of Maungapohatu, 20 January 1978.
46 O.S.: Horo Tatu, 24 January 1978.

[47] PBH, 30 December 1907.

[48] Tahu, NZH, 7 July 1916.

[49] O.S.: Paetawa Miki, 26 January 1978; Horo Tatu, 27 January 1978.

[50] O.S.: Boy Biddle, 5 December 1977; Horo Tatu, 27 January 1978.

[51] PBH, 4 July 1906.

[52] NZH, 15 July 1916.

[53] O.S.: Puti Onekawa, daughter of Rua and Pehirangi, 16 May 1978; Hillman Rua, 21 May 1978.

[54] O.S.: Te Huinga Karauna, 8 December 1978.

[55] O. S.: Puti Onekawa, 16 May 1978.

[56] NZH, 29 June 1916.

[57] Paul Clark, *'Hauhau': the Pai Marire Search for Maori Identity*, 1975, p. 79.

[58] NZH, 20 April 1908.

[59] AJHR, 1903, G-6, 33, 127; AJHR, 1907, G-4, 77, 119.

[60] O.S.: Purewa Biddle, grandson of Rua and Pinepine, 22 February 1978.

[61] Cowan, 'Rua', p.234: Isaiah 4, i.

[62] *Canterbury Times*, 16 February 1916.

[63] PBH, 7 April 1908.

[64] The song was first published by Margaret Orbell, *Maori Poetry: an Introductory Anthology*, 1978, pp.59, 93–94. We have corrected the transcription of the names of both women and, upon advice from Rata Takao, portions of the text and translation.

[65] O.S.: Iraia Rua, 7 December 1978.

[66] O.S.: Puti Onekawa, 21 January 1978.

[67] O.S.: Iraia Rua, 7 December 1978.

[68] Teka, NZH, 1 July 1916.

[69] Rua, NZH, 18 July 1916.

[70] O.S.: Paetawa Miki, 26 January 1978. This Covenant originally belonged to an English clergyman living at Whakarewarewa.

[71] Rua, NZH, 15 July 1916; O.S.: Mangere Teka, 20 May 1978.

[72] Rua, Court transcripts, Rua trial, p.267.

[73] Best, *Tuhoe*, I, 962.

[74] Alan Ward, *A Show of Justice: Racial 'Amalgamation' in Nineteenth Century New Zealand*, 1973, p.101.

[75] PBH, 30 December 1907.

[76] Beryl Gollner, 'Mountain of the Lord'.

[77] 5 July, no year. Transcription and translation: Rangi Motu. Collection: Dick Scott, Auckland.

[78] PBH, 30 December 1907.

[79] Rua, Court transcripts, Rua trial, p.298.

[80] Ledger, entry dated 10 April 1916. Transcription and translation: Rangi Motu.

[81] PBH, 30 December 1907; *Otago Witness*, 1 April 1908, p.33.

[82] O.S.: Henry Bell, 24 January 1978.

[83] PBH, 24 June 1907. And, according to W. L. Rutledge of Gisborne, he did keep money from land sales in the valley, substituting newspaper for the notes on the inside. Letter, 12 December 1964, donated to the authors by Bernard Teague, Wairoa.

[84] NZH, 4 April 1916.

[85] 30 December 1907.

[86] AJHR, 1907, G–4, 1.

[87] Numia Kereru, Akuhata Te Kaha, also on the block committee, and Te Pouwhare, to Carroll, 13 December 1907, MA 23/9.

[88] PBH, 8 August 1908; clipping [c. December 1908], Best Scrapbooks, M4, 35.

[89] *Daily Post*, Whakatane, 20 November 1976, p.28.

[90] NZH, 20 April 1908.

[91] PBH, 12 June 1907.

[92] *Otago Witness*, 1 April 1908, p.33; PBH, 30 December 1907, 7 April 1908; Numbers 6, iii.

[93] O.S.: Puti Onekawa, 21 January 1978; Iraia Rua, 7 December 1978.

[94] PBH, 31 December 1908.

[95] *loc. cit*.

[96] O.S.: Te Puhi Tatu, who married Whatu after Whaitiri's death, 22 January 1978; Mau Rua, 19 May 1978.

[97] Beryl Gollner, 'Mountain of the Lord'.

[98] For example, 'The Waiotahi Outrage', NZH, 24, 25 February 1910, which involved some broken windows on a settler's property. It kept the press active

for a week, until the report came in accurately.

99   Te Whaiti District Constable Occurrence Book and Daily Diary, 31 December 1907, NA.

100   *ibid.*, 12 May 1906.

101   *ibid.*, 31 December 1907.

102   PBH, 30 December 1907.

103   Cuttings [July 1908], Best Scrapbooks, M4, 32–3; PBH, 14 July 1908.

104   Depositions, p.33, Police File, P1, 1916/233, NA.

105   R. M. Smith of Taneatua, recalling a story told to him by Hine Ki Te Ao of Maungapohatu. *Whakatane Historical Review*, XI, 3 (September 1963), 171.

106   O.S.: Te Akakura Sherrin, daughter of Rua and Te Akakura, 7 September 1978.

107   PBH, 11 October 1906.

108   Cutting [c. December 1908], Best Scrapbooks, M4, 35.

109   Cutting [July 1908], *ibid.*, p.34: Revelation 18, xii–xiv.

110   Cutting [May 1906], Best Scrapbook, M4, 23: Revelation 19, xi.

111   *Hawke's Bay Herald*, 15 June 1908: Numbers 6, ii–v.

112   *Hawke's Bay Herald*, 15 June 1908.

113   Numbers 6, iii–vii.

114   O.S.: Ira Manihera, formerly of Maungapohatu, 10 December 1978.

115   O.S.: Horo Tatu, 27 January 1978.

116   Matthew 26, lxi.

117   Transcription and translation: Rangi Motu.

118   Timothy Cummings, Court transcripts, Rua trial, p.7, whereas Rua said that Cummings cut it for him before he went to Mount Eden prison, saying that it would be cut there anyhow (*ibid.*, p.269). Most newspapers, such as NZH, 8 April 1916, reported that his hair was cut in jail.

119   Numbers 6, xviii.

120   O.S.: Puti Onekawa, 3 December 1977.

121   O.S.: Te Puhi Tatu, 22 January 1978; Horo Tatu, 27 January 1978.

122   O.S.: Te Puhi Tatu, 22 January 1978.

123   O.S.: Nino Takao, of Whakarae, 18 May 1978.

124   PBH, 4 July 1906.

125   The list of Riwaiti is derived, in particular, from Te Paea Rua, 4 December 1977, 18 May 1978; Te Puhi Tatu, 22 January 1978; Paetawa Miki, 25 January 1978; Horo Tatu, 27 January 1978; Tawhaki Te Kaawa, 28 January 1978; and Hillman Rua, 21 May 1978. They do not always agree with each other, and it is clear that there was a core of about six who were absolutely dedicated.

126   Akuhata Te Kaha, 6 May 1897, Whakatane Minute Book, V, 190. Maori Land Court, microfilm, University of Auckland.

127   O.S.: Hillman Rua, 21 May 1978. The house bears the date 1930, but it is said to have been built a little earlier.

128   Rua, Court transcripts, Rua trial, p.298; Minutes of a meeting held at Ruatoki, 17 October 1910, transcription by courtesy of Jeff Sissons, University of Auckland. Mr Sissons is carrying out research for a Ph.D. thesis on the Waimana valley since European contact. His research will considerably expand our understanding of the Waimana valley communities.

129   PBH, 4 January 1911.

130   Rua, statement, 11 May 1916, Lundon mss.

131   O.S.: Harimate Roberts, 17 May 1978.

132   Te Kepa Tawhio, Court transcripts, Rua trial, p.332.

133   Rua, statement, 11 May 1916, Lundon mss; List of families living at Maungapohatu, December 1913, Maungapohatu Native School File, E 44/4, I.

134   Kereru, Akuhata, Te Pouwhare, to Carroll, 13 December 1907, MA 23/9.

135   Bell, p.125.

136   *ibid.*, p.119.

137   AJHR, 1915, H–31, 19.

138   O.S.: Mac Onekawa, 3 December 1977.

3.   THE LAW AGAINST THE PROPHET

1   *Hastings Standard*, 19 June 1908.

2   AS, 15 July 1916.

3   NZH, 15 July 1916.

4   NZH, 13 July 1916.

5   One of Te Turuki's supporters to Best: *Tuhoe*, I, 663.

6   Statement, 11 May 1916, Lundon mss.

7   Dyer, Court transcripts, Rua trial, pp.313–314.

8   Rua, Court transcripts, Rua trial, pp.270, 291.

9   *Rotorua Times* [sic] : *Rotorua Chronicle*, 26 January 1916, typescript copy, Lundon mss.

10   AS, 6 February 1916.

11   Rua, Court transcripts, Rua trial, p.285.

12   NZH, 8 May 1916.

13   Quoted Caselberg, p.112.

14   Rua, statement, 2 June 1916, Lundon mss; Tupu [Tana] Taingakawa, *Waikato Star*, 25 November 1916: ' "To them that choose to go, let them go." '

15   AS, 15 March 1916.

16   Cowan, 'Rua', p.235.

17   Makarini, Court transcripts, Rua trial, pp.133, 143.

18   Rua, Court transcripts, Rua trial, p.270.

19   Kereru to Herries, n.d. [February 1916], and Herries' annotation to it, 6 March 1916, MA 23/9.

20   Annotation, 6 March 1916, on Kereru to Herries, 9 February 1916, *ibid*.

21   As sung by Te Puhi, daughter of Tatu, 22 January 1978; transcription and translation: Rangi Motu and Pat Hohepa.

22   Court translation, NZH, 27 July 1916.

23   NZH, 28 July 1916.

24   NZH, 20 May 1915.

25   Depositions, pp.33–36, P1, 1916/233.

26   *ibid*., p.19.

27   *ibid*., pp.20–21.

28   AS, 13 June 1916; NZH, 25 July 1916.

29   AS, 13 June 1916; NZH, 14 July 1916.

30   Rua, statement, 2 June 1916, typescript, Lundon mss.

31   AS, 15 July 1916.

32   Rua, statement, 2 June 1916, typescript, Lundon mss.

33   Bressey, AS, 15 March 1916.

34   AS, 15 July 1916.

35   AS, 13 July 1916.

36   NZH, 4 July 1916.

37   AS, 30 June, 4 July, 13 July 1916.

38   NZH, 14 July 1916.

39   Petition and its translation, Lundon mss.

40   NZH, 4 July 1916.

41   Ngata, NZH, 20 June 1916.

42   Cullen to Herdman, 9 March 1916, P1, 1916/233.

43   Cullen, correspondence dated 25 February 1916 and 6 March 1916, P1, 1916/233.

44   Correspondence, 23, 28 February; 7, 28 March 1916, P1, 1916/233.

45   Tai Mitchell, AS, 13 June 1916.

46   Te Iwikino, AS, 26 June 1916.

47   O. S.: Paetawa Miki, 26 January 1978.

48   Depositions, p. 28, P1, 1916/233.

49   NZH, 5 April 1916.

50   AS, 21 June 1916.

51   For detailed evidence see, Philip Rainer, 'Company Town', unpublished M.A. thesis, University of Auckland, 1976, pp.213–214, 220–224, 260.

52   Cullen to Herdman, 23 March 1916, Pl, 1916/233.

53   *Evening Post*, 4 April 1916.

54   O. S.: Don Lochore of the *New Zealand Herald*, who shared a flat with him, August 1978; Arnold Butterworth, 9 December 1978.

55   NZH, 4 July 1916.

56   NZH, 7 April 1916.

57   *loc. cit*.

58   Norman Good, 'A Wonderful Journey into the Wilderness', *Journal of the Auckland-Waikato Historical Societies*, XXII (April 1973), 12.

59   William Bird, packhorseman, Depositions, pp.110–111, P1, 1916/233; Alexander McCowan, *ibid*., p.126.

60   O. S.: Tom Collins, 11 January 1977, 5 May 1978.

61   Blakeley, Depositions, p.54, P1, 1916/233; Tim Cummings, *ibid*., p.4.

62   Rua, NZH, 15 July 1916; O. S.: Mangere Teka, 20 May 1978. Probably John 10, xi: 'I am the good shepherd: the good shepherd giveth his life for the sheep.'

63   Rua, Court transcripts, Rua trial, p.279.

64 Depositions, p.95, P1, 1916/233.
65 *ibid.*, p.74.
66 Blakeley, *ibid.*, p.54.
67 Grant, *ibid.*, p.47.
68 Johnston, *ibid.*, p.65.
69 Tahu, AS, 6 July 1916.
70 Tutara, who hoisted it, NZH, 5 July 1916; Rua, Court transcripts, Rua trial, p.279.
71 Maloney, 'The Rua Expedition', p.66.
72 Depositions, pp.37, 43, P1, 1916/233.
73 Interview, *Evening Post*, 8 April 1916.
74 Cobeldick, AS, 11 July 1916; O.S.: Arnold Butterworth, 9 December 1978.
75 NZH, 7 October 1916.
76 O. S.: Harry Maisey, 20 June 1978.
77 Tori Biddle, NZH, 24 June 1916.
78 AS, 10 June 1916.
79 Depositions, p.134, P1, 1916/233.
80 See, H. E. Holland and R. S. Ross, *The Tragic Story of the Waihi Strike*, 1913, pp.101–102, 115, and the pamphlet, 'The Waihi Truth', cited R. J. Campbell, 'The Role of the Police in the Waihi Strike: Some New Evidence', *Political Science*, XXVI, 2 (December 1974), 35.
81 Cullen to Herdman, [4 April 1916], P1, 1916/233; also, NZH, 21 June 1916. Cullen said that the shot came from the gully, below the cook house.
82 E. M. Hellaby who, with her father, Walter Hutton, ran the accommodation house at Murupara in 1916. This was the nearest phone to Maungapohatu and it was from here that the first cables and newspaper reports were sent. *Daily Post*, 2 September 1970.
83 Court transcripts, Rua trial, p.252.
84 Holograph letter, 21 July 1916, and letter written in block capitals, received 19 July 1916, Lundon mss.
85 Tori Biddle, 9 December 1916, P1, 1916/233; Hare Rewi, packhorseman, undated statement, *ibid.*
86 O. S.: Eric Lundon, Lundon's eldest son, 20 July 1978.
87 Police Superintendent, Christchurch, to Cullen, telegram, 22 June 1916, P1, 1916/233.
88 Court transcripts, Rua trial, p.319.
89 To Lundon, 15 April 1917, Lundon mss.
90 Lundon's jotting of Cullen's statement, Lundon mss; Cullen, Court transcripts, Rua trial, p.91: 'Biddle told me Kingi fired the first shot'.
91 Depositions, p.47, P1, 1916/233.
92 *ibid.*, p.135.
93 Collins, NZH, 24 September 1971.
94 Court transcripts, Rua trial, p.254.
95 P1, 1916/233.
96 O. S.: Hillman Rua, 21 May 1978.
97 O. S.: Tom Collins, 5 May 1978, and quoted in NZH, 24 September 1971.
98 Court transcripts, Rua trial, p.85.
99 Birch, NZH, 20 June 1916.
100 Depositions, p.96, P1, 1916/233.
101 Rogers, Court transcripts, Rua trial, p.71. Rushton also observed that Toko had a 'long pistol', 'probably' a Mauser. *ibid.*, pp.67–68.
102 *ibid.*, p.51.
103 AS, 6 July 1916.
104 Brewster, Depositions, p.15, P1, 1916/233.
105 Tawhaki Te Kaawa, Toko's widow, recorded in the 'Mountain of the Lord'.
106 AS, 29 June 1916; Statement by Tori Biddle, 9 December 1916, P1, 1916/233.
107 Depositions, p.16, P1, 1916/233; NZH, 25 July 1916.
108 Cullen, Court transcripts, Rua trial, p.344.
109 Dyer to Herdman, 23 May 1916, Coroners' Files, 1916/561, NA.
110 Telegrams, Dyer to Cullen, [3 April 1916]; Dyer to Herdman, 4 April 1916; D. J. Cummings, 3 April 1916, P1, 1916/233
111 O. S.: Rangi Rakuraku of Tanatana, 3 December 1977.
112 Depositions, pp.116, 117, P1, 1916/233.
113 AS, 24 July 1916.
114 Wiremu Te Pou, one of the six, Court transcripts, Rua trial, p.195; Cullen, *ibid.*, p.93.

115 Huhana, NZH, 27 June 1916; Cullen, Depositions, p.51, P1, 1916/233.
116 NZH, 11 July 1916.
117 Cassells, Court transcripts, Rua trial, p.94.
118 Depositions, p.40, P1, 1916/233.
119 NZH, 4, 8 April 1916.
120 Telegram, 17 April 1916, P1, 1916/233.
121 Depositions, p.53, P1, 1916/233.
122 *ibid.*, p.97.
123 Cullen to Herdman, 20 April 1916, P1, 1916/233; Maloney, Depositions, pp.99–100, P1, 1916/233.
124 Depositions, p.126, P1, 1916/233.
125 O. S.: Te Paea Rua, 18 May 1978.
126 Cobeldick, AS, 12 July 1916; O. S.: Tom Collins, 5 May 1978.
127 Te Akakura, NZH, 3 July 1916.
128 NZH, 8 April 1916.
129 Williamson, Depositions, p.91, P1, 1916/233; List of men arrested, Lundon mss.
130 According to Cassells, 'About 24 natives were detained until Monday afternoon', but Cullen and others revealed that six had to be released to help with the burial of Toko and Te Maipi that afternoon (Court transcripts, Rua trial, pp.59, 93). Several men swore that they were kept prisoner for two or three days, in addition to the six who were finally taken out under arrest, so there are discrepancies.
131 Doyle, Depositions, p.78, P1, 1916/233; O.S.: Hillman Rua, 21 May 1978.
132 NZH, 8 April 1916.
133 Cobeldick, AS, 12 July 1916.
134 NZH, 8 April 1916.
135 O.S.: Tom Collins, 5 May 1978.
136 Police Executive Officer to authors, 9 May 1978.
137 Sheehan, Court transcripts, Rua trial, p.308.
138 Letter written in block capitals, received 19 July 1916, Lundon mss. This letter was received after the Maori complaints had been raised in Court.
139 NZH, 3 August 1916.
140 Mss draft of a petition from the people of Maungapohatu to Parliament, [1 May 1917], Lundon mss.
141 Statement given to Carter at Maungapohatu, 6 May 1916, by Te Iwikino and fourteen others, Lundon mss.
142 Makarini, Court transcripts, Rua trial, p.136.
143 Incomplete fragment, mss in the possession of Dick Scott. Translation: Rangi Motu and Merimeri Penfold. Lineation and punctuation added.
144 NZH, 18 April 1916.
145 NZH, 15 April 1916.
146 Chapman, 1 August 1916, 'Rex *V.* Rua', *New Zealand. Gazette Law Reports*, XVIII, 3 November 1916, pp.658–659.
147 The Register of the Auckland Supreme Court for criminal trials of this period has, in fact, survived: Crown Book No. 7, 1 June 1914–23 August 1917, Auckland Supreme Court. It lists all witnesses.
148 NZH, 4 April 1916.
149 AS, 3 August 1916.
150 NZH, 3 August 1916.
151 Covering letter sent to Charles Poole M.P., to the petition of 4 August 1916, Lundon mss.
152 An abridged version was published in the *Star*, 7 August 1916; the complete text, cited here, exists in the Lundon mss.
153 4 August 1916, Lundon mss.
154 AS, 7 August 1916.
155 Registrar, Auckland Supreme Court to Chapman, 16 August 1916, 'Case of Rua Hepetipa', ATL; Carter to Lundon, 5 August 1916, Lundon mss.
156 Carter to Lundon, 5 August 1916, Lundon mss.
157 NZH, 7 October 1916.
158 Makarini, statement, 11 December 1916, p.5, P1, 1916/233.(Corrected against mss version in Lundon papers.)
159 Biddle, 9 December 1916, P1, 1916/233.
160 23 April 1917, P1, 1916/233.
161 3 January 1917, P1, 1916/233.
162 Statement, [4 April 1917], P1, 1916/233.
163 14 October 1920, P1, 1916/233.

[164] 8 January 1917, P1, 1916/233.

[165] 11 December 1916, P1, 1916/233.

[166] 9 December 1916, P1, 1916/233.

[167] Typescript of Biddle's evidence given 4 December 1916, taken from *Rotorua Chronicle*, P1, 1916/233.

[168] Lundon mss.

[169] Carter, statement attached to letter dated 14 October 1920, P1, 1916/233; Cassells, Report, 1 May 1917, P1, 1916/233.

[170] NZH, 20 March 1917.

[171] NZH, 23 April 1917.

[172] NZH, 17 April 1917.

[173] 15 March 1917, Lundon mss.

[174] NZH, 29 March 1917.

[175] Lundon mss.

[176] Johnston, Depositions, p.73, P1, 1916/233; AS, 14 July 1916.

[177] Rua to Lundon, 8 June 1916, Lundon mss.

[178] 3 January 1917, P1, 1916/233.

[179] 13 October 1916, Lundon mss.

[180] Te Iwikino and thirteen others, including Teka, Tahu and Wiremu Te Pou, P1, 1916/233; Herries to Te Iwikino, 12 September 1916, *ibid*.

[181] Cullen to Tole, 11 August 1916, P1, 1916/233.

[182] 11 September 1916, 'Case of Rua Hepetipa'.

[183] 27 September 1916, *ibid*.

4.   IF CANAAN IS DESTROYED CAN THE NEW CANAAN ARISE?

[1] Report, 5 April 1918, Army, Defence Files 66/11, NA.

[2] Cassells, Report, 30 March 1918, Census and Statistics, 23/1/96, NA.

[3] *The Maoris in the Great War*, Maori Regimental Committee, 1926, p.17.

[4] Report, 9 March 1914, Maungapohatu Native School File, E44/4, I.

[5] J. A. Hanan, *ibid*.

[6] Ngata to Minister of Education, 5 April 1909, Waimana Native School File, E37/4/187.

[7] February 1916, Maungapohatu Native School File, E44/4, I.

[8] Interview with Pinohi, 9 August 1916, *ibid*. His reference to more than one school includes Ruatahuna.

[9] Bird to Director of Education, 31 July 1916, *ibid*.

[10] Dorrice Holland to Director of Education, 9 April 1917, *ibid*.

[11] Report, 26 May 1917, *ibid*.

[12] *loc. cit*.

[13] *loc. cit*.

[14] Quoted NZH, 22 June 1957.

[15] J. G. Laughton, *From Forest Trail to City Street. The Story of the Presbyterian Church among the Maori People*, 1961, p.17.

[16] O.S.: Rev. Lloyd Carter, missionary at Maungapohatu, 1931–1932, 18 July 1978.

[17] Laughton, pp.16–17.

[18] Laughton to Godber, 31 October 1931, Godber mss 78:12.

[19] Rua, Court transcripts, Rua trial, p.266; Hokimate, *ibid*., p.159.

[20] NZH, 8 April 1916.

[21] List of children and parents, December 1913, Maungapohatu Native School File, E44/4, I.

[22] Bird, Report, 26 May 1917, *ibid*.

[23] O.S.: Kiti Temara, formerly of Maungapohatu, 22 January 1978.

[24] Ngata, Notice of the general meeting of the Ringatu Church, 25–29 June 1938, Winks mss.

[25] O.S.: Miria Rua, 19 May 1978; Hillman Rua, 21 May 1978; Te Paea Rua, 8 December 1978; Puti Onekawa, 10 December 1978.

[26] O.S.: Te Akakura Sherrin, 21 December 1977.

[27] O.S.: Tuhimai Tiopira, daughter of Rua and Whirimako, 24 January 1978; Heta Rua, 18 May 1978.

[28] *The Press* (Christchurch).

[29] O.S.: Harimate Roberts, 17 May 1978.

[30] AJHR, 1919, H–31, Appendix A, p.35.

[31] Minutes of meeting held at Te Waimana, 10 February 1910, Ledger entry. Transcription and translation: Rangi Motu. On the meaning of the name

'Matahi' (lit. 'to open the eyes' with surprise) O.S.: Horo Tatu, 24 January 1978.

32 Laughton, p.17.
33 *loc. cit.*
34 Matahi Mission School File, E44/6, I.
35 O.S.: Horo Tatu, 27 January 1978.
36 O.S.: Hillman Rua, 21 May 1978.
37 O.S.: Horo Tatu, 27 January 1978; Hillman Rua, 21 May 1978.
38 O.S.: Harimate Roberts, 17 May 1978.
39 O.S.: Harimate Roberts, 17 May 1978.
40 Interview with Sister Annie Henry, *Wairoa Star*, 2 April 1969.
41 Report by Constable J. P. Willcocks, 3 June 1906, Waimana Native School File, E37/4/187.
42 O.S.: Rev. Lloyd Carter, 18 July 1978.
43 J. A. Asher, quoting Laughton, to Minister of Education, 1 July 1924, Maungapohatu Native School File, E44/4, I.
44 AS, 5 March 1927.
45 O.S.: Te Huinga Karauna, 8 December 1978.
46 'Maungapohatu Maori School History', typescript compiled by 'F.K.B.', p.9, APL.
47 PBH, 31 March 1927.
48 NZH, 14 May 1927.
49 AWN, 17 February 1927.
50 NZH, 14 May 1927.
51 *loc. cit.*
52 O.S.: Puti Onekawa, 16 May 1978.
53 NZH, 14 May 1927.
54 'Maungapohatu Maori School History', p.9.
55 Jeremiah 51, x.
56 Ledger, entry dated 3 February 1929. Transcription and translation: Rangi Motu.
57 O.S.: Makarini Temara and others, reminiscing in Tane Nui A Rangi, 21 January 1978.
58 O.S.: Norman Nicholls, 14 July 1978.
59 NZH, 19 March 1932.
60 R. Dickinson, *Rising Fish*, 1956, p.86.
61 *ibid.*, p.87.
62 Paulger to Godber, 21 June 1933, Godber mss 78:11.
63 PBH, 3 August 1927.
64 O.S.: Hillman Rua, 21 May 1978.
65 Dickinson, p.89.
66 *Dominion*, 21 July 1951.
67 O.S.: Hillman Rua, 21 May 1978.
68 AJHR, 1921–22, G–7.
69 Extract from Report, D. D. Dun and M. J. Galvin, March 1935, by courtesy New Zealand Forest Service.
70 Allan North, 'Modern History of the Park', *Handbook to the Urewera National Park*, 3rd ed., 1975, pp.29–31.
71 Shepherd-Galvin Report, 1936, p.6, MA 13/92, NA.
72 AWN, 2 February 1922.
73 PBH, 25 November 1908.
74 Rua to Shepherd, 28 December 1936, MA 13/92.
75 O.S.: Thomas Morgan of Taneatua (who helped to build Rua's tomb), as retold by his grandson, Bill Ormond, Auckland, 24 July 1978.
76 O.S.: Hillman Rua, 21 May 1978.
77 List of cream suppliers, Matahi to Tawhana, 1 June 1936 (Rua had 17 cows), MA 13/92.
78 O.S.: Te Akakura Sherrin, her daughter, 16 December 1977.
79 Letter from 'Tuhoe-Potiki', NZH, 19 May 1927.
80 Transcript of death certificate, Maori deaths 1937/87, ATL.
81 Currie to Godber, 26 January 1937, Godber mss 78:13.
82 Ezekiel 37, xii, xxi–xxii, xxiv, xxvi.
83 Dickinson, p.91.
84 Mark 15, xvii.
85 *Dominion*, 6 March 1937.
86 Quoted, *ibid.*, 28 April 1937.
87 *ibid.*, 25 February 1937; NZH, 22 June 1957.

88   *Dominion*, 1,6 March 1937.
89   O.S.: Puti Onekawa, 20 January 1978.
90   O.S.: Hillman Rua, 21 May 1978.
91   O.S.: Hillman Rua, 21 May 1978.
92   O.S.: Hillman Rua, 21 May 1978.
93   Currie to Godber, 16 July 1940, Godber mss 78:13.
94   Laughton, p.28.
95   John C. M. Cresswell, *Maori Meeting Houses of the North Island*, 1977, pp.70, 76.
96   O.S.: Miria Rua, 19 May 1978.
97   Huhana to Under Secretary, Native Department, 12 July 1923, Urewera Consolidation, MA 29/4/7, I, NA.
98   PBH, 1, 4 March 1937.
99   O.S.: Miria Rua, 19 May 1978.
100   Rev. Turuturu Ngaki, *Te Pipiwharauroa*, CXVII (December 1907), 10. Translation: Merimeri Penfold.
101   Eric Ramson, *Daily Post* (Whakatane), 20 November 1976, p.28.
102   O.S.: Mau Rua, confirmed by contextual associations, 19 May 1978.

Glossary

A glossary of Maori words used in the text without translation. (The meanings given here are appropriate to this book.)

Atua – supernatural being, god

Haka – posturing dance, usually in defiance

Hangi – earth oven

Hapu – segment of a larger tribal group

Hongi – greeting, by pressing noses together, whereby the 'breath of life' of the two souls intermingle

Huhu – larva of a beetle found in decayed timber and used as food

Hui – gathering

Huia – bird, prized for its white-tipped tail feathers, now extinct

Kai – food

Kainga – settlement, community, family home

Kaka – native New Zealand parrot

Karakia – prayer

Kehua – ghost, spirit

Kereru – native New Zealand wood pigeon

Kiekie – straw-like plant used for weaving (*Freycinetia banksii*)

Kiwi – native New Zealand flightless bird (*Apteryx*)

Korero – talk, speeches, discussion

Kumara – sweet potato

Makutu – (n.) black magic, curse – (v.) bewitch

Mana – prestige, vested with effective authority

Mangai – mouthpiece of God, a name taken by Wiremu Ratana

Marae – the complex of meeting-house and open space for speeches and ceremony, to which, in modern times, a dining-hall has usually been added. In original usage, the term applied specifically to the open space

Mate – sickness

Mere – hand weapon

Muru – legitimate plundering in compensation for an alleged offence

Noa – ordinary, unrestricted or free from tapu

Pa – fortified settlement, upon which, in post-European times, an unfortified community may have been built, as in the case of Maungapohatu

Pakeha – European resident of New Zealand

Papakainga – marae reserve

Pataka – storehouse, built upon raised supports

Ponga – tree fern

Poropiti – prophet

Rangatira – chief, leader

Taiaha – long wooden club used formerly for fighting and, more recently, for ceremonial challenges

Tangi – funeral, mourning ceremony

Tapu – under a religious restriction, 'sacred': the protective force of life

Tiki – carved figure, worn as a neck ornament, and usually made of greenstone

Tipuna – ancestor

Tohunga – expert, used often to mean an expert in traditional religious knowledge

Toi – tree (*Cordyline indivisa*)

Wahi tapu – tapu enclosure, 'sacred place'

Wahine – woman

Waiata – song

Whare – house

Wharepuni – sleeping-house, used communally

Works Cited

UNPUBLISHED SOURCES

Best, Elsdon. Scrapbooks, Alexander Turnbull Library.

'Case of Rua Hepetipa', typescripts, Alexander Turnbull Library.

Cassells, J. J. Report, 30 March 1918, Statistics Department, Census and Statistics 23/1/96, National Archives.

Crown Book No. 7, 1 June 1914–23 August 1917, Auckland Supreme Court.

Davies, H. G. Maori Manuscripts, III, Alexander Turnbull Library.

Dun, D. D. and Galvin, M. J. Report by Officers of the Lands and Survey Department and the State Forest Service on the Urewera Forest, March 1935, New Zealand Forest Service, Rotorua.

Godber, A. P. Papers, mss 78, Alexander Turnbull Library.

Grant, Andrew M. Report, 5 April 1918, Army Department, Defence 66/11, National Archives.

   Te Whaiti District Constable Occurrence Book and Daily Diary, 1903–1922, National Archives.

Hamilton, Augustus. Diary, January-August 1910, typescript, National Museum.

Justice Department. Coroners' Files, 1916/561, National Archives.

Lundon, J. R. Manuscripts, typescripts, and photographs relating to the trial of Rua and others from Maungapohatu, 1916–1917. Private collection, N. and E. Lundon, Auckland.

Maori Affairs Department. National Archives:

   Rua Kenana, MA 23/9.

   Shepherd-Galvin Report, 1936, MA 13/92.

   Tana Taingakawa and others, Petition, 7 October 1909, MA 24/8 (2).

   Urewera Consolidation, MA 29/4/7.

   Urewera Lands, General Committee, MA 13/91.

Maori Land Court. Whakatane Minute Book, V, microfilm, University of Auckland Library.

Maungapohatu Ledger Book, 1907-1929, Alexander Turnbull Library.

'Maungapohatu Maori School History', typescript compiled by 'F.K.B.', Auckland Public Library.

Native School Files. National Archives, Auckland:

   Kokako Native School, E44/4.

   Matahi Mission School, E44/6.

   Maungapohatu Native School, E44/4.

   Waimana Native School, E37/4/187.

New Zealand Broadcasting Service. 'The Mountain of the Lord', documentary edited by Tony Simpson, 1970.

Ngata, A. T. Notice of the general meeting of the Ringatu Church, 25–29 June 1938, Winks mss, University of Auckland Library.

Peeke Takotoranga Moni . . . O Rua Hepeti, Maungapohatu, ms 1207, Alexander Turnbull Library.

Police Department. Rua Expedition, P1, 1916/233, National Archives.

Rainer, Philip. 'Company Town. An Industrial History of the Waihi Gold Mining Company, Limited, 1887–1912', unpublished M.A. thesis, University of Auckland, 1976.

Rua Kenana. Transcript of Death Certificate, Maori Deaths, 1937/87, Alexander Turnbull Library.

Winks, Robin. Unpublished and untitled article on the Ringatu faith, annotated by Paul Delamere, Winks mss, University of Auckland Library.

PUBLISHED ARTICLES AND BOOKS

Appendices to the Journals of the House of Representatives: 1895, G–1; 1903, G–6; 1907, G–4, H–31; 1915, H–31; 1919, H–31; 1921–22, G–7; 1928, G–7.

Bell, James Mackintosh. *The Wilds of Maoriland*, London, 1914.

Best, Elsdon. *The Maori*, 2 vols, Wellington, 1924.
  Tuhoe: The Children of the Mist, 2 vols, 2nd ed., Wellington, 1972, 1973.

Bourne, George (Taipo). 'A Dusky Dowie: A Maori Prophet at Home', *Life* (Melbourne), 1 December 1908.

Campbell, R. J. 'The Role of the Police in the Waihi Strike: Some New Evidence', *Political Science*, XXVI, 2 (December 1974).

Caselberg, John, ed. *Maori is My Name. Historical Maori Writings in Translation*, Dunedin, 1975.

Clark, Paul. *'Hauhau': The Pai Marire Search for Maori Identity*, Auckland, 1975.

Cowan, James. *The Maori Yesterday and Today*, Auckland, 1930.
  The Maoris in the Great War; A History of the New Zealand Native Contingent and Pioneer Battalion . . ., Maori Regimental Committee, Auckland, 1926.
  'Rua the Prophet', *Wide World Magazine*, XXXVIII, 1916.

Craig, E. W. G. *Man of the Mist: A Biography of Elsdon Best*, Wellington, 1964.

Cresswell, John C. M. *Maori Meeting Houses of the North Island*, Auckland, 1977.

Dickinson, R. *Rising Fish; Catching Trout from Taupo to the Bay of Plenty*, Christchurch, 1956.

Good, Norman. 'A Wonderful Journey into the Wilderness', *Journal of the Auckland-Waikato Historical Societies*, XXII (April 1973).

Greenwood, William. 'The Upraised Hand', *Journal of the Polynesian Society*, LI, 1 (March 1942).

Holland, H. E. and Ross, R. S. *The Tragic Story of the Waihi Strike*, Wellington, 1913.

Koch, Rudolf. *The Book of Signs*, London, 1930.

Laughton, J. G. *From Forest Trail to City Street. The Story of the Presbyterian Church among the Maori People*, Maori Synod of the Presbyterian Church, n.p., 1961.

Maloney, Gerald. 'The Rua Expedition', *Whakatane Historical Review*, XI, 2 (June 1963). (Reprinted from *New Zealand Police Journal*, November 1937.)

Misur, Gilda Z. 'From Prophet Cult to Established Church; the Case of the Ringatu Movement', *Conflict and Compromise*, ed. I. H. Kawharu, Wellington, 1975.

North, Allan. 'Modern History of the Park', *Handbook to the Urewera National Park*, Urewera National Park Board, 3rd ed., n.p., 1975.

Orbell, Margaret. *Maori Poetry: an Introductory Anthology*, Auckland, 1978.

'Rex *V*. Rua', *New Zealand. Gazette Law Reports*, XVIII, 3 November 1916.

Smith, R. M. 'Rua Kenana', *Whakatane Historical Review*, XI, 3 (September 1963).

Ward, Alan. *A Show of Justice: Racial 'Amalgamation' in Nineteenth Century New Zealand*, Auckland, 1973.

Webster, Peter. 'When the King Comes to Gisborne – A Maori Millennium in 1906', *Whakatane Historical Review*, XV, 1 (April 1967).

Williams, John A. *Politics of the New Zealand Maori: Protest and Cooperation 1891–1909*, Auckland, 1969.

BIBLIOGRAPHIC NOTE (1995)

Since this book was first published some significant articles and books have appeared. They include:

Binney, Judith. 'Mangapohatu Revisited: or, How the Government Underdeveloped a Maori Community', *Journal of the Polynesian Society*, 92, 3 (September 1983).

Binney, Judith. 'Rua Kenana Hepetipa', *Dictionary of New Zealand Biography*, III, forthcoming 1996.

Binney, Judith. 'Two Māori Portraits: Adoption of the Medium', *Anthropology & Photography 1860–1920*, ed. Elizabeth Edwards, New Haven, 1992.

Binney, Judith and Gillian Chaplin. 'Taking the Photographs Home: The Recovery of a Maori History', *Visual Anthropology*, 4, 1991.

Hanson, Allan. 'Christian Branches, Maori Roots: The Cult of Rua', *History of Religions*, 30, 2 (November 1990).

Sissons, Jeffrey. *Te Waimana: The Spring of Mana*, Dunedin, 1991.

Note: In the earlier part of this century, the Tuhoe still maintained a patrilineal naming system: there was no fixed 'surname'. All Tuhoe are therefore indexed here under their own given names. Individuals who were part-European, or had adopted European surnames, are indexed by their surnames.